PRAISE FOR
The Soul of Discipline

"*The Soul of Discipline* offers practical tools for helping parents implement discipline that's respectful and effective, but the book is so much more. Kim John Payne offers a framework to guide parents in making decisions about why, when, and how to hold tighter reins as we build skills in our children, and why, when, and how to loosen the reins as we scaffold freedom."

—TINA PAYNE BRYSON, PH.D., co-author of *No-Drama Discipline*

"This book gets deep inside the challenge of getting along with children and teens and thinks deeply about what they need from us to become strong and self-managing. It elevates discipline to what it should be—a caring process of helping kids orient to the world and live in it happily and well."

—STEVE BIDDULPH, author of *The New Manhood*

"Kim John Payne provides a useful model for choosing our parenting stance—Governor, Gardener, or Guide—depending on the situation. Most powerfully, Payne begins with the radical view that children are not disobedient but rather disoriented. The upshot of this shift in perspective is that discipline is about helping children orient themselves effectively, not about controlling or chastising."

—LAWRENCE J. COHEN, PH.D., author of *Playful Parenting*

"*The Soul of Discipline* draws on Kim John Payne's years of gifted school and family counseling to show us with its clear and simple tone how to discipline without becoming our children's enemy. It is filled with memorable stories, dialogues that will engage your imagination, and great strategies. By the book's end, a new picture of parenting will live in you, one that will honor the soul of your children as you provide the structure, training, and guidance they need at each stage of their development."

—DEE JOY COULTER, ED.D., author of *Original Mind*

By Kim John Payne

Games Children Play

Simplicity Parenting

Beyond Winning
(with Luis Fernando Llosa
and Scott Lancaster)

The Soul of Discipline

The Soul of Discipline

The
Soul
of
Discipline

THE SIMPLICITY PARENTING APPROACH TO
WARM, FIRM, AND CALM GUIDANCE—
FROM TODDLERS TO TEENS

Kim John Payne, M.Ed.

Ballantine Books | New York

2021 Ballantine Books Trade Paperback Edition

Published in the United States by Ballantine Books,
an imprint of Random House,
a division of Penguin Random House LLC, New York.

BALLANTINE and the HOUSE colophon
are registered trademarks of Penguin Random House LLC.

Originally published in hardcover in the United States by Ballantine Books,
an imprint of Random House, a division of Penguin Random House LLC, in 2015.

LIBRARY OF CONGRESS CATALOGING-IN-PUBLICATION DATA
Payne, Kim John.
The soul of discipline: the simplicity parenting approach to warm, firm, and
calm guidance—from toddlers to teens / Kim John Payne.
pages cm
ISBN 978-0345-54869-6
Ebook ISBN 978-0-345-54868-9
1. Parenting. 2. Discipline of children. I. Title. HQ755.8.P39933 2015
649'.64—dc23
2015005743

Printed in the United States of America on acid-free paper

randomhousebooks.com

4 6 8 9 7 5 3

Illustrations by Katharine Payne

Book design by Casey Hampton

This book is dedicated to you, dear parent,
for the laughter and love you bring to your family.

Contents

Part 4: The Rescue Package: Taking the Pulse

Part 5: A Deeper Dive

Introduction

Although I have been a school and family counselor for more than thirty years, I have never met a genuinely *disobedient* child or teen. What I have encountered are myriad *disoriented* kids. When we do not provide our children with well-defined boundaries, they react by being difficult and defiant. They feel unsafe and unsettled, and we become frustrated and confused. Inevitably, our children sense *our* disorientation, which increases *theirs,* and a truly unhealthy, self-perpetuating cycle is activated.

As the imperfect parent of two teenagers, I am all too aware of the feeling of free fall we parents experience when challenging disciplinary situations arise. We grasp at any solid handhold to break our spiraling emotional descent, and although some parents think we can find solid ground in the advice of experts, who tell us to choose a parenting style and *stick* to it, I have my doubts about how well this works. Anything we stick to can become "stuck," and we cannot effectively enforce a rigid disciplinary method on our kids because they are constantly growing and changing, and their emotional needs shift with equal frequency.

Since the publication of my book *Simplicity Parenting* and the worldwide movement it spawned, the value of slowing down and simplifying family life has been affirmed by countless parents. The same idea applies to dealing with disciplinary issues. For instance, when our tween or teenager exclaims, "Don't treat me like a little kid!" we may well be off base, and our son or daughter may be right. But he or she may also be wrong. We may be directing our child appropriately at that moment. Complicated stuff. How does any parent know if he or she is on the right track?

The Soul of Discipline will explore such questions. In my view, it is critical when we discipline children that we "hold" them emotionally when things are too complicated or unclear. At other times—when they are doing well—we can relax our firm, caring embrace and apply a lighter touch. You may intuitively recognize this way of being present in your child's life. Let's explore how your intuition can become a practical, creative tool that can be used in a kind yet firm way to provide your child with the support he or she needs when difficulties arise.

The Three Phases

Underlying my philosophy of discipline is a three-tiered Governor-Gardener-Guide parenting approach—three phases of parental involvement that build on each other, three roles which can be used to appropriately calibrate how you respond to any and every challenging disciplinary situation.

Here is a quick overview of the three phases:

- The *Governor* oversees the early years—helping a child feel safe, control impulses, and learn to follow direction by showing him who is in charge. This builds healthy foundations for . . .
- The *Gardener* cultivates the flowering of the tween years and encourages a child to see that he or she is a part of a family in which everyone depends on one another. The parent is still in charge but now reaches out to a tween to hear how she sees things and what plans she may have. This naturally leads to . . .
- The *Guide* oversees the teen years. He or she knows the terrain ahead and listens to a teen as they plan together the best path to achieve his goals, hopes, and dreams.

The Governor-Gardener-Guide roles are an excellent way to adapt your disciplinary approach as a child grows, but you can also look at them from another angle—as a three-step process for supporting your child's specific *needs* rather than their age-related developmental *stages*. These stages can be described as:

- *Base* (Governor Principle): This involves building foundations that are broad and deep. The intention is to help a child of any age be able to control impulses, follow direction, and accept boundaries. Children are taught to direct willpower so that it is effective rather than the cause of trouble.

If this is in place . . .

- *Middle Ground* (Gardener Principle): When the foundations of impulse control are established, kids will become team players. They can make their plans while taking other family members into consideration. The intention is to help your child develop empathy, understand the feelings of others, and strengthen his or her social abilities.

If this is in place . . .

- *Top Tier* (Guide Principle): When a child has learned to accept appropriate boundaries *and* appreciates that others in the family have needs, he or she can build a path to healthy decisions. This is the time to encourage and guide his or her choices.

What this book will avoid doing is giving you a lot of seemingly sensible advice that builds a family situation in which you end up giving your kid too many choices and freedoms that he or she can't handle. A parent intuitively feels that this kind of situation is off base, and it sets you and your child up for a fall. Everyone feels frustrated, and your discipline is precarious and unstable.

But What If Things Are Already Hard?

So how does this help practically if your tween or teen is not doing so well at accepting your Gardener- or Guide-based discipline? For example, what if your teen wants the freedom to make big decisions but is disrespectful of how these choices affect others and is not accepting the sensible boundaries that keep him or her safe? The answer: "Hellooo, Guv'nor." You move your child back to the "base" camp of the Governor disciplinary dynamic to help him or her understand that freedom to choose is not an entitlement. The young person needs this shift in your discipline; otherwise things can spiral out of control. Your child needs to operate within a smaller and closer "family state." Once your son or daughter has understood who is in charge and that he or she must show consideration for the needs of others in the family, your child can again have more space. You're not going to be popular, but you will be happier feeling you are standing on sensible and solid ground, and most important, your son or daughter will now be operating within freedoms and responsibilities that he or she needs and can handle rather than you expecting too much from a child who isn't ready.

Tuning In Your Discipline and Support

This simple three-tier way to adapt discipline can also be used on a daily, small-scale level. One mother wrote in, "Everything can be going along fine with my thirteen-year-old, but then she flips out and is impossible. This used to go on for days, and I used to stand there not knowing what to do while everything seemed to be falling apart. Insisting on her making better choices seemed reasonable, but it was beyond what she was capable of at the time. Now I pull in the boundaries, go back to the foundations, and do the 'Governor' thing for an hour or maybe a day or two at most, and she is good to go and is a lot more considerate to everyone in the family."

The aim of this book is to clarify for you, the parent, the phases of a child's life and match them with the kind of discipline that meets and nurtures his or her needs. What this book should not do is make you feel you have to do things this way or leave you thinking, "Oh no, I've been doing everything wrong." Our kids need us to be family leaders, not the followers of the prescriptions learned from a parenting book, no matter how good the advice may be. Any book written by a "parenting expert" should come with a health warning similar to those that appear on cigarette packages. It should read, "This advice may cause your parenting self-esteem serious harm and can lead to Expert Opinion Dependency and a Family Leadership Vacuum."

How to Navigate This Book

As you read on, you will discover five sections. The first focuses on "The Big Picture." It examines "bad behavior" and why kids push back against us. It also shows you how parents can make discipline calm, firm, and warm. And most crucially, it will clarify how good discipline deepens our connection with our kids. We need not fear that by being in charge we'll alienate them.

Sections two and three explore in more detail the three parenting roles I've briefly described above. I have devoted a whole section (two) to the Governor role because it is the foundation on which the others are built. Necessarily, this material is more detailed, in-depth, and practical. It explains the five keys to healthy compliance, how to make transitions smoother, how to move from requests to directions, and how to help children avoid interrupting adult conversation as we build greater politeness and respectfulness in them.

Section four addresses the two questions that just about every parent asks at one stage or another: "Have I really messed things up?" and "Is it too late to make things better?" In both cases, the answer is a clear no. This section will put your mind at rest and provide you with a doable approach to easing whatever disciplinary situation you encounter. You will see how, step by step, you can match your disciplinary approach with the kind of boundaries your kid needs at any stage of his or her development.

Finally, section five takes you on a "Deeper Dive." In it, we will take a look at the disciplinary fads of the past sixty years and why they can undermine your loving authority and heartful connection with your kids. One chapter discusses how bringing greater simplicity and balance to our fast-paced family lives can improve our relationships and make discipline much less contentious. In this last section we'll also explore "Discipline in the Digital Age" and address crucial and ever more timely themes such as the effects screen media has on parental authority and on your relationships with your children.

And Just Before You Launch . . .

The things that are most enduring and effective in life are both profound and simple. Yet getting to this depth of understanding takes time and persistent revisiting. Over the last thirty years, during many hundreds of parenting workshops I've led, the question of how to calibrate and fine-tune discipline to resonate with specific ages and stages of a child's life has seldom been far from my thoughts. Although it started off as a jagged stone I rolled around in my hand, it is now smooth with familiarity. I have passed this stone on to many parents who have also held it and let it slide over their fingers. Our emerging understanding of how discipline can build a loving connection has transformed into a gem through our collective efforts. In these pages, I attempt to do justice to all the many kind and striving parents who have enthusiastically encouraged me to share more widely my work on the soul of discipline. Your children are lucky to have parents who take time to explore discipline, an issue which so completely defines family life. Happy reading, and blessings on your parenting path.

part one

THE BIG PICTURE

1

Disobedient or Disoriented?

How many times have we heard the expression "He's a lost soul"? We can sense when this is the case in someone close to us, such as a relative or friend, or even in a public figure in the wider community who causes us concern. To be lost and have no one to help us find our way is the stuff of nightmares.

No one likes to be disoriented, and few things in life are more unsettling. But children are particularly vulnerable when it comes to feeling lost and unsafe. We know there is too much coming at them all the time in today's frenetic world. Few adults among us have had to cope with the incessant stream of images, impressions, ideas, attitudes, and conflicting messages modern kids must navigate. We are, quite frankly, living in the midst of an undeclared war on childhood. Kids are exposed to too much and forced to grow up too quickly. As a result, disorientation and heightened anxiety have become the new normal.

So it's no wonder that troubling behavior surfaces more and more often at home and at school. As parents, we want to shield our children as much as possible, to provide a safe haven for them from the unrelenting buzzing and booming, the fever-pitched pace of modern life.

In this climate, disciplining a "disobedient" child can be quite challenging. We often feel like we are fumbling in the dark. We try so hard to say and do the right thing with the appropriate amount of energy and emphasis. We want to guide our children—to teach them how to behave and how not to behave. Our ultimate goal is to prepare them to handle themselves well as they set sail into modern society's often difficult waters.

Setting the Foundation— Understanding Disorientation

The way we perceive and approach misbehavior is the key to defusing our children's difficult and even explosive conduct. A critical shift in our approach to parenting takes place when we begin to understand that there is no such thing as a disobedient child, only a disoriented one.

In this chapter, we will examine our misconceptions about disobedience. If we can see our kids' challenging behavior as an attempt to orient themselves within the frenetic, confusing world they struggle to navigate, our role will shift from Disciplinarian in Chief or Crisis Management Specialist to Governor, Gardener, and Guide.

The Pinging Principle

Children, tweens, and teens orient themselves in a number of ways. They may read, play creatively, listen to a story, spend time in nature, delve into a hobby, or simply decompress while hanging out with family. These types of activities form a protective sheath between them and the hardness of the "real" world. They become the membrane through which kids process and digest all the good, the bad, and the busy things that happen in their lives. Engaging in these kinds of activities is not just a form of coping. It's how kids build resiliency and a burgeoning sense of self-esteem. When they can find a more centered and peaceful place within, they can let go and regroup their inner resources. What they are building is a sense of knowing who and where they are in their lives. When they can do this, they feel safe and well oriented.

But when there is too much going on in their lives, children lose their bearings and become disoriented. This can trigger a reaction that often manifests as challenging behavior. They push back against the world outside themselves. Unfortunately, the "outside" world they push against tends to be those nearest and dearest to them. It is so important to understand that their naughtiness or disrespect is not simply misbehavior but an attempt to come to some sort of balance in which they feel oriented and comfortable.

I call this the "Pinging Principle." Just as a submarine navigator gets his or her bearings by sending out sonic pings that bounce off underwater objects and orient the ship to rocks or reefs, our children send out "pings" in the form of challenging behavior. They nag, disrupt, or cry—seeking a reaction from us that will help orient them. This is their way of figuring out where they stand and what we want from them. In other words, the interplay between our kids' behavior and our adult reaction serves as a navigational system for them.

Understanding this concept is a real game changer. "When I recognized that my child was not just being naughty but actually feeling lost and pinging me, it changed everything," one parent of a young child told me. "Instead of just reacting to his behavior, I could now look for its source and understand it better." Another dad, with two young boys, said, "I tested this pinging idea. I watched each time my kids got antsy and fresh. Amazingly, just about every time it was because our family life had gotten a bit whacko."

"I Don't Take It Personally Anymore"

When kids "misbehave," it is only natural for a parent to run through a dog-eared catalog of self-doubt and recrimination. Some of the most common inscriptions on our personal parenting walls of shame are "I wonder what I did wrong in raising them?" or, for the guilt-wracked among us, who feel like untrained stand-ins, "Anyone else would deal with this better than me. Who am I to be doing this?" The Imposter Syndrome is particularly onerous. Like the Wizard of Oz, who makes great proclamations but feels small and unworthy behind that screen, we may feel unprepared, incapable, and lost just at a time when our kids most need us to be strong and oriented.

Feeling unmoored, we take our children's behavior personally. In a flash, we can shift from self-doubt and self-recrimination to angry reactions, punctuated by comments like "You will not speak to me that way, ever!" or "Do it right now, mister, or you will have me to deal with!"

Just about every parenting expert expounds on how we must stay calm in the face of bad behavior. Good advice, but how? Because unless we have a foothold on the "how," the cycle of self-blame will lead us right back to taking it personally. That catapults us to as far from calm as a parent can be.

When children are at their worst, we need to be at our best. Danny and Suzanne's story illustrates this well:

I met Suzanne at a parenting workshop I gave in Washington, D.C. She was struggling with a very defiant boy. Together we explored the difference between bad behavior and disorientation. "It was a real 'aha' moment for me when I began to see that my son Forrest's very difficult behavior was in fact a cry for orientation," she said. "Before we realized this, my husband Danny and I really struggled. We treated Forrest like a little adult, presuming that he had much more control over his behavior than he really did. We figured he knew what he was doing—that he was trying to wind us up. That led to all kinds of conflict and ugly scenes. We figured he should know how to stop, and we told him so. It might seem kind of crazy to get involved in a power struggle with a four-year-old, but that is exactly where we were."

Danny was at his wits' end too: "I'd get so exasperated. The more I insisted Forrest was making 'bad choices' about his behavior—that he should be capable of controlling himself—the more out-of-control he got. I can see now that his behavior wasn't bad; it was desperate. But back then I would get into these battles with him. You can't believe how personal it got. But I felt he was disrespecting me as a person, and it really pushed my buttons."

When Suzanne told Danny about the Pinging Principle, it made perfect sense to them both, but it upended their ingrained attitude toward their son and his behavior. "This new way of seeing the problem was scary and hopeful all at the same time," said Suzanne. "But the one thing it did immediately was to shift us away from taking Forrest's antics personally. You just can't take it personally anymore when your son has a meltdown if you've found a place within yourself to ask, 'What does he need to orient himself? What can I do to help?' In the few seconds we spend asking ourselves these questions, we move from being reactive and taking it too personally to seeing the underlying forces and staying much more centered, to becoming the kind of parents we always wanted to be."

Forrest still has occasional meltdowns, and he still pushes back. But Suzanne and Danny are relieved and grateful that the length and intensity of the difficult behavior has diminished to such a degree that it's "unrecognizable." Suzanne and Danny have undergone their own transformation: As Danny put it, "It's like I'm me now, not some weird person arguing with a four-year-old."

Does the Pinging Principle apply when a child is being deliberately challenging? The answer is yes. Even when children misbehave on purpose, they need guidance. Whether pinging behavior is conscious or unconscious, it is still a cry for help.

A woman we'll call Claire wrote to me about an experience she had when she was five years old. Her mother had just returned to full-time work after being an ever-present stay-at-home mom. Little Claire decided to go on an adventure. She walked to an abandoned warehouse four blocks from her home to explore "all the really good junk" she imagined she would find there. What's worse, she took her three-year-old sister with her. "I knew very well it was against the rules," she said, "but I did it anyway." A scary-looking man discovered them coming out of the building. He called out, "Go home, girls." They did just that, running all the way. Their parents were shocked when Claire's younger sister spilled the whole story that afternoon, and they watched the children closely for a long time afterward.

Reflecting on her actions, Claire said, "I am not sure if doing this was directly related to my mother going back to work, but I suspect I was feeling the need for their attention. I guess it was natural for my parents to worry after my adventure and make sure we stayed in the yard, but I certainly never would have done something like that again." The fact that Claire's parents were so attentive after their scare made her "feel safe again." Her willful disregard of the rules was quite clearly a call for attention and orientation.

Orientation Through Play

Any parent who observes their child deep in play knows how much kids try to make sense of what they have seen or heard through playing. Deep, absorbing play gives a child a sense of contentment and safety. Many of life's stresses reappear as games. Playing through these issues is how kids orient themselves inwardly.

As I walked by a group of eight-year-old children one sunny morn-

ing in May, I overheard them chanting a jump-rope rhyme. It went
something like this:

Soccer on Monday,
Playdates on Tuesday,
Ballet on Wednesday,
Soccer on Thursday,
Playdates on Friday,
Soccer on Saturday,
Sunday ain't no rest.

What stopped my heart about this seemingly innocuous rhyme is
that it didn't detail the overwhelming, overscheduled life of just one or
two of the kids on the playground. Every last kid had his or her own
individual jump-rope chant. And each song described a child's fever-
pitched pace of life. Music lessons, various sports, aftercare at school,
and homework were recurring themes. Here is another one that I
quickly jotted down:

Piano on Monday,
Swimming on Tuesday,
Tutor on Wednesday,
Piano on Thursday,
Swimming on Friday,
Shopping on Saturday,
Homework every day—no rest! [Here all the children shouted out.]

One child who moved back and forth between her mother's and
father's homes had an even simpler chant:

Mommy on Monday,
Daddy on Tuesday,

Mommy on Wednesday,
Daddy on Thursday,
Mommy on Friday,
Don't know Saturday,
Sunday maybe rest—phew!

One couple I spoke to returned from a checkup at the pediatrician's office expecting that their children would want to play a game of doctors and nurses. But the doctor's office had been frenetic and exasperating, and it had been clear that the staff struggled to keep up with the demands of the clinic. That's exactly the message the kids absorbed. Day after day they played a game they called "Health Security Office." They sat inside a big cardboard box "office" for hours drawing up forms on clipboards in their best tiny writing, with lots of boxes to check. Then they instructed their parents to wait outside a cutout window for long periods of time while they frantically answered their play phone. From time to time, the children would look up over their homemade eyeglasses and ask, "Yes? What?" in a well-practiced, annoyed tone. Thrusting clipboard and pen at the parents, they'd say, "Please read the in-suctions and answer every one of our questions!" This scene was repeated over and over until they had played the stress of the visit out of their systems.

When Normal Becomes Not So Normal

When overscheduling or an anxiety-inducing experience pushes a child off-balance, his or her own darling quirks—the very things we love about our child's personality at any other time—become exacerbated and suddenly annoy or even infuriate parents. One helpful tip: Consider your child's temperament. Extroverted personalities fall into either what I call "The Leader Type," a child who can become very dominant and controlling when off-balance, and "The Creative Type," a child who can become unfocused or even hysterical in this type of situation. Introverted types whom you might describe as "Easygoing" in other situations can become very stubborn and rigid when off-balance. If your child is a more "Intuitive" introvert, he or she may become overly sensitive and feel "victimized" by a harried pace of life. Whether your child is an introvert or an extrovert, stress affects behavior in very specific ways.

EXTROVERTS

The Leader Type—Can become very dominant and controlling.

The Creative Type—Can become unfocused and hysterical.

INTROVERTS

The Easygoing Type—Can become stubborn and rigid.

The Intuitive Type—Can become overly sensitive and feel victimized.

Sarah, a single mom with two children, consulted me about her daughter's inflamed temperament: "My thirteen-year-old daughter Lucy tends to be out there in the lead. A courageous girl who excels in sports, she is not afraid to work really hard. However, when we moved out of our house and town last year, she became impossible. I was at my wits' end because I was relying on her to pitch in and help, as I knew she could. But instead she became bossy and fixated on having everything done her way. Suddenly Lucy, who has always been a watchful big sister and my right-hand girl, doubled my workload with her demands and shenanigans."

I spoke with Sarah about the bigger picture and about the way children with certain personalities handle being overwhelmed. "That's when I realized that the move was stressing Lucy out and she felt lost," she said. "It helped me make sense of how and why she was acting out. Her natural tendencies, which made her very helpful under normal circumstances, had this shadow side that was now getting in the way. When I took a step back, I was flooded with sympathy for my daughter. She's a tough girl who does not easily admit to feeling overwhelmed. So it was hard to see what was really going on. I've seen her struggle a few times since. But I now know what she needs: her mom's help to find firm ground to stand on emotionally—even though she is being spiky. As a result, I'm much more likely to help rather than just react."

Understanding your child's temperament and how it can become inflamed can provide you with a framework for your parental instincts about your child's personality. But it's your actions that are critical here. When your child acts out, what she is really doing is crying out for orientation. And what is needed is your calm, reassuring hand to guide her toward reorientation.

Growing and Changing

We all know that kids go through various stages. Whether physical or emotional, developmental change can cause children to feel wobbly and act out a little or a lot. The new freedoms that each stage brings—and our kids demand—come with matching responsibilities, which they are not so keen to assume. Many kids look forward to these times of change. They see a whole new landscape of possibilities opening up, but deep down they can become unsettled by uncertainty. They have no road map to help them navigate this vast, scary new world. It's our job to provide them with one.

Children reach critical developmental milestones at ages two, five, nine, thirteen, and sixteen. Although much of a child's, tween's (nine to twelve years old), or teen's difficult behavior is rooted in developmental changes, this does not mean that a parent should excuse it. Understanding the underlying reason for this behavior—that your child feels vulnerable and disoriented—can be a big help as you struggle to provide the loving boundaries he needs to feel safe again and orient himself in this changing world.

Here's a quick overview of some of the key milestones and how they can play out emotionally and behaviorally:

Two Years Old: The Little Emperor

They are waking up to the world around them, discovering their own willpower and feeling a sense of omnipotence not matched by ability.

Five Years Old: "You're No Boss of Me"

They push away from the motherly fold, wanting to do things their own way, yet still needing a lot of help.

Nine Years Old: On the Cusp

They are leaving early childhood behind but are not yet fully in middle childhood. This phase is characterized by insecurities and pushback against family rules.

Thirteen Years Old: The Huck Finn and Pippi Longstocking Years

They are experiencing all the well-known hormonal changes, but it is also the age of breakout and discovery.

Sixteen Years Old: Closed for Reconstruction

A lot of energy goes inward as they try to work out who they are. While they are hypersensitive and emotionally raw, they are also capable of spectacular insensitivity toward others. They have so many decisions to make, and new responsibilities to consider, yet still want to have fun and be free.

———

If a child, tween, or teen is going through a lot of inward change, his or her emotional life will be shaken up and maybe even quite chaotic on bad days. The key point here is that in such hypersensitive phases, our

Pause Point

What disorients your child? What causes your child to get
bent out of shape or misbehave badly?

children need to ping us a whole lot more. At a time when all these
internal changes make them feel confused and uncertain, they look
for—and even demand—our help as they seek to reorient themselves.

It can be a big life change that disorients them or makes them feel
wobbly: moving out of a home or changing schools. But often it's a series of little things that build up over time. For example, you may have
chores to do after picking up your child from school: that shopping
you've been putting off, those errands that can't wait any longer, the
simple, time-consuming demands of daily life. How and why does this
disorient a child? Such short car trips can bother children and set them
off. They may start by being a bit antsy, but they often get worse
throughout the afternoon. This activity may be too "choppy" for a
child and lack the kind of predictability that kids need—that makes
them feel comfortable and secure. Most important, none of your chores
or errands is child focused. You may need to get these things done, but
can't some be done ahead of pickup time? Or maybe they can be clus-
tered into just two days instead of being spread out over the week. Can
you bring art supplies along so your child is creatively engaged while
sitting in the car or in a waiting room? Perhaps you can break up errand time by stopping to look through the window of a pet store or
taking a short walk through a park before soldiering on.

There are many possible solutions. But the key is to realize that the
child is looking for orientation and that a few changes in his or her

daily schedule stand a very good chance of making the difference. If such mini-shifts can settle a child and help you avert disciplinary battles, then stop and ask these two key orienting questions:

1. What is disorienting her and causing her to react like this?
2. What does she need to get her bearings back?

Taking Away "That Which Is Not David"

Discipline should not simply be about being punitive and corrective. It should be a definer of family values. Each time we discipline our children we will find firm ground under our parenting feet as we clarify what our family stands for. When we tell our kids, "In our family, we don't speak to each other like that; we just don't," it helps settle them. This is because we're doing two things at once: First, we're orienting them, and nothing orients better than an authentically stated, deeply held value. And second, we're creating a family-values pillar around which they can orbit. We are clarifying for them what our family does not do, what our family isn't.

Michelangelo was often asked how he could possibly have carved the statue of David out of stone. It was just too beautiful, too gorgeous and perfect. His response: He did not actually carve David. What he did was take away that which was not David. In other words, he didn't carve it; he revealed it. He had a picture of the archetypal image that he wanted to create out of the marble, and with that very clear image in mind, he set about taking away that which was not part of that image.

This provides us with a wonderful metaphor for parenting. Like Michelangelo, who created David by taking away that excess marble in which this glorious figure was encased, we, as parents, can help our children to become who they are or define themselves by taking away "that which is not of our family." By clarifying to our kids what our family does not do and does not say, we strip away all that excess behavioral material and reveal for them, in a clear and concrete manner, what is at the core of our family values.

This sets us on much firmer ground. Our discipline can now serve as guidance rather than simply as punishment. Otherwise, we get stuck in a heated, cyclic battle with our children. When we equate discipline with punishment, we may end up thinking we are being too harsh. Then we swing the other way and become too tentative with our discipline. The result? With all this waffling, we don't communicate clearly to our kids what we expect of them. Then when they don't follow our rules or requests (which were imprecise to begin with because we were unclear about how we feel about them), we overreact and become overly strict. This causes our kids to overreact in turn, sending us into Monster Parent mode.

Seeing discipline as parental guidance or "taking away that which is not of our family" rather than simply as punishment helps temper disciplinary interactions between parent and child. One dad I worked with says, "Everything changes after you get it that when you apply discipline you don't have to back off because you don't want to be punitive or come on too hard because you're fed up. I feel a wonderful new freedom when I swoop in." If your child makes a comment, uses a bad word, or does something that is not okay to a sibling and you correct and redirect him, you are chiseling away at that which is not of your family. Each time you do that you are revealing your true values as a family.

Considering core family values might seem like a lofty inquiry, but in truth it is quite simple. A good place to start is with one or two key values, such as respect or empathy. Because every time a child is disrespectful to you or a sibling or someone outside the family you can hold that up as an affront to your highest core value and return to that value again and again. Not just when the behavior is extremely disrespectful but even when it's just beginning to head off the rails. The saying "Don't sweat the small stuff" does not apply in parenting. Parenting is

Pause Point

What are the core family values that you want your child
to understand and embrace?

all about calmly and firmly noticing and acting on the small stuff. While
no one is suggesting we become neurotic nags, we must plant disciplinary seeds because "from little things, big things grow." When a child
steps over the line, departing from one of these key family values, it's so
important that we guide them back. They need regular reorientation.

If a child is pushing you and you feel that your family values are
being challenged, it's important to correct the child firmly and un-
equivocally. This does two things:

It immediately reorients the child.
It reinforces your family values.

Later in this book—specifically in the Governor, Gardener, and
Guide chapters—we will take a close look at this idea, and work
through practical examples of what is right for the stage and age of
your child, and we will apply them to guide your reactions. For now,
let's look at the larger picture.

Understanding Pushback

The principle of equilibrium and pushback is an important one. Simply put, pushback occurs when a child's inner and outer worlds
collide—when there is an imbalance of forces. If a child's inner world

is overwhelmed by demands or impressions from the outside world, he or she will act out or push back. Let's look at this in more detail.

The figure below represents a meeting place between a child's delicate inner world—his or her hopes and dreams, the unique shape of the person whom he or she is becoming—and the pressures and demands of the outer world.

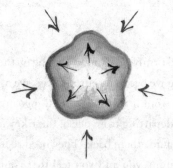

The arrows that point inward are all the things that are external to a child's life. For example, in any family, there is a series of small but consistent external events such as shopping, doctor's visits, or simply travel in the family car. We have playdates, lessons, all kinds of social gatherings, and sporting events. There may be childcare for some, and there's school and homework. All these things represent external forces—the arrows that point inward, to the center of the diagram. They are common aspects of family life related to the wider community and world.

Then there is the child within. This precious being emerges gradually over the years as our child becomes who he or she is. As our children grow, their inner worlds strengthen. They develop a sense of self, self-confidence, and understanding. These forces from the child's inner world, which move out and engage with the outside world, are represented by the arrows that begin at the center of the diagram and point outward. They are developed and strengthened by activities such as creative play and time spent with family and in nature.

There is a delicate, dynamic interplay between these inner and outer worlds. In a healthy, developing child, a cocoon-like sheath forms at the point where all the demands of the outside world (such as daily activities) meet the capacities and strength of a child's inner world.

This protective membrane separates the outer and inner worlds. When there is a balance between the two types of "forces"—when your child has downtime and engaged-with-the-world time—she becomes a flexible, resilient child. That's when something very special can grow inside that cocoon: a vibrant, multifaceted personality, nourished by burgeoning self-esteem, self-knowledge, and a developing clarity about life direction.

Behavioral pushback occurs when there is an imbalance between the inner and outer forces. Take a look at this second illustrative rendering of the concept. Basically, when outside forces have become too strong and a child feels overwhelmed, he or she will push back.

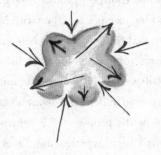

Once when I was working as a school counselor, a teenager we'll call Josh plopped himself down on my office sofa. He wrapped himself in the checkered blanket I kept there for kids to cozy up in and stared sullenly at the well-worn floor. "So, Josh, what's up?" I asked. "Well, it's like I can't do anything right," he announced angrily. "And today, like, I was late for school again. I had to go to the office to get a late slip again. And then there's all these classes and tests, and I gotta, like, drive all over the place with my mom all afternoon, and I have so much homework that I have to stay up until the middle of the night just to get half of it done. . . ." As he rattled off this laundry list of pressures and problems, it became clear that Josh was suffering from an acute case of "soul fever."

This was a kid drowning in emotional "overwhelm." Josh felt that everything was coming at him. When he erupted as a result and his teacher disciplined him, he felt the teacher's punishment was a personal attack. But his outburst had a perfectly logical foundation. He burst out because he was "fit to burst." And the teacher's discipline was just another of an overwhelming number of forces pushing in on him. I asked him if he felt like the world was closing him down. "Is what the adults are reading as you behaving badly just you trying to hold all this stuff back?" I said. This tall, strapping young man teared right up. "Exactly," he said. "That's exactly what it's like. I am not trying to make trouble. I am just trying to protect myself." When the people who loved and cared for Josh got together with him in one room and worked out a way to dial things back, his behavior improved noticeably. His comment was not unusual for a boy his age in its forthrightness. He was essentially saying, "If you respect me, I will respect you." What I found important to understand about his comment was that he had felt disrespected by the people who unwittingly played a part in the overwhelm he had been experiencing. Over the years, I would come to see this as a pattern. Young people do not philosophize or generalize about their stress when it all gets to be too much. Instead, they personalize it, and this understandably leads them to hit back at the people who they feel are responsible—us.

When you think about the pressures your child or teenager faces and when you ask them about those pressures, you may get a very interesting—and revealing—response. Again, our children are not simply being naughty. What they are doing is pushing back. We parents might describe them as "bent out of shape," but what's really happening is that they are suffering from an imbalanced life. The child or teen's inner world is subject to so much pressure from way too many outside demands that his or her delicate, emerging inner self gets bent out of shape.

It is critical for parents to realize what's going on, because if a child or teen's inner world is bent out of shape, his self-esteem will start to plummet. He will feel inadequate. In children, tweens, and teens, a sense of inadequacy can result in two distinct behavioral phases:

Fight Back

If the imbalance persists in their lives, they will at first fight back tenaciously.

Fall Back

But if the outer world keeps pounding and beating at them—overwhelming them—and Fight Back does not keep the world at bay, they will eventually retreat, becoming very defensive and inaccessible to their families and the world around them. Many seek harbor in the relative "safety" and "anonymity" of the online world with all its associated "virtual relationships." Relationships based in social media can be alluring to overwhelmed tweens or teens because these relationships allow them to develop a false sense of control over their interactions. And when a child is persistently pressured and experiences severe overwhelm, he or she may start to experience serious mental health struggles such as depression, addiction, or even disassociated aggression.

If the demands of daily life match the emotional capacities of a child or teen, something very different occurs. If a balance can be established between the outside world and the child or teen's inner (or emotional) life, she can develop and strengthen her emotional resilience.

The three key principles detailed below help develop and support a child or teen in day-to-day life as he or she grows up.

ONE: CENTEREDNESS AND ORIENTATION

The precious inner core of the child receives forces from the outside that his gentle and slowly developing inner self can meet and process. The core self of that little (or big) boy or girl is then oriented and forms an emotional pillar that supports him or her during moments of adversity and helps the child stay predominantly happy and calm.

TWO: EQUILIBRIUM AND BALANCE

If equilibrium and balance are maintained, a child or teen will have a much better chance to feel, "I have the forces within me to meet what is being asked of me."

THREE: SAFETY AND SECURITY

When there is a healthy balance between their demands and capabilities, children or teens sense that they can trust their environment. They trust the adults around them and feel safe and secure.

We all want our children to feel centered, balanced, and safe. None of us wakes up to a new day intent on causing imbalance or disorientation. But life happens. Because we are the drivers and schedulers, the people making demands on our kids' time (with the best of intentions, of course), we end up symbolizing, to varying degrees, the pressures that stress them out, the forces they struggle to cope with. And because we are the people closest to these developing souls, we are the ones they rail against. We are the recipients of the brunt of the back talk and other misbehavior. One might go so far as to say that in some families the child views the parent as the enemy rather than the protector.

The Child Under Siege

When a child experiences disorientation, he or she becomes fearful. External forces are overwhelming his or her inner life. There may be a long list of culprits: too many toys and books, too many after-school activities and sports, too many playdates, too much TV and computer time, too much adult information. When all these external forces are pushing in, the sheath or cocoon that separates a child's outer and inner lives and protects her as her emotional resilience and personality grow and strengthen is compromised. Sensing that she is in danger of becoming overwhelmed, the child (or teen) retreats and then lashes out or pushes back.

The sympathetic nervous system (SNS), which is responsible for switching on our fight-or-flight response, and the parasympathetic nervous system (PNS), which controls the relaxation response, engage in a delicate dance. Picture two teams trying to hold a rope between them while maintaining as little tension as possible—a tug-of-war in reverse. The fight-or-flight response and the relaxation response maintain a careful balance by making fine adjustments whenever something disturbs or threatens us.

The anchormen on these teams are hormones, the chemical delivery systems produced by endocrine glands. The word "hormone" comes from the Greek for "to set in motion," and they do just that. Some stress hormones don't know when to quit pulling, which can lead to all kinds of problem behavior. They can remain active in the brain for too long, injuring and even killing cells in the hippocampus, the region of our brains required for knowledge-based memory and openness to new learning.

Parents should try to be superconscious of when kids have been overwhelmed by the fight-or-flight mechanism. Providing your child with a balanced day that includes plenty of decompression points— such as play, reading, listening to stories or music, and rest—will help trigger the relaxation response and reestablish what brain scientists call metabolic equilibrium. If the child or teen can decompress after a stressful day, he or she will be much less likely to fight you or become solemn and stubborn.

Fortunately, pretty much every parent knows that hitting kids is not a great idea. But a parent who does hit a child, only to find that child appear defiant and remorseless, should understand that this posturing relates to the fight-or-flight response. When a child is hit, his body releases adrenaline, which substantially shuts down his pain centers. So it's not so much that the child is being defiant as that his mind and body have gone into overdrive and have prepared him for what is being read as a life-threatening situation. "Survival memory" is also switched on, which means that the child will remember this incident for much longer than we might imagine. The child may bounce back quickly, but he or she will develop an increased wariness of the parent. And here is the kicker: The same hormonal cascade is triggered in children who get shouted at aggressively. Shouting may have replaced hitting in many households, but the long-lasting effects are worryingly similar.

One couple met with me about their out-of-control four-year-old son. They described terrible tantrums in which he kicked, punched, and bit them. Outwardly, it was clear that the child was experiencing full-blown meltdowns. Inwardly, his nervous system was short-circuiting. His behavior was telling them, "Enough! I can't cope with all that is being asked of me. I need life to be quieter. I need more rhythm. I cannot cope with all this stuff that is swirling around me!" The child's tantrums—any kid's outbursts for that matter—can be summarized in four words: *"Too much is happening."*

"He fights us every step of the way," his exhausted dad said. "When is this going to end?" They were understandably scared that their son might be mentally unwell. The answer was simple, though surprising to them: "This will end when your son stops seeing you as the enemy, when he stops feeling he needs to fight back against you two in order to survive. When you cut back on things like playdates, and screen time, and adult conversation, which he can overhear and makes him anxious, he will very likely see you as the people in his life who quietly protect him. You will become his safe harbor again."

Sure enough, a few weeks after his parents simplified his life and cut out the things they thought were overwhelming the boy, he began to show signs of improvement. The wild, reckless behavior slowly decreased, and the tantrums got shorter and less frequent. The boy still pushed back, but much less frantically. "He still tests us, but not in that scary way he did before," said his mom.

Child in Flight—Parent in Fight

When your child or teenager is stubborn or sullen and blows you off with a quietly provocative "whatever," it can be maddening. Here you are trying to be reasonable, and your kid is disrespecting you. One very exasperated dad had this to say about his son: "It was like he was Teflon coated. Nothing I could say was sticking. It made me see red, really red."

This is a dynamic we all know too well: The kid crosses a line; the parent tells her to cut it out. The kid quietly does it again, and the parent begins to get mad. The kid walls herself up and "whatevers" the parent, and the parent explodes. A very common family exchange. But if it becomes a pattern, it can morph into a very destructive cycle: a kid in flight who triggers a parent into fight. Now the whole family is flooded with adrenaline and cortisol. The Romans called this *districtia,* which translates into "being torn asunder." When this kind of stress loop kicks into high gear, it can feel as though your family is being torn apart.

The Wonders of the Frontal Lobes

We want our kids to be reachable and teachable. For that, they need to have healthily developing frontal lobes. When a parent is able to be a quiet but steady gatekeeper or sentinel to what is and is not appropriate in a child's life, frontal lobes development can occur more fully. Good parental gatekeepers will have a healthy skepticism for so-called child-friendly marketing claims and want to see and review any material that is being marketed to kids before they allow their children to be exposed to it. While it may seem easier in the short term to go along with "what everybody is doing with kids these days," many of these toys, shows, and activities are dramatically age inappropriate. They can be oversexualized or express aggressive or even violent images or behavior. The brain's reaction to such material is to divert activity away from the frontal lobes and empathy development and into the amygdala or reactionary region of the brain. This makes talking to your kids about their behavior hard, really hard.

When a parent is able to guide his child without facing a lot of pushback, it is generally because the child is functioning from her more evolved brain or frontal lobes. In such a scenario, the child feels that life is safe and predictable. To be good gatekeepers, we, as parents, need to monitor the amount of stuff coming at our kids as we hold firmly to our core values. By standing strong and parenting in a conscious way, we are working out of our own higher, more evolved brain centers. We have, in effect, replaced a fight-or-flight survival loop that we can easily fall into with our kids with a more centered, connected dynamic. Awash in safety and love, family life can flow much more smoothly.

One of the best summaries of how brain science affects parenting and discipline comes from the work of Dr. Dee Joy Coulter, a neuroscience pioneer and the author of *Original Mind: Uncovering Your Natural Brilliance*. What Dr. Coulter does is compare a stress response (which comes from the amygdala) with a resilient response (which begins in the frontal lobes, also known as the "executive brain"), as presented on the next page. The italic text under each main point is mine and has been added as a series of practical examples and to show how they relate to discipline.

Let's consider what the frontal lobes are responsible for:

- They engage the will and activate initiative. *Your child will be better able to play for hours and take part in problem solving.*
- They regulate inner speech, which is needed for impulse control, reasoning, and creative language. *Your child will be better able to work through problems internally or take on board the directions you give by "self-talking" or reasoning his or her way through what could otherwise be confusing. Your child will learn to internalize your guidance so you don't need to explain things over and over.*
- They sustain alertness and concentration. *Your child will be better able to focus when you are giving instructions.*
- They foster cooperation even when things get busy. *Your child will be better able to handle transitions without melting down.*
- They see and attend to complex patterns. *Your child will be better able to see how an argument came about rather than just defend his or her way of seeing it.*
- They can process and act on multiple variables simultaneously. *Your child can better understand directions you give as well as figure out how to do what he or she needs to do.*
- They can think ahead, make plans, and anticipate consequences. *Your child will be better able to navigate away from conflict and discipline hot spots because he can see what will likely happen if he doesn't change his plans.*
- They are the only region wired to be aware of body-mind connections. *Your child will be better able to avoid hitting out impulsively without understanding what he or she did.*
- They are directly involved with all peak-performance states. *Your child will be able to get into, and remain in, the creative "zone" when engaged in play, academics, and especially social relationships.*
- They register feelings of compassion, empathy, social intimacy, and bonding. *This is the big one in terms of guidance and discipline.*

Your child will be better able to understand that her actions affect others. She will develop better relationships with siblings and, most important, open her heart to you as a parent and, through you, to the larger world around her.

When a child feels safe and can trust the emotional and physical environment around him, all these wonderful capacities have fertile soil in which to grow. When a child experiences her world as friendly rather than hostile and predictable rather than fragmented, the creative executive brain is freed from the primitive hold of the fight-or-flight response, which has one dominant priority: survival. In the "Deeper Dive" section of this book, you will find specific, easily applicable strategies to help you simplify and bring balance to your kids' lives. They will help you take a giant step toward developing these crucial frontal lobe capacities.

Flooding and Resiliency

To recap, our kids are likely to experience a fight-or-flight response—operating from their amygdala—when too much is coming at them: too many objectives; too many noises, distractions, and requests. They get "flooded" and cannot self-regulate. Alternatively, when our children can handle what is being asked of them, they are more likely to act from their frontal lobes. The table on the next page is a summary of Dr. Coulter's comparison of "flooding" with "resiliency" and what each might look like. The resilient child or teen can be guided and, when needed, disciplined without it becoming a big deal. The flooded child will very likely treat discipline and guidance as a threat. He or she will often react to ordinary instruction with exaggerated pushback.

WHAT IS RESILIENCY?

1. Ability to respond freshly to each situation.
2. Returning to a restful, alert state between events.
3. Ability to enjoy novelty and generate interest in emotionally neutral information.
4. Ability to engage socially and enjoy friendships, play, and humor.
5. Ability to accept positive feedback about one's performance.
6. Ability to "bracket" negative events. In terms of time: *It's only happening right now.* In terms of space: *It will only affect this aspect of my life, not everything.*

WHAT IS A FLOODED RESPONSE?

1. Reacting habitually; repetition and reenactment of archaic patterns of response.
2. Maintaining low-grade vigilance between events; rising to high vigilance for all events.
3. Becoming startled at novelty and only paying attention to emotionally charged, highly relevant information.
4. Social isolation, fixed routines, avoidance of play, inability to generate or respond to humor.
5. Rejecting praise and consistently seeing success as failure, as accidental, or as just not good enough.
6. Exaggerating the effect of negative events. In terms of time: *It's always going to be like this.* In terms of space: *It affects my whole life and contaminates everything.*

The Three Phases of Discipline

L ast summer my wife, Katharine, and I, together with our two teenage kids, rode across the United States on our motorcycles. There was lots of time on those long, rolling roads to gaze down from a rise and notice fields and fences appear and disappear from sight. As we meandered up Highway 1 from central California through Oregon, we became entranced by this beautiful, narrow road, which often clung high up to the cliff face. A quick glance down would reveal beach and roiling ocean hundreds of feet below.

Sitting by the campfire on one of those breezy summer nights, our elder girl wondered aloud why there were so often no guardrails on the sides of that precipitous stretch of road. She thought it strange because the drop off the side of the cliff was so sheer, and yet no barrier had been erected to help prevent us from falling should we veer off course. "Isn't it funny," she said, "how some fences can seem silly, like the ones we saw hanging in midair across creeks or deep gullies, and others, like guardrail fences, can help make you feel safe or afraid if they are not there?" Katharine and I looked at each other and smiled. Our daughter was right and astute on so many levels.

During our trip, we all wondered at the tenacity of wall builders. They construct fences and walls that march in straight lines across terrain that rises, folds, and bends, paying little or no attention to the contours of the land.

Seeing those fences suspended in midair across gullies and creeks made us laugh.

It also got me thinking about the way parents and kids interact, all the different types of walls and fences we construct in our relationships with one another. Such fences are often slapped together haphazardly and imprecisely.

A boundary, on the other hand, tends to take the terrain into account, moving with the shape of the land, giving definition without needing to be harshly defined itself. A boundary is noted on large-scale maps, whereas fences and walls are most often not. It's something stronger and more noteworthy than a wall, even though it is often invisible. In families, boundaries mold to and redefine the contours of our relationships.

All this musing about walls, fences, and boundaries, whether material or familial, reminds me of Robert Frost's famous line "Good fences make good neighbors" in his poem "Mending Wall." If that's the case, doesn't it follow that good boundaries make good families?

So here is the conundrum: Most parents would agree kids need boundaries, but we worry about the real risk that they will feel walled in and that we, the parents, will be walled out of our kids' lives. I must confess that in my relationship with my kids there *is* "something . . . that doesn't love a wall." We want to have fun and be close and loving to our kids. The thought of a wall between us seems wrong. And it is for this very reason that many parents are wary of, or even reject, boundaries. But boundaries are different from walls. A wall is fixed and permanent, whereas the boundaries of a living relationship are always in movement. They grow and adapt and then change again.

Boundaries Clarify—Walls Separate

Let's take a look at the role that the different phases of discipline play and explore how setting boundaries that are warm, clear, and changeable can help make your parenting journey much less rocky and arduous.

Smart, Responsive Boundaries

Understanding responsive boundaries is an essential starting place from which to explore a child's changing disciplinary needs. Simply put, the boundaries a parent puts into place in the life of a child or teen are most effective when they are firm yet responsive or flexible. They are helpful when they are neither too lenient nor too constricting. A boundary works when it orients both the child and the parent. The child, tween, or teen may not outwardly like the boundary but will inwardly feel secure because he knows where he stands. Boundaries help children feel safe.

The Dangers of Vague Boundaries

If a boundary is too vague or undefined, a child can "cross the line" and go into territory he or she can't handle. Although it might seem great to have no limits, sooner or later, a child begins to feel unsafe and disoriented in this situation. As we saw in Chapter One, disorientation leads to pinging, in which a child "sends out" a series of challenging behaviors in order to trigger feedback from a parent. This is not pleasant, and it need not happen with such intensity if boundaries are clearly defined.

When family boundaries are not clearly delineated, kids can get caught up in inappropriate stuff way before they have the ability to handle it. One glaring example: children who are exposed to highly sexualized and inappropriate content due to weak family Internet-use rules. It is disturbing how often this plays out in family dynamics around the world, even though parents recognize that vague boundaries carry a high risk.

Boundaries Change as Kids Grow

Flexibility and adaptability are critical to discipline that is simple and good. The Soul of Discipline approach is based on a clear understanding that boundaries change as kids grow up. This approach recognizes the need for *boundaries that define our family, not walls that separate us.* We need to keep in mind that boundaries expand and contract according to the specific needs of our child, tween, or teen.

Flexibility can also come to our rescue when we are confronted with an older son or daughter who has been allotted more freedoms but is experiencing a meltdown. In moments like these, we can adjust and tighten our protective embrace and restore freedoms later, when the crisis has abated.

I had a discussion on the difference between walls and boundaries with one parent who was experiencing authority problems with her two children. She later wrote me a moving, self-reflective email:

I thought a lot about our conversation over the last couple of weeks. The big realization I had is that what most deeply shaped my attitude toward discipline is not at all directly related to my kids, but to my own childhood experiences.

My parents seriously overregulated me as a kid. It was hard to fight back because we were heavily involved in a church, and it always seemed like they had God on their side. I often felt frustrated, unheard, and alone. When I left home, I rejected religion, and later, when I had my own children, I refused to set limits for my kids because I didn't want to box them in. Makes sense, right?

Then came my wake-up call. Because my parents were wall builders, I fiercely broke down any forms that I felt penned me or my kids in. Over the years, I have alienated many of my kids' friends' parents and particularly their school teachers. I convinced myself that I was fighting for their freedom, but what I now realize is that all this meant was that my kids are wild, unpredictable, and often disrespectful. That is not at all what I had in mind when I wanted freedom for them. I guess what I have done, in my determination to not be like my own parents, is confuse hurtful wall building with reasonable boundary setting.

I am working on not feeling embarrassed or guilty because that's not going to help me or my kids. But oh God, how could I have been so sure that my kids' teachers were so wrong? It's going to take a while to get the hang of this. But I am committed to becoming a boundary-setting partner with my kids' teachers and also in my own home. I know that I can now trust myself to know when a wall is being built rather than a good boundary being set.

Wish me luck!

W

Boundaries Expand as the World of Inner Speech Develops

When we have a big decision to make, we may go for a walk or sit quietly in our favorite chair and focus our attention inward. We seek to connect with that special inner voice that helps us work things through. This capacity for inner speech is what helps us regulate our emotions and impulses. When we have allowed ourselves enough time and space to have a "chat" (or inner chat) with ourselves, we can often resolve a conundrum and feel as though we can breathe freely again. Essentially, we have found high ground where the view of our lives is clearer, and the air is fresh and clean.

As children grow, they slowly develop this ability to engage in inner speech to guide their actions. If we, as parents, can better understand this developmental process, it will most certainly shed light on some of the very strange, frustrating, and even wonderful things children do. A mother of a three-year-old boy put it perfectly: "When I learned that inner speech balances impulsive behavior and that, at his age, my son's impulses were much stronger than his capacity for inner speech, everything changed for me. I calmed down a lot knowing that when he acted up he wasn't just being belligerent or defiant."

Inner speech has its own developmental process in which the brain goes through three major stages. These stages directly correspond to the three phases of discipline outlined in the introduction to this book. Let's explore these stages further:

STAGE ONE: THE YOUNG CHILD

The first phase begins when a toddler starts to speak. We notice that, though most of her speech is directed toward other people, the little child may babble away and occasionally say something like "I need to put Molly Dolly in her space suit now." What she is doing is guiding herself by talking things through out loud. How does this relate to behavior? At this stage, children don't yet have the capacity for *inner* speech, which is so vital for self-regulation. So they try to figure things out *aloud*. Keep in mind that a child between the ages of two and four can understand rules and even recite them for you verbatim, then turn right around and ignore or break them. "It's hard to realize that children are not yet able to regulate their own minds," says Dr. Dee Joy Coulter. "The brain cells which regulate inner speech also regulate motor impulses. Until the child is about four and has developed strong language skills, the speech powers of those cells just aren't capable of overriding the motor urges of those same cells."

Picture a pond teeming with large red fish and tiny blue fish. The wriggly red fish represent bursts of impulsive behavior. The calm blue fish help a child regulate and reflect on his or her behavior. Young children are equipped with a loosely woven neural net that can hold only big red fish. They may occasionally catch some of the little blue fish, but those tend to slip through and fall back into the water.

The key here is to realize that your young kids are not deliberately defiant. They are not consciously disobeying when they repeatedly drop food on the floor after being told not to. You may be certain they know the rules because you have told them again and again. But knowing them and being able to act on them are not the same thing. If you become frustrated and forceful and shout at a child who dumps his or her food on the floor repeatedly, your yelling doesn't increase the child's ability to self-regulate—to stop dropping the food. In fact, our antics can have very much the opposite effect. Scaring and shocking a child by yelling can delay the development of his or her inner speech. And it interferes with the bonding and attachment that is developing between you and your son or daughter. What's more, a child can become utterly confused because the adult is shouting *impulsively* about how being impulsive is bad and looks like a pretty scary person too while doing so.

STAGE TWO: THE TWEEN

A child from the ages of eight or nine to twelve is better able to hear his or her inner voice. It's not fully developed yet, but he can now think to himself, "I'd better not throw sticks and stuff down from this tree because my little brother can't look up and dodge them since he can only crawl, and my dad is just over there."

This inner-speech capacity also helps older children socialize. They can now begin to mull things over. For example, in a game of kickball, a ten-year-old may sense a potential conflict and avoid it by saying to herself, "Yesterday David got really mad when everyone said he was out. I am not going to say it now. Maybe I'll ask him about it later." Or it may be as simple as "Mom looks sad. She needs a hug." The key thing here is that the child between the ages of eight and twelve is learning to hit the pause button and engage in inner dialogue. This helps him or her to better understand family agreements and boundaries.

STAGE THREE: THE TEEN

The seeds of inner speech and reasoning, which first took root in the young child and started to bud in the middle years, come into full bloom in high school. Thoughts become more orderly as the teen begins to recognize sequences of events and figures out how to solve academic and social problems. The teen's reasoning may be subjective at first, but as time goes on, objectivity strengthens. It's impressive to hear teenagers say things like "I have been thinking about local versus organic food. Maria says that local is better because trucking food long distances is bad for the environment, but what about the gas that's used to truck in the pesticides used in the production of local nonorganic food? Doesn't that count?"

That neural net becomes more intricately woven and tightens as the young child grows into a teen. The net can now catch the smaller, calmer blue fish of inner speech along with those bigger, wiggly, impulsive red fish.

———

So how do we encourage this wonderful developmental capacity?

VERY YOUNG CHILDREN

At this tender age, children need to hear us think out loud to ourselves while at the same time signaling to them that we will help them do what is needed and accepted within the family. For example, when your three-year-old once again drops her food on the floor while sitting in her high chair, you've come to a crossroads. Do you go down the "angry, scary mommy or daddy road" or the road with the sign posted that says, THIS IS FRUSTRATING, BUT I KNOW WHY YOU ARE DOING IT? Armed with insight into why this just happened, it is possible for a parent to respond with "Oh dear, the food got on the floor again, and we all know it doesn't belong there. I think that tricky hand put it there. Hmmm, what can we do? I know—this bowl of rice needs to rest by me for now." Compare this with an irritated and forceful grab of the toddler's hand and angry voice saying loudly, "I have told you over and over *not to do that*! You know it is bad, *very* bad!"

FOR THE TWEEN

Dr. Coulter's recommendation is to "think aloud in front of our children, and honestly listen to them as they begin to talk about problems and ideas." This strategy is particularly helpful with tweens. For example, after listening to an eleven-year-old's plans for a sleepover with a friend, a parent may think out loud to her son, "Okay, I am not sure about how we arrange time for homework. I am thinking the answer might be to come home first for an hour, get it out of the way, and then be free of it. Seems to me that sleepovers can be so much more fun when there's no worry about getting into trouble the next day."

FOR THE TEEN

Teens are still impulsive, as we all know, but it is helpful to remember that they have access to inner speech. To help them access it, think out loud with them: "There are some gaps in my picture of what you are planning. Can you help me understand how hitchhiking there is better than waiting for the parts to arrive to fix your car? Can you think a little more about it and let me know after supper?"

———

As you can see from the examples given above, your tone and choice of words should change as the child grows, because you want to avoid being condescending. But the two currents that should run through our response to all ages are, first, modeling the reasoned behavior we hope to elicit and, second, giving them some time to develop their inner regulatory voice. The result of this? We stay calmer. They are drawn closer. And everybody is connected.

Governor—Gardener—Guide

Although developmental stages have been recognized by just about every child development expert in the past one hundred years, many parenting books—even some written specifically about discipline—make only occasional mention of the developmental appropriateness of different approaches to discipline. However, it is crucial to employ discipline within a developmental framework. Doing it any other way will trigger annoyance and anger in our kids. They will push back against us, because as teenagers, they don't want to be treated like babies, or, alternatively, when they are little, we may be asking too much of them, which frustrates them. There's so little disciplinary information out there that takes the changing needs of a child into account, yet this is exactly what effective discipline is all about.

I've described three important developmental phases above—the young child, the tween, and the teenager—but occasionally a metaphor fits a concept so well that we retain the meaning long after the actual words have faded from memory. Many parents have told me that, when they are in the middle of a tricky behavioral moment with a child, tween, or teen, my metaphor of Governor-Gardener-Guide

often comes to the rescue. Each word seems to accurately describe the
core of each of the three phases of discipline.

THE GOVERNOR PHASE: EARLY YEARS TO AROUND NINE YEARS OLD

In the Governor phase of parenting, we need to be the benevolent
Family Governor who knows the needs of our young son or daughter.
The Parent-Governor provides clear leadership and knows how to set
kind but firm boundaries that give a child a feeling of safety and well-
being. The parents in this phase of early childhood must do their best
to protect the "borders" of the family state as best they can by filtering
out aspects of life to which a young child should not be exposed. There
is really no way to do this effectively unless a parent is willing to be the
authority. The word "authority" shares a linguistic root with "author,"
and the Governor needs to be just that—the "author" of the family
values that enfold a young child.

THE GARDENER PHASE: NINE TO AROUND THIRTEEN YEARS OLD

A good gardener or farmer will watch and listen to what the earth is
saying or monitor the soil and its moisture content to know when to
plant and when to harvest. When is the right time to plant to be safe
from frost? When is the right moment to harvest so that the crops do

not turn out either under- or overripe? Patience and careful observation are necessary, but when the decision is made, it has to be total in its commitment. A farmer cannot sort of harvest a field of wheat. In the tween years, our kids need us to show them that we are listening, watching, and tuning in to their changing ways of being able to manage themselves. But they also need us to show them we're still in charge and responsible for each final decision.

THE GUIDE PHASE: THIRTEEN TO THE LATE TEENS

A guide knows the paths ahead. She has been helped, to some extent, by previous explorers who have mapped out their forays and shared their experiences. If they spoke clearly and sensitively, she most likely accepted their advice. Over years of exploring the terrain, succeeding and failing, the guide has made careful additions to her map, so while not complete, it is a good reference for any newcomer embarking on a journey.

A good guide also knows that there are many ways up a mountain and that a new explorer will have his or her own ideas about blazing new trails. This young explorer may also have special capacities to find routes through terrain that has previously blocked others. So when you provide guidance to your teen, you need to carefully balance your own experience with an acute sensitivity to the emerging life direction of your son or daughter. What the teen is mostly interested in is his or her own direction, *not* in hearing too much about your opinions. So when things go wrong, talk to teens about *their* direction and what helps and hinders them on that path.

When Development and Discipline Meet

One of the most frequent questions a parent asks about a son or a daughter's behavior is "Is this normal?" It usually comes mixed in with a hopeful "It *is,* right?" And yet, if it turns out that this questionable behavior is actually normal, then the parent may say, "Oh no, you mean that we have to put up with more of this?"

Understanding the capacities and limitations of children in each of the three phases will sharpen every parent's understanding of what is normal at each developmental stage.

To illustrate this, let's look at the three phases of child development. If you think of each phase as a basket (as in the illustrations for Governor, Gardener, and Guide), the key is to fit roughly the right amount of content (guidance or discipline) into the right vessel (developmental stage). Sounds hard. But it doesn't need to be if what is being suggested to you is simple and doable in the flow of regular family life. If the sug-

There's been a trend in the last decade or so to downplay the developmental stages of childhood, prompted by a belief that no two children are alike. That has a ring of truth to it, because as every parent knows, his or her child is unique. But if we reject the guiding wisdom and framework of the stages of development, we risk losing our bearings. Without realizing it, we can end up allowing things to enter our child's life that he or she is not even close to being ready to handle.

Fortunately, new brain-imaging technology has provided us with pictures that prove that developmental stages are real and that understanding the phases that all children, tweens, and teens go through is vital to nurturing their emotional health.

gestions come across as plain common sense, then we are on firm ground.

What you see on the right of this diagram is the stage of development of the child, tween, or teen. The Austrian philosopher and educator Dr. Rudolf Steiner explored three distinct capacities and phases of child development. Many influential child-development experts have also recognized these three overarching stages. Although the ages given are meant as a guideline—as, of course, children will develop in their own individual way—they do hold true for most kids. Here are three "baskets" representing the stages:

- **The Earlier Years (birth through around 8 years):** A life of action and movement—acting out of will—is typical of children in their first seven or eight years. It's all about impulse and what captures the interest of a child. It's great to see healthy children at this age explore the world intensively. There is so little separation between their inner lives and the world outside themselves.
- **The Tween Years (around 9 or 10 through 13 years):** We see this so often when things begin to change and the tween emerges. A tween at this age becomes more aware of his or her own feelings and, equally important, the feelings of others. He or she can be a better family team player now as new capacities for empathy begin to develop.
- **The Teen Years (around 13 or 14 through 19 years):** It's hard not to notice the new capacity for critical thinking about world events that leads a teen to question the values and motives of politicians, teachers, and, of course, parents.

You'll notice the baskets are different sizes. This illustrates which capacity is dominant at each age, which capacity is modestly present, and which is the smallest.

The Right Support at the Right Time

The Earlier Years (0–9)
Emphasis is on . . .
"I will decide."

THE GOVERNOR   The Gardener   The Guide

The Tween Years (9–13)
Emphasis is on . . .
"Tell me your plans. I will
listen carefully and then
I will decide."

The Governor   **THE GARDENER**   The Guide

The Teen Years (13–19)
Emphasis is on . . .
"Let's figure out how to
stay close to your hopes
and aims."

The Governor   The Gardener   **THE GUIDE**

Basket One

In the first phase—from birth to around the end of age eight and the beginning of age nine—children are action and exploration oriented. When they are toddlers, this is poignant, as we bear witness to their charming, funny, and utterly exhausting investigations of everything around them. It's all felt, tasted, smelled, and sized up with such serious intent, before being dropped on the ground when the next object of sensory research is sighted. It's at this age that we "spot" our children. We let them explore but move in quickly when they try to touch a rusty can lid with their fingers. We don't ask toddlers to consider possible tetanus complications. We make the obvious decision that the rusty can is not a safe plaything, and we remove it. Even if the child howls, no parent would cave and give it back. The same dynamic still applies to a child who is seven or eight years old, but the "voicing" of it changes as no eight-year-old wants to be talked to like a baby. We can feel tinges of the "tell me your plan" stage of the Gardener coming up as this earlier phase ends, and there will be times when taking that approach feels like just the right thing to do for an eight- or nine-year-old, but it is not yet the dominant, day-to-day discipline and support strategy.

What is fundamental to this exchange is the parent acting out of the "I will decide" principle. It's simple, healthy, and intuitive. No matter how many parenting books and experts tell us to give a child choices, parents have a basic gut intelligence about when not to negotiate. Even if a parent wants to allow limited choices, it is still the "*I will decide* to give my child limited choices" mode. It's still a Governorship.

Basket Two

In the second phase, from about eight or nine through around thirteen years old, the mantra is "Tell me your plan, and then I will decide." If you are in a two-parent or two-partner family, then it may be "Tell us your plan, and then we will decide." Kids love this because you're asking them how they see things. They're a little smarter now. They can see the world as a little more separate from themselves. This means they can start to make plans while taking others in the family into consideration.

One dad told me, "When my child was twelve years old, she just loved telling Mom and Dad her plans. She loved the fact that we would listen carefully to her picture of what she had in mind and take it seriously when deciding what we would do as a family. It seemed to satisfy something deep inside her."

At around ten or eleven, there is a beautiful balance. The child is clearly not a teen, no matter how much he wants us to believe he is, and yet the lovely and dear early childhood phase is fading. Most kids have not yet fallen fully into the heaviness of puberty—though it is on its way—and there is still a skip in your ten-year-old's step. This is why the middle basket—the largest—is like the midpoint of a seesaw. There are still some situations in which a parent needs to move in with firm, Governor-like boundary setting, but there are other moments when your twelve-year-old shows a flash of wisdom and maturity that signals to you that you can briefly be more Guide than Gardener and dole out more responsibility to your Buddha-like tween.

As your son or daughter grows up and enters the tween years, you may feel a bit sad that he or she is no longer your baby, but it is thrilling to see how capable your child is becoming. You can relax a little. There will be fewer nights spent sitting anxiously beside your fevered child. She has stronger forces to help her get through her illnesses. But something intuitive inside many parents knows that, although their children are stronger and more capable, they are still not ready for the big wide world. If we quietly stand by the bed of a sleeping nine-year-old child, we can still see that he is young and vulnerable, even though his toes now peep out from under the end of the blanket that used to cover him completely. Children this age are not little ones anymore, but they surely are not ready for the teen world, in which they will need more mature judgment to navigate the media-driven, overt sexuality; images of violence; and other assorted teenage temptations. So is there some kind of sensible middle ground?

Basket Three

This third phase is all about the slowly emerging direction a teen wants to take in life. The frontal lobes region of the brain becomes more active. This executive area of the brain helps teens clarify their ability to think their way through a situation. This is why the basket holding the compass bearings to achieving your teen's life direction is now the biggest and overshadows the other two.

Many teenagers can use critical thinking like a sharp chef's knife to slice up a situation and see all its facets. This can sometimes be frustrating for a parent, as this ability is often coupled with a lot of "dissing" and criticism. It's helpful to remind ourselves that negative criticism is just the lowest rung on the ladder of self-discovery and that our job is to help develop the dissing into a greater capacity for critical thinking in later teen years.

When guidance issues arise, the "Let's figure out how to stay close to your hopes and aims" approach is most effective. The wording may vary, but the gist will be the same. A parent is saying to a child, "This is about your hopes and path in life, and the main way I can help is to keep things moving in that direction and to step in when things wander aimlessly or into dangerous territory."

This way of working with a teen is golden. If you have a teenager at home now, have a conversation with her about her delicately formed ideas about the future. Then gently remind her of these hopes when things get hard for her with friends, at school, or with something that is happening in the family. This helps reorient your teen and moves you into cooperative territory. There is certainly still a young child–like pushing of the boundaries of healthy compliance going on, and also a tween-like exploration of how one can be a team player in the family, but thinking is now king.

In this third phase, both parent and teen are working with choices. Some choices a teen makes are insightful and well reasoned while others are spectacularly unrealistic and troubling. We're dealing with a developmental dichotomy: critical thinking and independence emerge one day, offset the next by confused and convoluted teenage thinking. At times, they surge forward with their plans and aims making determined solo runs. At others, they edge close to us, seeking shelter from a storm of expectations and responsibilities.

APPROXIMATE AGE	BIRTH – 8	9 – 13	14 – 19
What Develops?	Will	Feelings	Critical thinking
Key Capacities	Action	Planning	Choices
Inner Speech	Impulsivity dominates over inner speech	Impulse is balanced with inner speech	Inner speech dominates over impulsivity
Boundary Pushing	"You're no boss of me"	"I don't care about others"	"I'll do it on my own"
Parent Role	Governor	Gardener	Guide
Parent Response	"I will decide"	"I will listen and decide"	"We will decide"

Dealing with such unexpected setbacks, surviving squalls, and finding a way back to the path when lost all make a teen stronger. But, doubtless, teens truly need your parental guidance to help them navigate these tricky times.

One Stage Leads to the Next

With luck and some good guidance, your teen has gotten pretty close to his goals because the choices he made were mostly good ones. And when he did make a bad choice, he was able to accept suggestions and change course because he had learned to be a team player when he was in his tween years. He developed impulse control in his earlier years because, when he needed them, he met with loving but firm boundaries. He wasn't allowed to always do what he wanted, when he wanted it. And because of this, he has developed a strong will. Willpower and cooperation are essential if he is to get through whatever tough times lie ahead. A teen who didn't learn in her early years to respect boundaries and who did not develop good impulse control is likely to follow many false paths.

Teens make healthy choices because they've learned that their actions affect other people as well as themselves. They were taught this in the Gardener phase when you focused so strongly on social skills, when they learned that the adults around them listened to their plans but still gave them direction when it was needed.

There are many critical decisions that need to be made in the later teen years, so it's important that your guidance has helped your teen get to the developmental high ground and so be able to see the landscape ahead and choose a plausible direction. It may be which career to pursue, what college to attend, or which trade or interest to follow. These are the big decisions we hope we are preparing our children for as we work to understand the phases of development they are going through and try to provide the necessary boundaries they need so that they can grow to be strong, sensitive, and courageous individuals as they move out of the home garden and into the world.

part two

∞∞∞∞

THE
GOVERNOR PRINCIPLE

3

The Governor: The Five Essentials to Healthy Boundaries and Compliance

As parents, we are our children's first teachers. And though we may feel underprepared for this daunting responsibility, we try our best, knowing that the foundation we put in place needs to be deep, wide, and strong, so that what we build in later years has a solid and well-defined footing.

There are three distinct phases or "terrains" to navigate in our kids' journeys to adulthood. This chapter focuses on the first, which spans the early years—from birth through around eight or nine years of age. During these formative years, children are "mucky." They love to play in the soil, make tunnels, pile rocks, and build forts and especially to stay close to the earth. It's easy to observe how absorbed they become in pushing, placing, and shaping the objects they find in nature.

There is, in fact, something foundational about the way children this age pour all their energy into play and exploration. They instinctively know to play close to home or near a parent so they don't have to be distracted by concerns about their personal safety. Playing in this way—deep in the mud, down among the rocks, but within the comforting pale of parental protection—helps strengthen their willpower.

During this first developmental phase, everything we do to help make our kids feel safe and clear about who is in charge affirms this sense of safety and trust in their world. We are the kind but firm Governors of the "family state."

Healthy Compliance Builds Willpower and Good Governorship

Many parents have bought into the belief that if we give our young children a lot of freedom and myriad choices they will develop strength of character and willpower. Many are even wary of presenting themselves as authority figures within their own family: They worry they will squash the will of their child by introducing boundaries and providing direction. However, there is a significant difference between a Malevolent Dictator, who forcefully bends others to his or her will, and a Benevolent Governor, who acts out of caring to bring safety and calm to the family state.

Over the years, countless frustrated parents have approached me and said, "I have such a strong-willed child." What I suggest to them is that strength of will is often misunderstood. Perhaps their child is not *strong willed* but willful or *will filled*. In truth, a strong-willed child can learn to ease his interactions with his family or express his desires in a productive way. Strength of will is not so much about getting your own way as it is about being able to control impulses until the time is right.

Children who struggle with willfulness, on the other hand, are trapped in an internal (and eternal) cycle of trying to get their own way. When this bottled-up will bursts out, it causes friction with the parents, siblings, and friends who form the child's outside world.

Seven Differences Between Willfulness and a Strong Will

Strong Willed: Is flexible and can subtly adjust what she wants in order to keep moving forward.

VS.

Willful: Sticks rigidly to a course of action that gets her stuck.

———

Strong Willed: Is aware of others in the family and will look for where their needs align with his and reach out to them to keep from getting bogged down.

VS.

Willful: Finds himself more and more isolated and frustrated as he pushes harder to have his own way. Sees parents, siblings, and friends as obstacles rather than allies.

———

Strong Willed: Is clear about what she wants but is willing to get there one step at a time.

VS.

Willful: Has to have all that she demands "right now."

———

Strong Willed: Can bounce back quickly from a setback.

VS.

Willful: Becomes sullen for long periods and feels victimized.

———

Strong Willed: Stays focused on what he is doing or creating and can even come back to a task day after day.

VS.

Willful: Has short but intense bursts of energy that are often followed by aimlessness and exhaustion. Will lay claim to an area or toys he has long since stopped playing with if anyone else shows an interest in them.

Strong Willed: Focuses her willpower on creating play situations that include others. Is able to balance having the "funnest" time with the urge to be the boss. If she realizes she is being too bossy, she can dial it back a bit.

VS.

Willful: Needs to control and dominate almost all situations. If she is met with resistance, she increases her forcefulness and prefers to engage in conflict and risk losing friends rather than back down.

———

Strong Willed: Has a hunter's sense of timing and can "go for it" with total commitment and energy when he senses the time is right.

VS.

Willful: Will often do sort of the right thing, but at the wrong time, in the wrong way, at the wrong volume. Misses obvious cues that he is annoying or upsetting people and that it's time to stop.

———

How do we help a child if he or she is stuck in a state of willfulness, then? To be sure, most children move continuously between these two dynamics, but problems surface when their inner world (of needs and desires) becomes dominant and they become habitually willful, forceful, and controlling.

Limits and Boundaries Pave the Way for Compliance

Limits and boundaries instill feelings of safety, trust, and, above all, orientation in your child. Compliance to a parent's direction further solidifies your child's orientation. The compliance I refer to here is very different from the "blind obedience" many children experienced growing up in the fifties and sixties. Your child must not be forced to accept an edict from a rigid, overpowering authority. Soulful disciplinary compliance is firm yet loving. Furthermore, it is vital to a child's social

Pause Point

What are the roadblocks to better compliance at home?
And how can I get past them?

and emotional health. In learning to comply, a child accepts his or her parents' warm but unwavering direction and develops inner flexibility.

When a child in a playground is told by Mom or Dad that it's time to go home, a balancing act begins in his or her mind. "I want to keep playing" (my needs) rubs up against "I'd better do what Dad is telling me to do" (our needs). When the child learns to comply with his or her loving parent—whose goal is not only to raise a strong, caring child but also to get home in time for dinner—the child shifts away from the smaller sphere of self-centeredness and entitlement and toward a wider one of flexibility and social awareness.

As you'll recall from the introduction of this book, a child will not have to provoke or ping you into setting boundaries if they are made clear from the onset. When a child knows where she stands with respect to parental limitations, she is not spurred to negotiate incessantly. Clear and consistent boundaries provide a firm foundation for healthy compliance.

Some parents tell me their challenges are rooted in the blind-obedience parenting they suffered growing up. This realization is the first step in clearing such an obstacle. As one parent said, "I realized that, in order to parent more effectively and be able to set boundaries and handle my kids, I have to get beyond my own biography." Once you can develop an inner dialogue or self-talk, things can begin to change. Say to yourself, "I'm not going to be tripped up by what my parents did. I won't react to their extreme approach by being a lax doormat parent. I know it's best for my four-year-old if I insist on compliance, knowing that when he turns nine I can loosen the reins a bit, and again when he is a teen."

Anticipating your roadblocks can help you put things in perspective and make your parenting go a lot smoother. One parent said to me, "Well, my roadblock is that I can insist on compliance, but my partner in all this, my ex-husband, is an anything-goes guy. What do I do?" The best thing we can do in such situations is accept that we cannot control everything. When our kids are away from us, they are beyond our sphere of influence, and it's okay if they aren't disciplined completely consistently between parents. Remind yourself, "They may be able to get away with things at their dad's house, but none of that goes here." The fact that kids have to recalibrate when they come back into Mom's home—that they learn to shift their behavior according to their environment—is not a bad thing. In fact, it's a key part of their development into flexible, open-minded people.

Fostering this kind of inner dialogue may sound easy. It's not. But if you can develop constructive self-talk, figure out roadblocks, and deflect them, you will be in a much better position to parent effectively. If you'd like advice on techniques, post a question on the Soul of Discipline social-networking pages. Talk to other parents in your community about your roadblocks and theirs. Find out what they think and what works for them. It's important to be proactive. Anticipate possible challenges and draw up a plan to redirect them.

Five Essentials of Healthy Compliance and Governorship

Most parents would like their child to follow directions without getting bogged down in major negotiations or pushback. It makes life a lot easier and more fun, and, luckily, it's not that complicated to achieve.

There are five essentials to healthy compliance. Ronald Morrish describes four in *Secrets of Discipline,* a book that fully supports the parent being in charge. I've added a fifth to help make things a little more doable.

When you are about to give a direction to a child, stick to these five essential steps:

1. **Pause and Picture:** Pause, allowing your child a moment to orient herself. Even more important, center yourself as well. Picture yourself giving your child a direction that she fulfills well. Allow yourself to imagine success.

2. **Start Small:** Give your child an instruction that is in his or her doable range.

3. **Stay Close and Calm:** After giving an instruction, move in close to your child. You can give older kids a bit more space, but little ones respond well to a parent's physical proximity. Remain calm, collected, and centered. If you cannot remain calm, return to the Pause and Picture step.

4. **Don't Negotiate—Insist:** Don't get drawn into explorations of whatever angle your child can dream up to avoid doing what you have said. Insist quietly and calmly. Be a broken record. Your voice should be monotone but clear.

5. **Follow Through:** In our age of distraction, in which multitasking seems to be a grown-up word for ADHD, this can be a challenge. But it is vital to remain focused after you have given an instruction. Stick to it.

A Closer Look

Let's take a deeper look at the Five Essentials. Kids have an intuitive sense when it comes to knowing if a parent really "means it" when he or she is giving a directive. Your voice and presence will help your child *sense* your Governorship so that, in that moment of cost-benefit analysis when he weighs whether to comply with or ignore your instruction, he will more often choose compliance.

Developmental psychologist Gordon Neufeld uses the phrase "collect then direct" when speaking about guiding children. Most people interpret this to mean that you need to connect with your child before giving a direction, and that's certainly part of it. However, it's important to take a step back and connect with yourself as a parent *first*. If you take a moment to understand your own needs and feelings before giving an instruction, you are much more likely to stay calm, be kind, and stand firm.

Self-talk is critical to self-connection. You may even find it most useful to speak to yourself out loud (when no one is around, of course), or you can self-talk inwardly, especially since finding time alone is no easy feat for any parent. Even the bathroom becomes a public space when you have a young child.

One of the brain-based or cognitive benefits of self-talk, particularly when you feel anxious or uncertain about how to handle an unfolding disciplinary situation or an instruction that forces your child to transition from one activity to the next, is that it moves you away from your fight-or-flight response and into the part of your brain that processes speech. When this speech center is activated, your anxiety lessens, and a broader view of possibilities opens up.

Here are some examples of effective self-talk strategies:

"Do I really need this to happen?" one mom asks herself. That filters out some of the unnecessary instructions that she would otherwise give. If yes, she proceeds.

A parent who was told by his partner that he often gave directions that were too complex and demanding now pauses first and asks himself, "Is this instruction reasonable?" before calling it out.

Another dad confided that he often gave his young children instructions that were too complicated for a child to properly understand:

"My wife would look at me with gentle mockery in her eyes. 'Okay. You're stuck with that one. Do you need a hand?' she'd say." Now, he imagines his wife's voice guiding him toward simpler instructions.

As parents, our attention is pulled in so many competing directions, especially if we are caring for more than one child. But timing is everything, isn't it? One mother I spoke with always makes sure to ask herself, "Is this a good time and place to give this instruction?"

Defiance (or pushback) is often most pronounced when your timing is off. Context is key. As the colorful 1950s comedian Red Skelton put it, "Any child will run an errand at bedtime." It's not always possible, but try to choose an appropriate time and place before you provide guidance, and your child will be at his or her most receptive.

One mother took the importance of context truly to heart. Her key self-connecting question was "Can I limit distractions while we go through this?" She had four children and a busy household, so she got very practical. Every time she gave her daughter a "must do" instruction, she would take the girl to a staircase and have her climb to the "instruction step," which had previously been established and never changed. Since that staircase was one of the only places in the house that was screened from everything else, they could speak privately. She'd say, "Now then . . ." and pause as they sat there for a moment. Then she would give the instruction. What was so impressive was that both daughter and mother always came out of their stairway huddle looking calm and oriented.

Another mother, who worked full-time, told me she felt "out of whack" when she came home each day. She would blast forth a series of commands and questions as soon as she walked through the front door: "The house needs tidying." "Why was food left out on the counter?" "The table needs to be set." She didn't like the person she became in those moments. She felt like a space shuttle miscalculating its reentry point as it returned to earth from a mission on a faraway planet. "Everyone felt the heat as I exploded into the home atmosphere," she told me.

Pause Point

Ask yourself, "What is my own key self-connecting question?"

The solution she came up with? To pause for a moment each evening before walking through the front door. "There's a little playground across the street from our home," she said. "I would sit on a swing and sway back and forth for no more than a minute or two. I'd ask myself out loud, 'Are you feeling balanced?' Even if the answer was 'not really,' just stopping and asking myself the question helped a lot." That moment of self-talk helped her orient herself. She found that after quietly connecting with herself she could better control her reactions when she walked into the house. More often than not, she was able to approach her family with understanding and receptiveness instead of frustration and aggression.

If you are not sure, take a few days, and observe the moments when you come close to "losing it" or when your child ignores a direction you give. Why is the child defiant, or why does he or she blow you off? What would help you be more centered in those moments? Is there a pattern that you can identify? Once you understand when and how you are internally disconnected—and what you need to recover—your interactions with your kids in which you give a direction will improve. Simply put, to give a direction, you need to have a direction.

1. PAUSE AND PICTURE

Imagine your ideal scenario and then step into it. When we ask our kids to do a chore, we are too often instantly overcome by a "here we go again" sinking feeling. Rather than be stymied by premeditated defeat, imagine the job done successfully. Run a mental video from start to finish. See yourself and your child taking the compost out, emptying the bucket, bringing it back inside, washing it out thoroughly, and putting it back in the right place.

Athletes are taught to visualize successful outcomes at pivotal moments: to run a race in their minds, for example, and picture when they should break out, the turn they need to make, and so on. Parenting, like sports, requires you to be at your best and most creative in the pressure of the moment. And while no one will hand you a trophy at the finish line, the knowledge that you anticipated and ingeniously handled a tricky disciplinary situation is worth a dozen gold medals.

Imagine the outcome you hope for. Visualize laughter, cooperation, ease, or anything else that is important to you. Nothing too complicated. Don't worry about appearing goofy, because no one knows you're doing it. Before you say, "It's time to get in the car" or "It's time to come to the table," pause and imagine this scenario flowing in a natural and relaxing way.

On the Balcony and on the Dance Floor

In *Leadership on the Line,* authors Ronald A. Heifetz and Marty Linsky recommend that leaders get off the dance floor of daily life and up onto the balcony, where they can see the bigger picture and reflect upon it. Parents also have to occasionally step out of the fray to understand what's really going on. The key is to move back and forth frequently between the two realms. We often spend a great deal more time on the proverbial dance floor responding to the incessant needs of our kids. The Pause and Picture strategy ensures that we take a few more moments on the balcony each day. Things go a lot more smoothly when we have a balanced perspective on our family life.

2. START SMALL

Starting small involves three key concepts:

a. Doability.

The first concept is doability. If your kid has difficulty complying with instructions, start by choosing tasks that are not likely to cause a lot of pushback. For a month or so, while he or she gets used to following your directions more regularly, stay away as much as possible from hot-button issues. There will, of course, be times when you have to instruct on touchy issues, but what I'm talking about here is giving yourself time so that this way of giving directions feels familiar. Practice the things that are less controversial first, and build from there. It usually takes a couple of weeks for a child to get the message that a shift is occurring and that she must now do what her parents direct her to do.

b. Break it down.

If you meet resistance, break a task or instruction down into its component parts. For example, when you are working on improving compliance in your home, avoid saying things like "Let's set the table," as this is a broad and vague request, even though you may feel you are being perfectly clear. Instead, try "We'll put the forks out first. Can you remember which side they go on? That's not so easy." You're making it fun. You're warm, but you are also being as granular as possible. If such advice seems obvious, please forgive me. Over the years, I've found it remarkable how many parents issue grand instructions and only start to break them down into smaller parts (in a very frustrated tone) after they are ignored.

It's much better to divide a task into smaller parts before things go wrong. You might say to a child, "We're going to set the table now, but you know what? We're going to start with the forks." Then, if there's still resistance, try redirection involving your child's interests. Perhaps it's summertime, and you've just hauled him or her away from a game of making little waterways in the mud out back for a paper boat. If you involve water in the table setting, your child will instantly relate to the task. Say, "Let's see how many cups of water it takes to fill a jug." And then: "Can you place a cup full of water by each place mat?"

A certain kind of humility is required here. And you must trust the process. I hear parents say, "Look, I just want to tell him to set the table and be able to get on with it." But how often does it work just like that? The compliance muscle needs to be built up and exercised regularly. Eventually you will be able to say to your child, "Please set the table" and almost never have any trouble.

c. What can I influence? What is beyond my control?

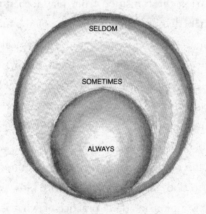

Looking at this diagram, most parents can instantly identify areas where their authority is strongest and weakest. If we try to exercise authority in areas where we do not have much of it, stress and self-doubt will result. Build your confidence by knowing what is in the "always" zone, where there's almost always compliance, and practicing techniques that are in the "sometimes" zone. Here are some examples of things that fall into each zone:

1. **Always:** Directing a young child to come and sit on your lap when you are about to read a story—it is nearly always a comforting moment for you both. You draw a child close and seldom meet resistance.

2. **Sometimes:** Asking children to clean up their jigsaw puzzles or tidy their room—both are tasks that have to get done but aren't necessarily as fun as reading, playing, or making the creative mess.

3. **Seldom:** Whether your child repeats inappropriate language that he or she heard at day care or school is seldom within your control.

Start small, and build a strong base of compliance first. Eventually your areas of authority will expand. For example, you may seldom have control during the transition from play to bedtime. Even after you've finally tucked your child into bed, he or she may call you with all kinds of unnecessary requests. Before the typical "bedtime skirmish" begins, give your child a series of small instructions that you are pretty sure he or she will comply with. For example, if he loves helping you fix things, ask him to be your assistant as you set out the tools for tomorrow's mending project. If she has a gift for caring for animals, have her help you brush the dog. These easy-to-follow tasks will bring the two of you closer together right before the bedtime transition. This slipstream connection between parents and kids will extend into harder areas. It is a bite-size daily practice of what is known as "Attachment Theory," in which a child forms a bond with the parent who nurtures and protects him or her. Here, we are using it as part of our daily Soul of Discipline practice to build authority and direction within a family.

Remember, you are not giving up on the "seldom" column, but it's most important to first focus on the instructions that will build up warmth and connection. Countless parents have reported that within

Pause Point

Finally, it's important to identify which instructions are most likely to be followed. Take your time, and be as practical as you can.

1. Which of my directions are ALMOST ALWAYS followed?
2. Which of my directions are SOMETIMES followed?
3. Which of my directions are SELDOM followed?

weeks of applying the Five Essentials, their "almost always" list has grown considerably.

3. STAY CLOSE

The four Stay Close principles are:

The Proximity Principle
Stay close to the physical location where you expect your direction to be carried out. Kids can be slippery little customers, outa here in the blink of an eye. If you give a direction and walk away, things seldom work out as hoped.

The Siphoning Principle
Step in to help when needed to ensure that your direction is being acted upon. Step away when your child is getting into the flow of the task you have given him or her. If your child's focus starts to wane, move in again, but don't stay too close if you don't need to. Experiment with this. See how far away you can go and how many times you need to return to get things moving again. You are giving your child attention

and support but also withdrawing when things are going well. This gives him the sense that he can do more and more on his own and be successful.

The Scanning Principle

Get on with your own to-do list, but remain within earshot and view of your child. That way, he or she feels your presence and notices that you are also working. This creates a sense that you are getting things done together, which counterbalances a child's "I don't want to do this" stance.

The Imitation Principle

Young children learn so much from watching us and copying. There are "mirror" neurons in the human brain that help a child not only imitate an action but also understand the intention of a parent or sibling. "When you see me pull my arm back—as if to throw the ball— you also have in your brain a copy of what I am doing, and it helps you understand my goal. Because of mirror neurons, you can read my intentions. You know what I am going to do next," University of California, Los Angeles, neuroscientist Dr. Marco Iacoboni told *The New York Times.* In an article titled "Cells That Read Minds" (January 10, 2006), Dr. Iacoboni explains, "When you see me perform an action—such as picking up a ball—you automatically simulate the action in your own brain." Dr. Iacoboni further explains that mirror neurons work best in real life, when people are face-to-face. Virtual reality and videos are shadowy substitutes.

If you've just given a direction to a child, don't immediately turn away to your computer or phone. Resist the urge to check email or answer a text. Because when you do that, you are modeling distracted behavior to your child. She will perceive you as being wishy-washy. And accordingly, she will mirror you by responding vaguely and distractedly to your request. Kids learn and grow by imitating, so it's hardly fair to get frustrated with them for being so distracted when we lack focus ourselves.

4. DON'T NEGOTIATE—INSIST

No negotiation, no justification, no deviation, no repetition. If you give direction to a child, there is no need for any of that. When you dither, you throw the door to negotiation wide open. So it should be no surprise when in walks what we in Australia call a "bush lawyer"—an amateur attorney who wants to argue every point and analyze every little thing you say.

"Shouldn't we let our kids ask questions?" you might ask. "Isn't it good to encourage them to discuss and debate?" Yes. Of course it's healthy for kids to develop their own plans, strategies, goals, and desires. But negotiation with a young child is the right thing at the wrong developmental phase. Including him in planning and decision-making will be completely appropriate in a few years, when he is a tween (and even then, there's a big difference between talking plans with an eleven-year-old and getting mired in negotiations). Young children are simply not equipped to handle that kind of power. It gives them a false sense of entitlement and triggers fear and insecurity because it makes them feel like no one is in charge.

Jack Petrash, who wrote *Covering Home* and is the former host of Pacifica Radio's *On Parenting,* talks about the importance of flat-line responses: He explains that parents should just take the flat line with your child. You don't have to be warm and bubbly. You don't have to be cold. Aim for somewhere in between. Guide your child with a mantra-like unchanging tone of voice.

You might say, "No, Jon, we pack up our toys like this" as you place a block in the block basket. Then again: "No, like this. No. We are not going to question why. We do it like this." This is not repeating the details of the instruction and getting into long explanations, it's just calmly and lovingly insisting on the direction you gave.

Never Repeat an Instruction

What parent has never said—in an exasperated tone—something like "Why do I have to tell you this over and over?"

Rather than repeat an instruction over and over, say something like "No, no, we do it like this. No, no, no, Sophie, like this. No, no, dear, like this." Be very wary of one-sided conversations that go like this: "Would you please pack up your dolls?" "I have already told you to pack up your dolls." "If I have to tell you one more time to pack up your dolls, there will be trouble, young lady!" When a child ignores your instruction three or four times, your authority *and* your relationship are undermined. She perceives that she has a choice about when to listen to you and when to ignore you. And when this happens, parents often fall into a negative pattern. They get more intense and threatening in order to elicit the sought-after response. This can lead to a relationship dynamic in which the parent has to appear aggressive and angry in order to get anything done. Some parents tell me they just jump straight to being forceful since they know that nothing gets done when they are kind and gentle.

Just as bacteria become resistant to overprescribed antibiotics, the child who is habitually spoken to in an emphatic manner may develop an immunity to coercion. The parent then has to ramp up the dose of forcefulness needed to break through to the child.

Being coercive is *exhausting*. We become exhausted and feel like parental failures when we have to spend so much of our time stuck in a "current" of coercion. It's not really who we are or want to be as parents. And yet it's a very common parent-child interaction pattern. The good news is that this cycle can be broken. We can dial things back using the Five Essentials. We need to focus on quietly helping kids do what is instructed rather than saying the same words over and over and hoping for a better outcome as we repeat them more and become more assertive with each repetition.

When You Get a No Response

If you have given a direction that your child has ignored or resisted, use the two previous steps in the Five Essentials: start small and stay close. After you've asked your daughter to clean up and she's said, "No, I won't," move in closer and make the task smaller by saying, "Let's pack the dolly clothes up first, and we'll deal with the furniture later." That works much more effectively than force. Whatever you do, don't repeat the direction again and let things escalate into conflict.

Defiance and the Problem with Giving Consequences

If you try breaking it down into small tasks and getting closer and are still getting no as a response, your son or daughter may be really stuck. Stick with the Five Essentials. It can be really tempting to throw up your hands and say something like "If you don't clean up this mess, I will pack all of your toys away, and you won't see them again." You may think such a dramatic approach will spur compliance. But it won't.

How Consequences Undermine Compliance:

1. They throw the door to negotiation wide open.
2. They give the child a choice. She may run another cost-benefit analysis and decide that, rather than give in to you, she will give up the dolly clothes.
3. They create a win-lose situation: The child has succeeded in having you clean up the clothes, which you did as you took them away (child victory number one). She also most likely suspects that, if she nags you enough, you will relent in a day or two and give them back (child victory number two). Now

you've lost twice, and what's worse, you've spun into an ineffective disciplinary cycle.

Why Does This Make Us Exhausted? If a child says no and is in an escalating defiant state, it is very unlikely that talk will help shift the situation. We've all fallen down that rabbit hole. The more you talk, reason, shout, plead, and shout again, the more your child digs in his or her heels. Children use very little energy in simply disobeying you, whereas you may go on an energy-burning tirade that leaves you exhausted, depleted, and even resentful.

Economy of Engagement When your child is stuck in reckless defiance and you're getting that sinking feeling, remember the power of Pause and Picture. Take a moment to exhale, and take charge of yourself and the situation. Say something like this to your child: "I can see that you are stuck. I know that doesn't feel very good. We'll come back to tidying later, but for now we'll sit here and take a break." The child may not show it, but he or she will be relieved by this change of energy. During this pause, picture the task you set for your child being done well. The moment you pull yourself out of the "forcefulness current" and focus on a positive image, you move from your "fight" brain into your collaborative, creative brain. What's more, your child can sense this shift within you and will feel safer and more relaxed, and he will unfreeze from the defiance he has become stuck in.

Sit for a couple of minutes if you need to, though this may be a long time for a child. After you feel calmer, resume the task. But reduce it to what is doable. The key here is to return to your instruction calmly and firmly to ensure that it is followed. You are the Governor of your family state. Your word is law. You'll be pleasantly surprised that, after only a few episodes of calm but firm insistence, your child will respond when his or her parent has set a boundary and given an instruction and will not be blown off track.

5. FOLLOW THROUGH WITH LOVING TENACITY

Following through is critical to foundational discipline. But it's not always easy in the chaos of daily life. It all comes down to your ability to focus and stick to your word. I call it *loving tenacity*. When you stand your ground in disciplining your child, you are not only helping him or her learn about boundaries and flexibility but modeling following through as well. Your child then senses that you are someone who can be trusted.

Parenting is about prioritizing multiple individual tasks rather than multitasking. If you are working through a difficult disciplinary situation and are moving in a positive direction, don't lose focus and move on to something else before your child has fully complied with your direction. There is hardly anything more important in the world than following through. Say something like "That was hard, Josh, but you cleaned up well even though you didn't want to at first. You were very helpful. Now you can go outside and play."

You have done the hard work to help your child comply with an instruction. You made it doable and reasonable, you stayed close by, and you broke the habit of negotiating. You quietly insisted that what you say needs doing must be done.

Parents often wonder, "What if you're doing all this compliance stuff and dealing with one child, but you've got two other kids in the house?" When you're working through a situation in a warm but firm way with one child, the other children often sense a change of climate in the house. As one mom said in a workshop, "It not only makes things quieter, but the others come around, watching me focus on whoever needs it at the time. They seem drawn to us and are interested because they can usually see that whoever is being spoken to has crossed the line." She added with a smile, "They assure me that they're good children and that they would never do what their brother did."

Transitions That Work

So many parenting flash points occur in moments of transition. Say you need to pull your child away from something he is doing. You feel guilty because he was enjoying himself or hesitant because you anticipate his unhappiness and anger. Kids pick up on these feelings, making the transition even more difficult. And many of these moments occur in public places such as the playground or a store with a play space. All eyes are on us as we struggle through public meltdowns, so you can add acute embarrassment to hesitancy and guilt.

Transitions become troublesome when we try to take our kids away from an activity before connecting with them and the activity that they've become so absorbed in. First connect; then direct. Young children do not see themselves as separate from the environment they live in. It's why they touch, taste, smell, feel, and gaze at everything around them with such intensity. They have not yet developed the ability to stand back and look at the world in an impartial way. Children pour themselves into play. They become one with the scene, structure, or game they have created. It's beautiful to witness this happy, unselfconscious concentration. The most problematic transitions come when a parent tries to move a child quickly from a state of connectedness to what they were engaged in to a situation that is vague for them and they have little relationship with where they are being directed to go or what they are being told to do.

Imagine a child is playing in the mud and sand, making rivers and streams to direct the water she pours in. There are twig bridges, pebble roads, and a mud dam. Dad has enjoyed spending time helping but is also aware that they need to pick up his older child from school and get everyone home before the low-blood-sugar skirmishes begin. He has already given his customary five-minute warning. But that only spurred his daughter Mazy to gather an even bigger pile of rocks and twigs. Dad now anticipates some pushback and says with firmness,

"It's getting late—we have to go now." Mazy resists. She says she hasn't finished yet. He responds that he told her five minutes ago that they would need to go. Her stubborn stance signals to Dad that the only way to get going is to pick her up and carry her crying to the car. He wrestles to buckle her seat belt. People are watching. When they are finally under way, he says, seething inside, "Mazy, that was very naughty. If you can't finish up your game when I tell you to, then we are not coming to the playground anymore." Mazy lets loose a deafening howl.

Such transition drama sounds all too familiar to many parents. But transitions do not have to be harrowing. These practical techniques can help make them much less arduous:

YOUR WORLD–MY WORLD–OUR WORLD

Understand how self-involved children become. Rather than crash into their world waving our agendas, bring them back gently. First your world, then my world, and lastly our world.

Your World:

A child's world is a space all of her own. She may be reading a story or playing with her dolls. If you want to prepare her for a transition, approach calmly and sit beside her quietly. Some parents like to do something of their own while they sit, like lace a shoe, knit, or sharpen a pencil. That way you aren't interrupting. You are sharing the moment. Your child may look up and say, "It's, like, a robot. The robot's got these killer ants. And the ants are going . . ." And with that story, you connect with your child. Even if neither of you say much, she is very much aware of your presence. This step usually only takes fifteen to thirty seconds.

My World:

After you have connected in this manner, a child will be much more open to the fact that you've got a world too. Infants tend to be easier to enfold within a parent's energy, as they still are in or want to inhabit this protective sphere. From about age three or four, things start to change as children seek to become more independent. Starting at this age, they need a bridge to cross to their parents' world. Say something like "Yes, a flying robot can do a lot. We'll set the table when I'm done making the salad." Such words form that bridge. You've acknowledged your daughter's flying-robot-versus-killer-ant worldview, but you've also signaled to her that you are cooking supper, and both of you will set the table when you finish your clearly explained task.

Our World:

You have now laid the groundwork for a successful transition. Not only have you connected with the child, but you have also connected the child to the next part of the day. If you had simply told her what to do and insisted that she respect the parameters of your world, she would have experienced a sharp transition, felt disconnected and disoriented, and likely pushed back. All it takes is a few seconds and a matter-of-fact sentence or two. For example: "Okay, let's park your cars back in the garage, and then we're going to fill the water jug." Or "Come, let's fill the water jug and see if you can carry such a heavy thing all the way to the table by yourself."

A tip here: As you refer to the water jug, start pulling it out of the cupboard. A young child relates much better to seeing and doing than to words alone. The same strategy can be applied to an older child, though your tone, of course, will be different, since older kids bristle if they feel like they are being talked down to.

What About Time Warnings?

Some parents think that time warnings can help transitions. "We're going to set the table in five minutes," they'll announce. And then they'll say, "Two minutes until we set the table." Time warnings often backfire. Very few little children have the brain capacity to understand something as abstract as time. When they are faced with it in the form of an ultimatum, they're apt to handcuff themselves to their Legos or go back to feverishly digging a hole to store supplies for the long siege ahead. Time warnings do little to help connect children to the next part of their day. There's no picture that they can create to associate with "five minutes" to give it meaning.

Doesn't All This Take a Lot of Time?

One mother I worked with was highly skeptical about how much time the Your World–My World–Our World strategy could save her family. She worked as a systems analyst (or efficiency expert—yikes!) at a blue-chip company. But after using the technique, she saw "significant time savings," and what's more, she noticed "a better mood throughout the day." She realized you might save a few minutes in the short term when you force a child to transition quickly, but you invariably set off a cascade of refusals and hours of bad-tempered resistance. The net result: much more time lost. What parents like most about Your World–My World–Our World is that transitions that were once the source of endless aggravation become moments of warmth, tenderness, and connection.

Make Transitions Rhythmic

There are some transitions you can predict and plan out and, of course, others you cannot. You may know that you need to get your kids into the car every weekday to take them to day care or school. Building a routine around this transition can be extremely helpful. When a transition is rhythmic, the child's inner clock and muscle memory adjust to it quickly. The child does not need to think about the transition and figure out how to navigate what, to him, are the complex steps involved in getting to the car.

One mom told me, "My daughter is such a magpie. She doesn't purposefully try to drag transitions out and make them unbelievably frustrating. It's just that she always gets distracted by half a dozen shiny objects along the way." When this mother made her transitions predictable and rhythmic, she found that her daughter's distractedness decreased because she was "carried along by the familiarity of the drill."

A few practical ways to do this:

Little habits. Do all the little things to prepare for the transition exactly the same way every day. For example, place the lunch boxes in the same place on the counter; hang the backpacks on exactly the same pegs, with corresponding shoes underneath facing the same way; and so on. This may seem pedantic, but it's astonishing how much that kind of repetition and familiarity helps children feel safe and transition more smoothly.

Time. Make the transition at the same time every day.

Hum a little song. It may sound strange, but quietly singing or humming helps shift your child (and you) into the brain center that promotes cooperation. That's why we often join in with a song we know. Don't worry if you don't meet concert standards! It will still be soothing. And it's helpful to hum the same song for each transition.

One father's experience underscores how effective rhythms are for transitions. "Ever since we started focusing on rhythm, it's like the kids go on autopilot, and we just make the change," he said. "You cannot believe how much easier this is than the nag-filled skirmishes we suffered through every morning."

I hope this chapter has helped you understand that the current parenting trend, which assumes that a young child has the emotional and decision-making capacities of a teen or adult, is misguided. When a child is given too many choices, serious behavioral problems result. If you take time to absorb and put into practice some of the healthy, sensible, and doable alternatives in this chapter—such as the five essentials to healthy compliance—you will establish firm ground under your parental feet. In the next chapter, we'll delve deeper into healthy compliance strategies, exploring ways to develop and strengthen impulse control and lay the groundwork for the future development of vital skills such as empathy and perspective taking.

4

Practical Strategies for Building Healthy Compliance

Many parents take issue with the idea that a child should "comply" with directions. They worry that if they take too strict an approach, they risk becoming *disconnected* from their child. This is a reasonable concern. Severe, inflexible parenting often creates emotional fissures between parent and child, which can widen and worsen over time. The key to healthy compliance in parenting, though, is to be warm and kind but also firm in your authority. When you are quiet and grounded in the conviction that your instruction is fair and reasonable (and will be carried out), you strengthen your connection and relationship with your child. Kids who are parented this way feel safe and know instinctively that they are in loving, authoritative hands.

To teach your children healthy compliance, start by helping them learn to control their impulses and delay gratification. The importance of these twin pillars of self-control is underscored by the well-known Marshmallow Test, whose results are unambiguous.

Forty-five years ago, hundreds of four-year-olds were given the ultimate test of willpower. They were stuck in a small room with a marshmallow or another yummy temptation and given a choice: devour the treat immediately, or abstain for fifteen minutes and be rewarded with two. Most of the kids agreed to wait, but many could not follow through. Some ate the marshmallow within the first minute. Others delayed gratification for five or even ten minutes before succumbing.

The children who succeeded in waiting for the full fifteen minutes devised ways to distract themselves from the temptation before them: They sang, talked to themselves, and covered their eyes. Years later, researchers found that the kids who had been able to delay their gratification in the original study were less likely to struggle with drug addiction, obesity, or behavioral problems than their snack-gobbling counterparts. The delayers also scored an average 210 points higher on their SATs.

Any parent would hope his or her child falls into the successful-delayer category. A parent who realizes her child lacks strong impulse control might fear that he will struggle throughout his life. The good news is that the researchers discovered that even children with under-developed impulse control can change as they grow up. How can we help shape this tendency so that it does not remain a lifelong obstacle?

"NOW" Demands

If your child wants something *"now,"* let her know the *w* always drops off when she wants to know the answer right away, turning "now" into "no." One dad told me, "The worst parenting decisions I make, the ones I really regret later on, are when I respond too quickly to a demand from my son."

We have gotten so used to living in an "on-demand" world that we are in danger of letting it spill over into our relationships with our kids and what they expect from us. Teachers and school counselors will tell you that the number one reason kids get into trouble at school these days is poor impulse control. Help your children exercise their "waiting muscle" when they demand an instant response. You are not giving them a hard time but building up an essential skill. Little by little, request by request, they will grow stronger as they learn to wait for your response.

Our kids are stepping into a world in which an increasing number of jobs will be contract based or part-time. Many of them will need to be self-employed self-starters. Patience and a good sense of timing will be critical skills in such a competitive future. They will need to be able to wait until they see an opportunity and then seize it. Children used to learn this ancient skill when hunting. If you didn't know how to hold back, to wait quietly, and if you had poor timing, you went hungry. Impulse control was linked, in the most basic way possible, to survival.

If a child can't connect the ability to control impulses with accomplishment, he will become weaker willed as he grows up. And more important, he will become *more* rather than less dependent. This puts an entire generation of children at risk and turns child development on its head.

It is up to us to stem this tide. Every parent wants his or her child to grow stronger and more autonomous. With the exercises and techniques provided in this chapter, you can build your child's healthy compliance. If you do the groundwork day by day, you can help your children learn to control their impulses.

When a child pushes you and you give in, she gets the answer she wants and learns to do it again and again. Children who do this make sure to catch their parents by surprise because a distracted parent is much more likely to say yes. Changing that habit will take some preparation. Start with a brief conversation with your child. Say something like this: "From now on, Toby, if you ask me a question, I'm going to take the time I need to give you an answer. If you want an answer right away, you will get one, but it will be a no, and I will mean it."

When we show children on this basic level that we need time to pause and think, we are modeling exactly what it is we are asking them to do. We might say "Just wait a few seconds" or "I'll sleep on it," but either way we are not only asking that they develop patience and good timing but also practicing it ourselves. If we do this effectively, they will begin to mirror us.

Serial Interrupters

Never allow a child to interrupt an adult conversation. Unless someone is bleeding, choking, or vomiting, they must not break in. Helping our kids learn not to interrupt adult conversations is critical to teaching them impulse control and getting them to exercise their waiting muscle on a daily basis.

To illustrate the all-important workout plan for this muscle detailed below, let's meet Sophie, interrupter extraordinaire. Sophie is six. And boy does she hate to wait. Sophie believes that the moment she has something to say everything and everyone must stop and listen. She insists on being heard. The adults in her life have reinforced her sense of absolute entitlement by always breaking off mid-conversation and turning to her (even kneeling down) to collect her pearls of wisdom. This has happened so often that she truly believes her needs are supreme, when very often what she has to say can wait.

Here are four simple steps you can take to help your child break the habit of interrupting and in doing so improve self-control, timing, and impulse control:

STEP ONE

When your little serial interrupter approaches you, hold your hand up in the universal signal for "stop" and make no eye contact. Don't look at her. The message is clear. Keep having the conversation with your spouse, your friend, your colleague, or the teacher. Don't break from conversation; just put your hand up (high enough that she can't give you a "fresh" high five).

STEP TWO

Keeping your hand firmly in the stop position, carry on with your friend. Say something like "I'd love to hear more about that, Margaret. Sophie is getting better about waiting, but excuse me, Margaret. I'm sure she must have something important to say. Otherwise, she would not want to interrupt." Now you have made your child wait for about five seconds.

STEP THREE

Now that you have modeled simple politeness in excusing yourself from your conversation with your friend, affirm your child with a "Thank you for waiting, Sophie. It's not so easy to wait." It should be a very matter-of-fact, no big deal, no Fourth-of-July-fireworks thank-you.

STEP FOUR

Listen. Say something like "Sophie, dear, tell me your story *briefly*. Remember, not a long story, as Mrs. Brown [Margaret] is kindly waiting." If Sophie is not successful in keeping it brief, don't hurry her along, as that may make her lose track and go right back to the beginning. Pack a runaway story up with a closing reflection, something like this: "Okay, I get it. It seems like Dylan has really been bothering you. Oh dear. You stay with me here while I visit with Mrs. Brown. We'll sort this out in a moment." Or if you're lucky, it could be "Why don't you give playing with Dylan a rest and go over to the sandbox and see if anyone's left a spade you can dig with?" (though only if you've noticed that there actually is a spade).

Now it is important to turn back and round off your conversation. Don't rush it, but don't go on and on either, as that really discourages a child. Give it another ten or fifteen seconds. If Sophie's in the sandbox, let her go. But if she really pushes, then just dust off the "now" response: "Sophie, love, do you want a 'now' answer? Because I've got one ready right here, and you remember what it's going to be." Then turn back to Margaret, and finish up your conversation.

Let's imagine all that worked, because it's simple, doable, and commonsensical. Hooray! But nothing is *that* simple. It takes a bit of time to break a habit, particularly one as ingrained as interrupting. You probably won't have to wait long for another interruption. The good news is that when the next one happens you don't have to remember anything other than the simple four steps outlined above. There is one crucial difference, though. This time, Sophie will have to wait longer. Extend her first wait from five seconds to about twenty seconds. And after a few twenty-second waiting periods, try thirty seconds. One dad I worked with on this technique told me, "It sounded a bit like puppy training, and that put me off. But honestly, I was willing to try anything that could help me handle my son's constant interruptions. What stunned me was how quickly he learned to wait until it was a good time to ask me something. It's embarrassing when I think how long I put up with something so frustrating that was relatively easy to fix."

A mother of nine-year-old twins said, "They no longer cut across our conversations. What they do is circle us, at a distance, waiting for a break in the conversation so they can tell me what they need. My friends were blown away by how respectful my kids are." Another dad shared what his five-year-old said when he spoke to him about not interrupting: *"I hate it when people won't stop talking when I am erupting!"*

So what is going on when you use these steps?

- You are modeling respectfulness toward your friend right in front of your child.
- You are modeling focus and attention by having only one conversation at a time.
- You are teaching a child that he or she will not lose your attention by waiting.
- You get a chance to quietly (and publicly) affirm your child for his or her ability to be patient.

Lastly, a key question: What's in it for the child? The simple answer: your undivided attention.

The Attention Wars

Attention is one of the most critical assets we can employ when laying the groundwork for our children's healthy development. But in today's fast-paced world, maintaining focus is particularly hard. Our attention is often split. And perhaps our biggest daily challenge centers on how we use screen media, particularly our cellphones, while we parent.

This isn't some abstract social issue emblazoned across a glossy magazine cover. We are interrupted daily, even minute to minute, when we are with our kids—each time the phone rings or a text message chimes. When we receive that alert, how we respond is sending a clear message.

In that moment, what is more important—the phone connection or the connection with your son or daughter? The message that millions of kids receive dozens of times each day: *The screen is supreme.*

The bottom line is that when we check our phones, email, and texts incessantly in the presence of our children we are disrupting our connection with them. As we obsessively try to stay connected with the outside world, we inadvertently sever the parent-child pipeline—the most important one of all. So it should come as no surprise, given how we behave around them, that our kids interrupt right back. Often, they aren't really being naughty. Rather, they are fighting fiercely for our attention against stiff electronic competition. What better way to make themselves visible than to be goofy or fresh to force a response? Our kids feed on our attention, and if they can't get it by being normal, they will act abnormal. We have set up a problematic cycle here that is reinforced daily.

THE FIRST ATTENTION WARS CYCLE

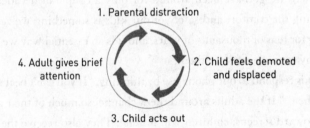

1. Parental distraction

4. Adult gives brief attention

2. Child feels demoted and displaced

3. Child acts out

The Troublesome Truth About Screen-Distracted Parenting

Little kids live in a world of *doing*. And as the old saw goes, *actions speak louder than words*. Kids pay attention to our actions much more than they do to what we say. It's what they base fundamental critical judgments on, about who is and who isn't safe to be with. A parent who postpones checking his phone and focuses his attention on his family sends a powerful, positive, reinforcing message of safety.

It's very hard, of course, for us to resist that primal tap on the shoulder: the text message alert or the phone buzz. Responding immediately connects very deeply to our basic survival instinct. With each ping or vibration, a potent mix of hormones, including adrenaline and cortisol, is released, and our inner voice calls out in a slightly panicked tone, "Oh no! What's wrong?" We feel compelled to meet the potential danger (even though we know that most of the time there is nothing at all to worry about). Relief floods through us when we confirm that there is no danger, and the phone now becomes a source of relief and pleasure. What an emotionally complex little device we keep in our pocket at all times!

When that alert sounds, what do we value most? Our need to answer to relieve our anxiety or our child's sense of security? It's as basic as that. Excuses like "Oh, that's just the way it is nowadays" can obscure our primal duty to our children. Phones that accompany us everywhere we go have been around for only a couple of decades, but ensuring the comfort and safety of our kids is something we've been doing for tens of thousands of years, and it is an essential way we build healthy connections with them.

Kids respond to our phone use by thinking, "If you can't beat them, join them." If the adults around them channel so much of their attention toward screens, children will imitate. They also receive the message that *screens provide comfort.* Screens are a panacea. They offer escape.

The outcome of this redirection of attention and interaction is a stark erosion of family life. Parents who check out by plugging in fail to provide their kids with feelings of security and safety. And when you redirect that energy away from your children, you risk abdicating your position as central authority and nurturer in their lives. Parental influence fades each time you disappear into a virtual world of friending and cyber connections.

The Relationship Vacuum

Children who feel displaced due to a parent's preoccupation with screens go through four stages:

STAGE ONE

"See me!" (Child-Initiated Reactive Attention Seeking): The child will act out and try to provoke adult response.

If this is unsuccessful . . .

STAGE TWO

"Whatever." (Ambivalent Attention Seeking): The child copies the parent and now gives her primary attention to the screen instead of to her relationships. Sad? Yes. But understandable. And underneath it all, a child may hold the hope that she can revive her connection by "parallel playing" (an early play stage) with her parents—using screens next to them—or may think, "They will miss me and be sorry."

STAGE THREE

"Hear me!" (Adult-Initiated Reactive Attention Seeking): You may now presume that things have improved because your son or daughter is no longer acting out. Home life may suddenly seem a little easier. However, you're bound to become frustrated, forceful, and even angry when your child ignores your requests. Your child may either continue to hold on to her blasé attitude, or she may reestablish her relationship with you because you are paying attention again.

However, either way . . .

STAGE FOUR

"I am the boss." (Inverted Authority): Your child steps into the leadership vacuum created by your preoccupation with screens. His subconscious strategy has worked. The tables are turned. You are now sidelined and risk losing your standing as the central authority in your family. Your child intensifies his relationship with the virtual world in order to maintain the safety he experiences by filling the leadership and power vacuum with his relationship to the digital device.

Simple Hope

There is still hope in this otherwise unhealthy interpersonal dynamic. Since we are the ones who kick-started this cycle by withdrawing too much of our attention from our children, we have the power to change it. The tricky part? We have to be conscious and courageous enough to stand up to the new normal: the highly *distracted* parent. No big announcement needed. Nor should we douse ourselves in mea culpa. We *just need to do it,* to place our connection with our family well above our connection to screens.

Here are some strategies that parents have found very helpful:

Ten Ways to Avoid Screen Distraction

1. **Anticipate:** If you are expecting an important message, tell your child ahead of time. Let him or her know you don't like breaking away and that this is an exception.

2. **Plan B:** If you suspect you may need to take a call when you are with your child, set him or her up with a simple activity while you are engaged. Try to make the call brief by agreeing on a better time to chat or promising to email back. Tell your child that if he or she doesn't interrupt your call, it will go even more quickly.

3. **"Thank you":** Give your child a quick and simple affirmation for waiting: "Thank you, Jenny. It's not easy to wait, and you really helped Mommy a lot."

4. **Respect the call:** Briefly tell your caller or texter, "Great to hear from you. I really want to focus on this, but I'm with my kids right now. I'll call you back in X minutes." This demonstrates respect for both your caller and your kids.

5. **Post-call reconnect:** Make it a family habit to do something nice with your child after you've interrupted your time together. It doesn't have to be anything grand—just a little cuddle or comment about the way his picture is turning out or how her jump shot is really improving.

6. **Glance and return:** If you cannot unplug completely, allow yourself to glance at an incoming message. But unless someone's reporting that his or her hair is on fire, tell your child, "It can wait until later." This way you not only keep track of your messages but also communicate clearly that you are not pulling away from your son or daughter.

7. **Sneak checks:** Before checking your phone, make sure your kids are thoroughly engaged in an activity—and unlikely to need your help—or otherwise entertained by your partner or friends.

8. **Phone-free times:** Decide on certain times of the day when unbroken time with your child is paramount, and shut your phone down completely during those times: perhaps after-school check-in, homework time, meals, bedtime, or all of these. Commit fully. No quiet ring or vibrate alert; just turn the device off. Some moms and dads give their friends and colleagues a heads-up about phone-free family time. Others specify their whereabouts on their voicemail greetings. One example: "Hi. You have reached Lesley's voicemail. If you are ringing during office hours, I am probably in a meeting. If you're calling after hours, I am likely with my kids. Either way, I will call you back

as soon as I can." One mom who did this was told by a number of people that they really liked the being "with my kids" part of her greeting and that they were going to do the same on their own voicemail message.

9. **Don't even look:** If the phone rings or vibrates, say out loud to your child, "Oh. That can wait."

10. **Include your kids:** If your child has his own phone, make sure to set clear boundaries about its use. He should know to put it away when the family has company and particularly when he is spending time with you. This will be a lot easier if you are both following similar guidelines.

Doable Quality Time

Some parents try their best to carve out *quality time* with their kids. We tend to imagine hours spent in the park or playing in the yard. While it's great to strive for this, it's not always so easy to pull off. We can end up feeling guilty and apologetic when that long-awaited morning outside evaporates because we are called into work, the refrigerator is empty, or we are submerged by the myriad other demands of modern life. How do we make quality time more doable? Undivided attention is golden. But we may not have big blocks of time to give to our children. If we can sprinkle our kids with small but concentrated doses of attention throughout the day, we establish continuity as we strengthen our connection.

Respectfulness and Courtesy

Helping children learn to be respectful builds three essential qualities that are the hallmarks of future social success:

1. **Impulse control:** Respecting that another person may act differently.

2. **Empathy:** Respecting that another person may feel things differently.
3. **Perspective taking:** Respecting that another person may think and see things differently.

University of South Australia professor Ken Rigby is a world-renowned expert in the field of children's social lives. He has written terrific books about bullying, teasing, and their effects on child development and learning. He has found that children who get targeted or target others lack the three qualities mentioned above. Kids who avoid being bullied and refrain from bullying others are more capable in these areas.

It's not hard to fathom that a child who is capable of imagining another perspective or respecting someone else's emotional response would be a good brother, sister, son, daughter, or friend. Thoughtfulness and empathy in a child is not a weakness. In fact, it takes strength of character to be able to pause and listen before acting. As Dr. Daniel Goleman points out in his seminal work, *Emotional Intelligence,* studies have clearly shown that the development of these abilities leads to sustained future success in the workplace and throughout adult life.

The big question, of course, is, *how do we build these qualities in our kids?* The answer is in brain science. The first quality that can be developed is impulse control. Little children will learn self-control if the adults around them have the right tools and the resolve to use them. What little children *cannot* yet do is understand and act on a level of more refined empathy or perspective taking. These two higher abilities develop later, in the tween and teen years.

When parents say to a young child of four or five, "How do you think that must have felt for Amanda?" they are met with sullen silence. And if they probe further? "Come on. How did Amanda feel when you did that?" the child will most likely give the parent a blank stare and say something like "I don't know." Or, at best, "Bad?" According to brain science, the child's response is spot-on. We are the ones who are off base by asking for a higher degree of empathy and perspective than is possible at this age. What we should be concentrating on instead is helping our kids strengthen their impulse-control musculature. We explored this at the beginning of this chapter, but it bears repeating. We must begin by developing compliance in our children and setting boundaries that help orient them, and build from there. Only then are we asking our children to strive for something that is within their developmental grasp.

Sweating the Small Stuff

One effective way to teach your child the importance of respectfulness is to sweat the small stuff. You can insist daily that they behave respectfully in all the little ways. No big lectures needed. Simply stand firm when the line of respectfulness gets crossed. What you are doing is teaching your child a new language: the language of respect. It's conveyed in words and actions and taught like any other language—slowly, over time. When you engage with your child continuously in this way, he or she will develop a healthy fluency in this new language.

They say the devil is in the details, but when it comes to respectfulness, the angels are in the angles. The angles are the many ways you show your child each day what is important to you. Every time you insist on respectfulness or true courtesy, you are exercising his or her waiting muscle. Every time you pause and ask your child to reframe some comment, put-down, or mannerism that is disrespectful, you strengthen his or her impulse control. Every time you insist on table manners or pull your child aside and say, "No. We don't use the word 'stupid' in our house; we do not say that in our family," you are teaching him or her the language of respect and encouraging impulse control, little by little. It's a beautiful, doable thing. And most important, it's something that builds upon itself. What's more, there is nothing people value more than genuinely respectful children.

When you teach children respectfulness, you are also developing their empathy and perspective taking. Getting started when kids are little gives them a foundation to build on. It also means that you have figured out a way to present and insist upon respectfulness that will continue to develop as they grow into tweens and teens. And yes, it *is* perfectly possible to have a respectful teenager (at least most of the time).

The Gifts of Rhythm and Anticipation

What have rhythm and anticipation got to do with impulse control, healthy compliance, and discipline in general? A rhythmic life is a predictable one. Knowing what's coming next comforts kids. Daily rhythms prepare them for chores, transitions, and other activities that build compliance and impulse control. Anticipation does the same. When children look forward to something over days, weeks, and even months before they get it, they learn to hold back the feeling of needing to have everything *right now*. Much of the force of impulsiveness stems from the sense that there is no tomorrow, so children think, "I better get what I want today." When children feel secure, tomorrow seems worth waiting for because they know what to expect. A more predictable life is a more secure one.

RHYTHM

Rhythm and predictability offer children four advantages:

1. **They provide a sense of flow in time, as opposed to being lost in space.** There is no better way to help a child control her impulses than by providing her with a sense of the flow of time. This makes her feel safe and oriented. The rhythm of daily

events, such as bed, meal, snack, and story times, secures a child in that flow.

2. **They allow for decompression moments.** Impulse control issues and behavioral pushback flare up most often because kids are bursting from an overwhelming day. Think of how a child behaves when he's been stuck in a car for long hours on a road trip. The context and confinement of the day have been too much for him, and he lashes out. A rhythmic and predictable day provides kids with moments of excitement and activity but also moments of rest and recuperation. For example, if a child who is in school knows she will have reading time at the after-care program or at home later, she can look forward to that quiet, relaxing moment. It functions as a safety release valve.

3. **They promote a sense of safety and security.** Rhythm is key to developing a child's belief that "I am safe. I know what my world is all about. I know what's going to happen later on this evening." When a child pictures a small event that he or she knows will happen, and then it actually happens, the child feels affirmed and grounded. This prevents his or her brain from firing up the fight-or-flight response, which leads to behavior outbursts and discipline issues. A safe child doesn't need to fight the world or live on high alert for most of the day. Rhythm is the key to relaxation.

4. **They provide a sense of orderliness and the passage of time.** Rhythm and predictability reinforce for a child the sense that there is order in the world, that there is a *right* time and a *wrong* time for everything. So if you provide your child with a rhythmic, predictable life and then say to him, "This is not the right time, my love," your words mean something. He has already experienced, on a daily basis, that there is a right time and a proper order in which certain things should happen. As a result, postponing something makes sense to him, and he will un-

derstand when you say something like "I know you want to play ball, but right now it's time for lunch. We'll go outside later this afternoon." One mother I worked with said to her creative, fashion-conscious little girl, "Oh dear, Missy [the dog] does look very nice, but it's not time to dress her up in her diaper and necklace. It's actually time for you to brush your teeth, so that we can have our *Hairy Maclary from Donaldson's Dairy* bedtime story." She found that her daughter complied more easily when given these specifics because it not only gave the child a simple instruction to follow, but it was an instruction that was very familiar. Such orderliness helps children grasp the passing of time. Many discipline issues arise because an adult presumes a child can understand time in an abstract way. When we recognize that our children perceive time differently—not as units linked to hour markers on a clock, but as times of the day when the same things happen again and again—we will get much more cooperation, experience easier transitions, and have a lot more fun.

ANTICIPATION

How does the lost art of anticipation help create healthy compliance?

Anticipation builds trust. A child learns that when he or she waits good things happen. That may sound obvious, but how many kids believe it nowadays? It signals that adults are in charge, and they follow through on their commitments. When you explain to your child, "I know, love. I can't play with you for the next two evenings, but on Saturday morning, we're going to have a great time at the playground," he or she understands. You have provided a picture of an upcoming activity, an anticipatory gift: the dream of playing ball with Dad or Mom or maybe Frisbee with the dog. The fun event now stretches over three days, far from the demand for instant gratification when your child insisted, "Daddy, I want to play ball right now, and afterward ice cream. Can we do it now, pleeease?"

Occasionally responding to that kind of request is fine if you have the time—there's nothing wrong with spontaneity. But consistently dropping your plans and doing something because a child wants it *right now* sends all the wrong signals. On the other hand, just telling a child that you will do something with them at some point later is not advisable. Vagueness is not an effective way to build up anticipation.

Anticipation has been a wonderful way to exercise the waiting muscle for one family I know. "The whole 'now' thing was really bothering us," said the mom, "so we decided to put more emphasis on waiting and anticipating. Now my daughter asks all sorts of little questions that signal to us that her imagination is growing in a lovely way. My husband and I feel that doing things this way has great value, because for every day we do something nice, we get a week's worth of imagination buildup." Mom and Dad were accurate in their judgment that anticipation provides great value. Imagining something can feel just as rich as actually doing or getting it.

In Conclusion

This chapter has provided you with a disciplinary base upon which you can establish loving authority and ensure that your child feels relaxed and safe. When you support your child with kind but firm boundaries as you teach him or her healthy compliance, you strengthen this behavioral foundation. Your child can then more easily handle the give-and-take needed to make good friends and maintain healthy relationships with siblings. And from this place of clarity and strength, she can grow, launch out into the world, and return to your calm home full of warm predictability and the surety that after a busy and complex day she can wrap herself up in the warm blanket of loving authority that boundaries bring.

5

Directions and Instructions vs. Suggestions and Requests

Mona looked exhausted and defeated. "Getting my three kids out the door to school each morning is like trying to herd butterflies!" she exclaimed. "It's not that they're rude or curt, though it sure does seem like they are blowing me off sometimes. They're just super self-absorbed."

Rather than spending hours talking concepts and strategies in my office, we arranged a morning-rush-hour home visit for later that week. Mona's partner left early for work each day, so the burden of preparations and departure was hers to bear alone.

I noticed immediately that, although Mona was polite and upbeat with her kids, they responded to her dismissively. She was clearly frustrated and perplexed. "I try to model respectfulness to my kids," she told me, "but the more polite I am, the more indifferent they become!"

What Mona didn't realize was that she communicated with her kids by peppering them with requests and appeals. She had developed a habit of beginning many of her interactions with her kids with phrases like "Would you like to . . . ?" or "Why don't we . . . ?" Yet no amount of coaxing or cajoling moved things along. Her suggestions were so often ignored that she had become tentative, even resigned. She let her kids keep doing whatever they were doing rather than insist they look at her when she spoke to them. The more she failed, the more heroically she redoubled her efforts to be mindful, flexible, gentle, and polite—inwardly seething the entire time. What's worse, this unhealthy dynamic was making Mona physically ill.

It was, of course, heartwarming to see a parent try so hard to cultivate respectfulness in her children. But Mona's efforts were misdirected. We met in a café later that afternoon for a much-needed cup of tea. "You have lovely kids, Mona," I began. "Really. And take this to heart. It may look like they are being disrespectful, but I think that the heart of the problem is how you communicate with them."

The solution for Mona was twofold. First, she needed to understand that her flexibility in allowing her children to continue with their activities while she spoke to them was counterproductive. It was paramount that she make sure they put down their books, remove their earbuds, and give her their full attention to create enough space for her to connect with them. She should calmly ask them to stop what they were doing and look at her, because she was going to tell them something they needed to know. Second, she needed to completely overhaul the language she used with them. Suggestions and choices needed to be replaced by simple, clear, firm instructions.

We discussed how this could still be done politely and respectfully. Mona agreed to try to create the conditions to hold her kids' attention and the language that would convey her needs to them directly.

I visited during morning rush two weeks later. Things had changed dramatically. Mona was still polite, but she was also direct. "Emma, just a moment," she said. "I got something for your lunch box which you need to know about." When twelve-year-old Emma looked up,

Mona made eye contact with her and continued, "I got those sweet apples you asked for, but they are big. You will need to find a container that fits. Please do it now, honey."

In interaction after interaction, Mona first "collected" her kids' attention, then "connected" with them, and finally delivered a simple direction. She confided that when she had first shifted to this Collect-Connect-Direct practice, she'd had her doubts, but it had felt natural, and to her relief, it clearly worked. "It was like a fog cleared and my kids knew exactly what I needed them to do," she said.

In this chapter, we will examine how to best communicate in order to ensure cooperation and healthy compliance from your children. We'll examine the neurological reasons kids don't respond well to suggestions and requests and why they function much better with warm but firm directives. We'll also learn several strategies parents can employ immediately to guide their kids more effectively.

Exploring the Issue

As you can see from Mona's experience, how you communicate with your child has a resounding impact on the likelihood that he or she will take you seriously and comply with instructions. The art of being a Family Governor is about issuing "executive orders" that are certainly spoken in a caring way but are also clear and uncomplicated. How often have we said something like "Shall we all get into the car, dear?" or "Honey, we should probably get going now. It's getting pretty late" and watched with surprise and growing frustration as our little boy or girl decided whether to get in the car or keep playing? As one exasperated mother we'll call Janet put it, "My kids don't seem to understand that I am not actually *asking*. I am politely requesting. It just blows me away that they don't get this."

It actually makes perfect sense. Suggestions live at the far left end of the Choice Spectrum. A suggestion is the softest approach to calling a child to action because it opens up a broad range of choices. A request is a bit more clearly formed since it implies that you want something to happen, albeit somewhat obtusely. But it still leaves the child a big open space in which to choose *not to do* what you are "inviting" him or her to do. And at the end of an exhausting day, it doesn't really matter whether you suggest or request—both leave your child confused and you, the parent, drained of authority.

What Janet is grappling with when she does something like suggest that it might be time for her daughter to get into the car is a popular style of parenting characterized by gentle, communal, inclusive approaches to decision making. The child is intimately involved in what is happening. He or she is provided with detailed explanations about when and why things need to be done and has a considerable amount of control over the outcome.

Suggestions and requests (polite or otherwise) give young kids too many choices and too much decision-making power at too early an age and are likely to confuse a child and frustrate a parent. In fact, younger children thrive when given clear directions or instructions, because those are much better suited to their needs and more appropriate to their age and capabilities. This becomes clear when put into practice, but the best way to understand it is to take a close look at how a young child's brain works.

The Brain Maze of Suggesting and Requesting

A Family Governor speaks in a way that helps a child feel safe and oriented. Children get confused when we don't say what we mean. This has a lot to do with their developing brain capacity. When you make a suggestion or request, a child relates it closely to being given a choice, and when a child processes a choice cognitively, he or she utilizes the area of the brain that handles what feels safe and good rather than what is right for others. The big picture *is not* front and center for children under a certain age. So a child who is not responding to suggestion is not being selfish or naughty, though it may appear so. He is still in a process of self-discovery. He doesn't fully relate his inner vision (or imagination) of a choice he has been given to the repercussions of either complying or pursuing his own interests. When a parent asks, "Who would like to help clean up?" the child gets caught in a choice-pleasure-imagination loop rather than an action-consequence one. He senses that, while his mother's words and tone suggest that she is *asking* him if he wants to do something, underneath it all, Mom is really *telling* him to do it. This ambivalent messaging creates a brain maze of uncertainty and contradiction. Your child may be able to find his way to doing what you are suggesting, but you have chosen a slow and indirect route.

Judge and Jury

To understand this better, let's zero in on how the brain develops in young children. Scans of the developing brain show us that the orbitofrontal cortex section—which plays a central role in judgment and decision making—is developmentally immature in a five-year-old child. We can see it become decidedly more mature as the child ages. As children grow into their tweens and teens, this region of the brain becomes more active and appears increasingly dark in imaging scans. This area of the brain is mainly responsible for three key kinds of judgment that we will explore briefly below.

Considering Long-Term Consequences

The first kind of judgment relates to the comprehension of long-term consequences. When we suggest things to a child using language like "Would you like to get into the car?" the child processes that question as "Would getting into the car be fun?" So Mom says, "Alexa, would you like to get in the car, dear? We need to go and pick up Adam, and after that there's some shopping to do, and, oh, we don't want to get home late!" Mom is trying to be kind, thoughtful, and inclusive, but Alexa is not thinking about Adam. She doesn't care about shopping either. Or getting back home in time to get supper on and avoid a late bedtime. And she is decidedly uninterested in the fact that a late bedtime translates into grumpy, difficult children the next day.

Alexa is thinking, "Do I want to get into the car? No! It is much nicer here in the sandbox!" It's that simple. The region of Alexa's brain that handles big-picture stuff and links actions taken right now with what may or may not happen later is *simply not well developed* at this stage. Being in Governorship of our family means we can be responsible for holding the big picture rather than expecting our children to do something they cannot.

Adapting Actions in Order to Take Others into Consideration and Becoming Emotionally Flexible

The second and third types of judgment for which the orbitofrontal cortex is mainly responsible involve the modification of our actions to take others into consideration and the development of emotional flexibility. Before the age of four or five, kids' brains just can't make these two types of judgments. Because their orbitofrontal cortex is still forming, they don't fully grasp cause and effect, nor have they built up the emotional flexibility to be able to quickly recognize other people's needs.

Every parent has seen his or her child completely engrossed in some activity, whether it is digging or painting or chasing friends. Kids demonstrate a kind of focus that is both deep and, frankly, almost rigid. You may believe that asking Johnny to understand the dilemma you are in and to consider your feelings is reasonable, especially given all that you do for him every single minute of every day, but your needs have disturbingly little impact on Johnny's decision-making process or emotional concerns. Your plea for empathy falls on deaf little ears. You may think, "Oh my goodness, am I raising a sociopath or something? Johnny doesn't care about anyone but himself, not even his own mother!" But this is not the case at all. The answer is much simpler. The area of Johnny's brain responsible for empathy just hasn't developed yet. If you were to look at a brain scan of a child's five-year-old brain, you'd see that the orbitofrontal cortex—the critical area for empathy—is not very active. By nine or ten years old, it has darkened and expanded (indicating activity).

The Mismatch Cascade

A child's brain can process suggestions and requests. But it takes time, and the responses are most often slow and diffuse. Parents, on the other hand, make hurried suggestions like "Shall we get ready to leave the house?" because they want to move things along. Things stall. The parent tries to make the child understand that not everything orbits around his or her needs. Now the child runs the *suggestion* through the choosing loops. This, again, takes time, *and* the parent may interpret the child's mental process as purposeful stalling and selfishness rather than the slow movement of thought through underdeveloped neurological loops. I call this the "Mismatch Cascade."

Here is a concrete example of the Mismatch Cascade in action:

The parent asks the child if she would please do something.

Then . . .

The child appears to be distracted and stalling.

Then . . .

The parent's frustration begins to boil over, and he or she tries to hurry things along.

Then . . .

The child resists because she is still processing her response to her parent's suggestion.

Then . . .

The more the parent repeats the suggestion, the more the child feels confused because she can see that she is not in sync with her parent.

Now . . .

This makes the child feel increasingly unsafe, misunderstood, and disoriented, and there is nothing more likely to trigger a meltdown than overwhelming feelings of disorientation.

And finally . . .

The parent and the child have unwittingly strained the attachment between them. No one planned it this way. If the popular parental approach of giving little kids choices, requests, and suggestions rather than clear instructions is so wholesome, then why does it produce this unintended result that feels so uncomfortable at a gut level? We want to strengthen our bonds with our kids, not damage them.

You might say that a negative experience you've had is not that significant because it was only a little flare-up. But these mini-battles tend to repeat themselves and escalate when left unresolved. And more important, all these little daily exchanges slowly develop and solidify the relationship between a child and his or her parents. You want connecting moments that are positive, not a series of ruptures and meltdowns that drive a wide wedge of mistrust and misunderstanding between the two of you.

Here are three things you should know about parental requests that will help you stand in loving Governorship:

1. If you are going to make a suggestion or request, be aware that you will have to give your child the time needed to consider it and respond.
2. The response you get may not be at all what you were looking for.
3. If you want to go somewhere or do something specific, avoid using suggestions altogether.

Seven Reasons to Go on a
No Request–No Suggest Diet

When kids are *asked* over and over, dozens of times a day, what they want or if they want to do something, instead of being told to do what they should do, they get confused and upset. This is epitomized by seven comments I have heard request-generation kids make discussed below. After you read them, you will be inspired to go on your own No Request–No Suggest Diet to limit the damage you do to your children.

1. Bait and switch: *"If you don't do what they want, you get into trouble even though they ask if you want to do it or not."*

    What a telling comment. They ask you, but unless you choose what they want you to choose, you get into trouble.

2. Anxiety: *"I get really nervous when I try to figure out what to say."*

    This comment came from a little girl who was very anxious. She was trying to be cooperative and find the right answers to the many suggestions phrased as questions she received each day. But when I asked her point-blank, she said all the questions made her nervous and upset. As soon as her parents came to understand the negative impact all their suggesting had on their daughter, they began to give her directions instead. Her anxiety faded, and she began to feel much more grounded and secure.

3. An iron hand in a velvet glove: *"Are they really asking or just telling in a nice voice? It's sort of scary."*

    When you say, "Would you like to get in the car?" some kids kind of figure it out. But they're not always sure what your intention is. Are you asking, or are you telling? They know you want them to get into the car. Your inner will says, "Madison, get into the car. We're running late," but out loud you are asking, "Madison, would you *like* to get into the car?" Such duality can be quite scary for kids: They see a wide schism between what's going on inside us and what we say when we come at them with an urgent suggestion.

4. Role confusion: *"It's like you're the boss, but you're not."*

The child is confused by conflicting messages. One six-year-old we'll call Tommy told his friend, "It's like my mom is really nice and asks me what I want. And then I tell her, and then she gets mad." Tommy could sense that his mom was trying to be a good parent by politely requesting things and offering him choices. So Tommy made the decision that he thought he was supposed to make, but when his mom got angry, he was left puzzled and hurt. One moment he was asked to make an adult choice and thought he was being promoted to big-time decision-maker, and the next he'd been shoved back into his little-boy role. It was all very confusing for a young child, as you can imagine.

5. School-home train wreck: *"I always get picked on by my teacher. She's always telling me to do things, and it has to be done her way."*

Eight-year-old Lisa wasn't feeling very good about school. She wanted to do well. The teacher and her parents certainly wanted her to succeed. But there was a discipline and guidance culture clash raging. Lisa's parents were mainly request-suggest types. Her teacher, with an entire class to keep on track, was a no-nonsense instruction-and-direction disciplinarian.

Your child will very seldom encounter a teacher who says, "Third grade, who would like to put their pencils away?" or "It might be nice if we all line up at the door." Any teacher who speaks to children this way will have a colorful but brief career in education. Teachers don't speak or act this way because they know that it leads to all kinds of problems. To put it bluntly, you've got to get your kids used to directions and instructions if you're going to send them to school.

6. I do it my way: *"Other kids think I'm bossy, but I just know how to do it."*

When we raise children on a steady diet of requests and suggestions, we risk setting them up for a long list of friendship failures. Kids who are used to being asked what they would like to do by an adult tend to try to dominate other children because they are so used to things going their way. As they assume their accustomed role of decider, they inadvertently alienate kids who have learned to compromise and share decision-making power.

7. The Lonely General: *"I don't care if I don't have friends. I'd rather do what I want."*

There are legions of Lonely Generals in our school playgrounds. Such kids come from request-choice families and tend to have trouble opening up to other kids' suggestions. Social flexibility is critical to healthy relationships: Kids must be willing to roll with the "funnest" ideas rather than insisting rigidly that everyone adhere to their way of playing. Nowadays any group or class of children is populated with a good number of kids who come from request-choice families. When these children come into contact with each other, conflicts and power struggles bubble forth. Such children find it very difficult to back down, and after spending some time in stalemates, they walk away from social activities entirely, preferring to rule over an army of one.

But they often are unhappy, feel unappreciated, and blame the other children and the teacher for not understanding them. They may truly long to play with others, but no amount of social engineering and teacher supervision can soften their resolve. The answer to this conundrum lies with the parents. Mom and Dad can help a child to learn to follow directions and not feel the need to make all the choices.

Exploring the Solutions

COLLECTING AND CONNECTING

Discipline is a dance between a child and an adult, and it works smoothly only when the two partners move together willingly. Let's take asking a young man to dance as an example. Before you approach someone to ask him to dance, you've probably watched him and noticed if he is sitting forward and looking out at the dance floor, eager to take part. If he is, you can approach your potential partner with confidence, hold out your hand, and ask him to join you. Alternatively, if you see that he is sitting back, eyes downcast, looking hesitant or withdrawn, you approach much more cautiously and sensitively. You might sit down beside him and engage in light conversation to feel things out and perhaps build up some common ground before asking for a dance. You certainly wouldn't just haul him out onto the dance floor and pull and push him against his will.

Good discipline and guidance are employed similarly. The parent should adjust his or her approach according to the child's state of mind. Sometimes we can be direct and unvarnished, while at other times our kids sorely need us to proceed slowly and gently. This emotional attunement can help build a stronger connection, especially when a child is feeling vulnerable and anxious because things are not going well.

This is what Gordon Neufeld, co-author of *Hold On to Your Kids,* calls the art of "collecting and connecting," and its importance cannot be overstated. If we first collect and connect to a child who is feeling disoriented, the direction we give is much more likely to be followed. If the invitation to dance is well considered, there is immediate engagement, and even though there is a leader and follower in the "dance of discipline," a flow develops that has a beauty all its own. A Family Governor accepts being in the lead, but that does not mean there is not ease and a fun-filled and loving relationship with your child, who feels safe and "held" when he or she follows.

Here are a few things to do or avoid that will help you to collect and connect more directly. And don't forget to enjoy the dance!

PARALLEL PARKING

If things are not going well and you get the feeling that your child is likely to either implode or explode at your first word, listen to your instinct, and sit down beside her. Take care not to position yourself directly opposite her as this will be perceived as a challenge; sit facing the same direction. One of my favorite things to say in these moments is "Hmmm, this is hard." It's a neutral, truthful comment. It makes it clear that you are not imposing but that you understand that she is having a tough time. Wait for your child's posture to shift or even soften just a little bit. Even then, it's best to say very little. You've helped your child collect her emotions and connected with her quietly. When your kids get used to you "parallel parking" beside them in this way, things get sorted out much more quickly than when you battle and the situation escalates. They intuitively associate your calm approach with safety and security. They trust that all will be well. You can parallel park even more effectively when you are doing something nonthreatening such as peeling potatoes or mending a sweater. My favorite: Pick up a beloved children's book and casually thumb through it.

BODY LISTENING BEFORE EYE CONTACT

We all know that body language is a big part of how we communicate. Far too often, parents insist on eye contact with their child when they are in a difficult disciplinary situation. While it may seem that this is what it takes to be a Family Governor, we risk becoming more of a dictator when we force a child to look at us. It's best not to do that first. In such moments, we tend to see the child's eyes harden as they display resentment at being forced to look up. Things tend to escalate from there because we feel disrespected, even though our kids claim they were doing what they were told. Another type of connecting, such as the parallel parking described above, works best. After you've parallel parked, even though the child may be looking down, his or her body language may show the first signs of softening or "body listening." At that point, your request for eye contact is much more likely to be successful, and you may sense your child's emotional arms reaching out to you as his or her eyes soften.

AVOID ON-THE-FLY SUGGESTIONS AND REQUESTS

On-the-fly requests usually fall on deaf ears and often lead to escalation, so it's best not to make them at all. Of course, we all use them at times, because life gets frenetic. Just be aware that when you ask a child to do something while you are on the move, in a hurry, or distracted by competing demands on your time and attention, you are inviting disciplinary problems and should proceed carefully. Just ask Joyce.

Joyce is trying to get three children out to the car and off to school. "Melanie, *Melanie*! Shall we all get into the car now? Timmy, why don't you pack up your blocks? Come on now, Brendan. If the label is prickly, would you like to turn the sweater inside out?" Joyce is doing her very best to stay calm and functional during this dreaded part of her day. She grabs her bags and the dog, gets out to the car, and starts it up. Phew! Then she turns and looks into the backseat. No one is there. The kids have spun away using some form of suggestion-avoidance aikido.

So Joyce gets out of the car and starts back toward the house. With each step, her walk more closely resembles the menacing stomp of a character in a Clint Eastwood shoot-'em-up. Inside, she finds Melanie quietly reading a book. Brendan is dressing himself in an entirely new outfit more suited for the beach than this cold, windy day, and Timmy—sensing the need to fortify himself against the coming barrage—is surrounding himself with another course of blocks.

Kids love on-the-fly suggestions, particularly if they are shouted out from another room, because they are an invitation to do absolutely nothing. Our children have a sixth sense that they use to figure out when we really mean something and when we don't. In the unlikely event that they are not sure, they run a cost-benefit analysis and most often decide to ignore our suggestions and requests.

That's why on-the-fly requests can so often be ignored by children. Parents need to find a few minutes, no matter how chaotic the day becomes, to *pause, collect, and connect* with their children. For example, Joyce might say, "That is one of your tallest towers, Timmy. You can see a long way from that tower. We will leave the tower but pack away the other blocks now because it's time to put our coats on." Having acknowledged Timmy's creative efforts, Joyce has provided him with a clear path to compliance and stays with him for a few moments to ensure it.

GIVE TWO-BY-TWO INSTRUCTIONS

A two-by-two instruction is a proclamation that you, the Family Governor, issue with *two feet* on the ground and your child no more than *two feet* away from you. If you sense positive body language, you can also insist on eye contact as you issue your directive.

Some parents like to get out of a busy family traffic zone if they are about to utter an edgy instruction. At such a moment, take your child to a quieter place. Make sure your feet are solidly on the ground—literally. One dad told me he wiggles his toes before he gives an instruction to make sure he is grounded. A mom said, "I sense my feet growing roots down through my shoes and into the warm earth before

I give a direction." It may sound silly, but that physical grounding will have a huge impact on your mental foundation for this conversation.

The bonus for two-by-two instruction users? For every ten two-by-two instructions you give, you get one twenty-footer free. You can call up the stairs, "Boys, it's time to go now!" and they'll come down promptly, because they now know that, unless they do, you're going to do one of those weird two-footers again. With time and consistency, kids figure it out, and you can be a bit more flexible. But if things go downhill again, and your kids stop responding to your more relaxed instructions, just circle back to the two-by-two approach. Children sense that when they comply regularly you give them a little more space, and when they don't, you move in tight. This calculated flexibility prepares the ground for the broader transition from the Governor stage to the Gardener stage.

Directing: Giving Direction via Directions

In this chapter, we have gone over the pitfalls of making suggestions and polite requests or giving directives disguised as choices. Now let's look at the benefits of *giving directions*. Remember that there is no such thing as a disobedient child . . . only a disoriented one. Replacing suggestions with directions is a key part of orienting a child because it helps him *get his bearings*. You are the forest ranger that your lost, frantic child bumps into in a vast national park, a smiling guide who says, "Don't worry. You're not the only one this has happened to. It's easy to get lost in these parts. Follow me, and I'll show you the right path." Relief floods through your child as the kind, experienced ranger leads the way. She knows these paths well. And your child is thankful that the ranger did not once make him feel stupid. He is most grateful to the ranger because she gave him simple directions and helped him on his way. She did not say, "Weeell, there are three routes you might like to take, and you can see which is best for you. The first way is west of here, and it's a little rocky and difficult, but the views are great. The second way is faster but involves a known bear-attack zone. The third path involves following the river, but you gotta keep sort of east of the fork a few miles ahead. I better be going now. Best of luck, kid." Though parents may not realize it, we often leave our kids lost in a forest thick with choices, suggestions, and requests when all they really want is a clear direction.

Here are six helpful tips for giving clear directions:

1. Clarify expectations. *"This is the way I want you to do it."*

   A good direction explains what you are expecting. This sounds basic, but requests and choices don't do that and can easily confuse a child. He or she is not really sure what you expect.

2. Be empathetic but firm. *"I understand it's hard for you, but we are going now, Shanti."*

   A direction can be kind and empathetic. In no way does it have to be steely and hard-edged.

3. Clarify family values. *"No, no, Miguel. That is not a word we use in our family. We try to speak kindly."*

   Taking lots of chances to clarify the values you hold dear as a parent each day is good practice—for both of you.

4. Create a feeling that you and your child are going in the same direction. *"It's just the way we do it, Sophie."*

   Even if Miguel is wavering from being in rhythm with his family by putting a sibling down unkindly, his parents' clear directions create a strong current that he can slip back into; he can now flow with his parents rather than swim against them.

5. Be authoritative and warm. *"Lights out when you finish that page, Elisha. You have a big day tomorrow."*

   Clear direction assures a child that there is a warm but authoritative hand at the wheel. In other words, a child knows that there's someone in charge of the direction of the family. As an example, let's consider a story that one mom told me about her daughter Joni. After being over at a friend's house, Joni said, "Mom, you know, Caitlin's mom kept asking, 'Would you like to go to bed?' And Caitlin was like, 'No. Soon. Yeah. Okay, soon.' Then the dad came and asked Caitlin too. It was weird. It got really late, and we were both so tired in the morning that Caitlin was cranky and got into a huge fight with her dad. I'm so glad you don't do that. You would have just told us to go to sleep and made sure we did."

6. Prepare for an instruction. *"This is the way I want you to pack up, love, because we are going to pick Danny up soon."*

Directions help simplify and clarify transitions. Suggestions and choices cause a transition logjam.

Instruction Creates Inner Structure

Instructions provide structure and direction. They break complicated actions down into smaller, more doable steps for a child.

To better understand the difference between an effective instruction and a confusing suggestion, consider the following series of choice-laden suggestions that have been reworded as unambiguous instructions:

- Suggestion: "Lisa, would you like to get in the car?"
- Instruction: "Lisa, it's time now to put away the bike and get in the car. Let's put the bike back in the shed, and make sure to close the door."

- Suggestion: "How about you tell me what you would like for breakfast?"
- Instruction: "It's Sunday. Pancakes day! Let's get the ingredients out now."

- Suggestion: "How about we all clean up now?"
- Instruction: "It's time to clean up. Let's start with the boxes."

- Suggestion: "Are those kind words? Would you like to think about an apology?"
- Instruction: "Something must be bugging you. You may read your book right here until you're ready to tell us what is up and we put things right with Anna."

- Suggestion: "Shall we all put our coats on?"
- Instruction: "Please put your coats on now. And now your boots. That's it."

Where We Are Going *and Then* How We Will Get There

A direction . . . helps a child get a sense of the big picture. A direction is the Governor setting out the family priorities that give form to the day and help the child understand where this part of it is going. Giving a child an overview helps him feel safe and prevents him from going into a fight-or-flight state and resisting you. The brain center responsible for perspective is not well developed in a young child, so he needs your help to understand what's happening.

One stay-at-home dad who was wrestling with defiance realized that the big picture was missing for his four-year-old daughter. "It was like she was lost in space," he said. "And when I tried to transition her, she got very upset." He started to give her clear directions before any kind of transition or instruction. "I became Chloe's road-mapping brain. I filled in for her while she slowly learned to do it for herself. It helped so much that she became a different kid."

An instruction . . . gives a child the smaller picture of how to get where he or she needs to go and what is expected of him or her in a practical sense. That's where practical instructions save the day. While it's good to give a directional overview, if we go no further, the young child will not know what is expected of her and become confused and then defiant or distressed. A parent may say, "Goodness! I told her we need to get to the bus. Why can't she just cooperate?" Children up to the age of five or six need help understanding exactly how to proceed.

It's essential to give instructions in the right order. We all know that if we are tasked with putting together one of those flat-packed, "easy"-assembly pieces of furniture, unless we follow the instructions step by step, we have no chance of ending up with something that looks even vaguely like the photo on the box. The same is true for kids when it comes to any multistep task. So pause before you give a direction, and put your instructions in a sequence that makes sense and is most likely to work for your child. It's easier than you would think to mix up the sequence of instructions when we are right in the thick of a discipline and guidance situation.

Be careful not to overwhelm your child by rattling off too much of the sequence at once. Don't expect him or her to remember the whole thing. It's better to give "leapfrog" instructions.

Try something like this: "Good, Imran. Now that we are almost finished packing the lunch things away, we can start to clean the counter off with the big blue sponge." Then a minute or six later, continue: "There. The counter is almost done. Now we'll stack the dishes over here."

Take care not to finish one part of the instruction and then give yet another—that is, the instructions should flow into each other. Otherwise, you can lose momentum and give the child the false impression that he is finished and should be allowed to play.

You may be thinking, "That sounds like a lot of work just to get the lunch packed away and the dishes done!" but once you get into the habit of giving instructions like these, it becomes second nature. You create a flow of activity, things take a lot less time, and, most important, you get closer to your child.

One grandmother who gave a lot of welcome support to her daughter Sarah told me, "Sarah would often say to me that Isabelle [the granddaughter] would get with the program much more when she was with me and that everything got done more quickly without the usual upsets. Sarah and I figured out that Isabelle did this because I am a very systematic person, and it calmed her to have no doubt about what I expected from her." She added with a bright smile, "It doesn't make her love me one bit less, and anyone can learn to be systematic if it's going to prevent all that shouting and crying."

A Direction Followed by an Instruction

It's not difficult to train yourself in this approach. You give a child the big picture first and then the little steps necessary to get there. It sounds something like this:

Direction (big picture): "Dion, we are going to leave soon because we have to pick your brother up early today."

Instruction (smaller picture): "Come and help me put your lunch in your backpack, and then we need to get our coats on. It's gotten really cold today."

Q: What if they say no?
A: Never repeat a direction. Get specific about the instruction.

Parents often repeat suggestions over and over. You hear parents saying in a frustrated tone, "Why do I have to ask you ten times?" One mother told me that her quick-witted, risk-taking child once responded to that question, "Because I don't have to listen to you the first time, since I know you're going to say it nine more times. That gives me a lot more time to play Lego, Mom." Even though she burst out laughing at the time, it was a major wake-up call.

If you have given a direction to your son or daughter and been met with a sullen no (spoken or unspoken), resist the temptation to repeat the direction again in a louder voice. The child probably doesn't have a hearing problem, so raising the volume will not help.

Here are ways parents can train themselves to use visualization techniques the way athletes do when preparing themselves for competition:

Consider these three options:

1. **Down and back:** When a child is defiant, some parents sense an upward movement of their energy or emotions. "I feel the heat start to *rise,*" they say, or "I can feel the *up*set starting. I tear *up* because it is so difficult," or "I get *out* of myself, and I don't like it." Other parents use terms that suggest a forward moving or assertive reaction: "It's like we are going *headlong* into conflict," or "I tend to move into con*front*ation," or "I can feel that I am getting *pushy.*" Disciplinary problems clearly involve energy and spatial direction. The answer to dealing with these issues is simple and intuitive: Rather than go "up" and get "out" of yourself, practice trying to go "down" and "back" into yourself.

2. **Heavy cloak and brooch:** When you are about to get too far into "front space," being *pushy* and *confrontational,* bring up an image of a gorgeous, full-length damask or velvet cloak that is fastened in the front with a heavy, pure gold brooch. It pours itself over your shoulders and cascades down the full length of your back and legs and trails onto the floor. Each time you take a step, you feel its weight behind you.

3. **Lion's paws:** When you feel yourself going up and "out" of yourself with frustration, imagine your feet as big, soft, wide

lion's paws. Place your feet slightly wider than shoulder width apart, and flex your toes and move your feet so that they soften and widen, giving you a fabulous, deep, rich connection with the earth.

Some parents practice these images inspired by the movement disciplines known as Spacial Dynamics and Bothmer movement for a few minutes each day so that when they need to use them in a moment of escalation they have them right at hand. Other parents can retrieve a helpful image without preparation or practice. Either way, the magic of this exercise is that the parent does it in the moment in order to change a potentially negative exchange with his or her child.

After you have used the visualization technique, try the Five Essentials of Healthy Compliance detailed in Chapter Three. Move in close; break a task down into smaller, more doable bites; and pay extra attention to the "Insist" step. This means there is no negotiating, just a warm but very firm insistence that what is being instructed will be done.

Don't be drawn into justifications or conversations. Here are some approaches you can try: "No, no. I am not going to explain anything, Joshua. We are just doing it like this." "It's hard, I know, but we are going to do it this way." "Yes, we can talk about it afterward, but first we need to do it this way."

Too Many Words and Too Little Meaning

Fashions and styles take hold in parenting just as they do in any other aspect of culture. A major trend at the moment involves *explaining* everything to babies, toddlers, and young children. We have become preoccupied with our words. One elderly neighbor recently told me, "All my son seems to do is talk and talk, and all his kids seem to do is *not* listen."

Smart Speaking Is Not the Only Type of Intelligence

Popular parenting magazines have misinterpreted solid research with simplistic headlines such as "The More You Talk to Babies the Smarter They Will Be." Well, of course we want our kids to be smart. And "smart" may be catchy in a headline. But it's not exactly accurate. What the research does point to is that children who have an active verbal engagement with their parents will likely develop good language skills. But to claim that good language skills are all there is to being smart is not smart at all.

In his book *Multiple Intelligences,* Howard Gardner lists verbal skills as one of many forms of intelligence including logical (mathematical), interpersonal (relationships with others), intrapersonal (knowing yourself), naturalistic (being sensitive and insightful about the natural world), kinetic (being well coordinated, for example, good at sports, acting, or dance), visual-spatial (the ability to visualize with the mind's eye), existential (spiritual), and musical.

The problem is that many parents have been led to believe that *simply* talking to our kids will ensure they are successful. This is a worryingly simplistic view of what it takes to raise a well-rounded and genuinely intelligent child. Parents (and teachers) tend to overload this particular aspect of their relationship with their kids, and before long, nattering becomes an unconscious habit.

It's About Speech That Connects

These short, glitzy articles often fail to point out what the research underscores: It is the *quality* of interaction, not just the *quantity* of words a baby hears, that affects language-skill development. In an interview about her 2013 Stanford-based study, lead researcher Dr. Adriana Weisleder said, "Toddlers learn language in the context of meaningful interactions with those around them." When well-meaning

Pause Point

THE W-A-I-T SOLUTION

If you find yourself talking too much with a child and you are beginning to lose track of what you are trying to communicate, try the W-A-I-T solution, which my colleague Davina Muse recommends. Ask yourself:

W = Why

A = Am

I = I

T = Talking

Doing this can help you pause and get back to what you really wanted to communicate. It often helps you use a lot fewer words that communicate a whole lot more.

---

parents flood toddlers with torrents of words, the words become babble, and none of that "meaningful interaction" takes place.

After a parenting workshop, one mother wrote the following: "I did not have my first baby until my midthirties. I am a grade school teacher, so I had read a lot and was particularly interested in giving my baby a good start with language skills. However, the more I followed the popular advice to speak as much as possible to my baby, the more she seemed to be tuning me (and my many words) out. It was quite upsetting. After your workshop I decided to speak less but try and fill the words I used with meaning and, when I could, connect them to movements and little jobs and chores as you suggested. Now when I speak, my little one looks at me and comes running to me. I know this sounds basic, but I sometimes cry with relief because this did not happen when I was talking all the time."

All of this well-meaning but misdirected overtalking can be quite detrimental. It plays a large role in kids switching off or disconnecting from their parents. And if children do not attach to and bond with their parents in a healthy way, all kinds of behavioral problems can ensue, as any child psychologist will tell you.

Actions Lead and Words Follow

Little children have a wonderfully rich understanding of the movements and gestures of other people. They learn through watching and copying. We get a clue to how deeply our child absorbs our movement habits when she grows up and we see that she uses pretty much the same body language as us. Brain science tells us that young children can even sense what it is we want or, as one report in *The New York Times* put it, "read our minds" by watching our movement.

Words are important, of course. I am by no means suggesting they are not. On the contrary, words are so important that we need to make the best use of them to help our children develop good language skills. We can do this by linking words with purposeful movement, which is how a child really absorbs and understands the words we are using.

If we link giving a direction or instruction with movement . . .

1. We are playing to a child's neurological strength.
2. The child will be much more likely to "get" what it is we are speaking to him or her about.
3. We give a child the cue to what we would like him or her to do.
4. Children mirror what we are doing in their own minds and then can motivate their bodies to follow.

Here are a few tips for how you can use action and movement to help a little child follow your direction, followed by some examples:

1. First, pause and connect after you have moved in and before you give an instruction. Slow down, and face the child.

2. Avoid speaking over your shoulder (see "Avoid On-the-Fly Suggestions and Requests" above), or into the cupboard, or as you are going out the door.

3. Give the instruction when you are close to the child (two to five feet away).

Action: The parent moves toward the door, takes the child's hand, *pauses, and then . . .*

    Instruction: "Laurie, now it's time for us to get into the car."

Action: The parent takes out a skillet, a big old frying pan, says, "It's Sunday. That's Pancake Day!" *pauses, and then . . .*

    Instruction: "Let's get out the big mixing bowl and a good spoon."

Action: The father brings the basket (a big, familiar one) to the play area, *pauses, and then . . .*

    Instruction: "It's time we cleaned up, Lee."

Action: The mother approaches a child from the front or the side, picks him up (not startling him by unexpectedly scooping him up from behind), *pauses, and then . . .*

    Instruction: "We don't hit in our family. You were so gentle with your sister all this time, but hitting is not gentle. Something must be upsetting you. You may look at your book right here next to me until you're ready to make up with Lily."

Action: The parent puts his own coat on, begins to hold out the coat for the child, *pauses, and then . . .*

    Instruction: "One arm goes in here, Elizabeth. Now the other. There. Now let's do up this tricky zipper."

Following is an overview of the critical, comforting, and grounding value of purposeful movement and actions for a young child. Such movement signals to a child your Governorship without the need for words.

- Actions and movement create a visual and a bodily cue. Young children are visual and physical. When we use movement to communicate with them, it strengthens the meaning of our words.
- Purposeful movement and actions clarify that a parent means what he or she says. They show that you yourself are following through with the direction or instruction that you're giving.
- Actions make clear that a child is a part of the flow of family activity, not separate from it. Purposeful movement brings connection, whereas arguing and shouting, and having a child shout back at you, create a separation.
- Actions give a child something to imitate, which is crucial because children thrive on imitation. Their brains are wired for it. And when you move first and speak second, a child can really follow you.
- Actions create a sense of "we" and help satisfy children's intense need for safety and trust in us as parents. As Erik H. Erikson points out in his book *Childhood and Society,* without this security, children cannot easily move on to other important developmental stages. He explains the essential qualities a child can achieve in each stage, alongside what can happen if each capacity is not developed. Not every child moves along at Erikson's ideal pace, of course. For some children, establishing safety and trust can come much more slowly because of the environments they grow up in. Much of their movement into higher social and emotional development will be inhibited until each capacity associated with earlier phases has been achieved.
- Erikson's stages of development:

1. Learning Basic Trust Versus Basic Mistrust (Hope, birth–18 months), which leads to . . .
2. Learning Autonomy Versus Shame (Will, 18 months–3½ years), which leads to . . .
3. Learning Initiative Versus Guilt (Purpose, 3½–5 years), which leads to . . .
4. Industry Versus Inferiority (Competence, 6–12 years), which leads to . . .
5. Learning Identity Versus Identity Diffusion (Dependability, 13–20 years)

Rejection-Based Discipline

Every parent has used a time-out when his or her child has behaved badly. While this might be a tool to keep in your parenting skills toolbox, it is dramatically overused and can risk the child feeling scared of a banishing dictator rather than safe with a loving Governor. It suggests to a child that an effective way to solve a problem is to send it away. If we give a child regular time-outs, we are reinforcing this message.

Rejection is a powerful, primitive message to send a child because it triggers a primal fear that he or she is being cut off from the group. It activates the brain's most basic fight-flight-freeze-flock survival response—the most vulnerable of feelings to activate in a child because kids intuitively know they are dependent on our protection and care to keep them safe and alive.

Here are a few key concerns about the overuse of time-outs:

- The child will use the time to get more upset at you and move further away from accepting what he or she did was wrong.
- The child will disassociate from her actions, and when you ask, "Why did you get a time-out?" (as prompted by many parenting

books), the child will answer with a shrug or say, "I dunno." Or she will say the words she thinks you want to hear.

- The child will feel like he is bad, and even though you assure him that it is his behavior that is the problem, he will have a hard time accepting this because he has been sent away.
- The child will deflect the blame onto a sibling or onto you.
- The child will deny what happened and even lie about it.
- The child may seek revenge on her sibling who she feels got her into trouble.

Perhaps the biggest concern associated with rejection-based discipline revolves around what it can set in motion for the future relationships of our sons and daughters. In their future marriages and partnerships, we want our children to be able to take the rough along with the smooth. We don't want them to encounter a problem with a partner and reject him or her without making a serious effort to work things through. If we want our kids to connect deeply to their future friends, colleagues, and partners, we mustn't overload them with the message of rejection.

This does not mean, however, that we ought to be soft on discipline. We must hold a child accountable for his or her actions. In fact, children are much more likely to be able to see the implications of their actions, and be open to correcting things, if we have not blamed, shamed, and isolated them.

Some alternatives to rejection-based discipline:

WE-DIRECTIONS

A lot is written about redirecting children when they are struggling and even becoming defiant. Redirection involves shifting a child away from a potentially difficult situation toward a space from which he can gain perspective and return to himself. However, many parents (and teachers) have found that children refuse to be redirected, and a difficult situation they hoped would ease with redirection actually worsens. The main reason this happens is that the adult unintentionally communicates to the child that he or she is being sent away. **Redirection works most effectively when the redirection is transformed into a we-direction.** Phrases like "Let's both . . ." or "We need to . . ." or "Come with me and . . ." or "I wonder how our . . ." are often deployed in a successful we-direction. We are reaching back here to an old, reliable concept: "Actions lead and words follow."

Here are some examples of everyday we-directions:

- **Distraction for cooperation:** "I wonder what is going to happen to poor Eeyore in our bedtime story tonight. Let's hop-hop out of the bath now and get ready."
- **Change the environment:** "Oh dear! It's not helpful to speak to your brother like that. Let's get these leaves raked, and we can sort things out later so that he feels better."
- **Acceptable alternative:** "Oh, Molly. Scissors are not for cutting curtains. I'll show you how we can cut this paper and make some lovely shapes to hang up."

Avoiding the Downside of We-Directions

While we-direction and distraction can be especially helpful for toddlers and young preschoolers, it may discourage older children from using their problem-solving skills. To avoid this, use the we-direction to help a child out of a stuck or escalating situation; then, when the time seems right, talk calmly to the child about what was happening and discuss how things could be done better. If it feels possible, once you connect with a child through a we-direction, lead him back to the situation that was causing the problem and take some simple steps to put it right.

When you we-direct your child away from a difficulty, you risk assuming responsibility for resolving the issue instead of helping your child work it out. You don't want your son or daughter to think he or she can act recklessly and that you will swoop in and make everything right (that would be Snowplow Parenting). Another risk: Your kid will blame you if the problem is not sorted out to his or her satisfaction. So again, you need to establish a good connection and then return to the problem and engage your child in solving it. Just remember, the younger the child, the more the solution should be based on "doing" rather than just talking.

Take care not to insist on punitive alternatives such as isolating your child to a room or giving her a chore to do on her own. And even when you are we-directing, be careful not to set yourselves too big and complicated a task. The aim is to help a child return to himself *and* connect with you.

DADD

Disapprove—Affirm—Discover—Do Over (DADD) is a very effective strategy that orders and organizes what parents often say and do anyway. This approach is calming when things start to go south. Your tone and intention assures your child that you care for her and love her, even though what she just *did* or *said* was not at all helpful. It's a strategy that allows a parent to be firm and direct when sorting out a problem and, at the same time, build an even stronger connection with his or her child.

Considering character type and temperament is an important part of working things through. This approach works best when it is tailored to the individual child. Timing is all-important in DADD practice, and a great way to ensure your timing is right is to get to know the individual tendencies of the child. If it is tricky to determine a child's temperament, consult the list below.

Ask yourself, "Which temperament least describes my child?" Through the process of elimination, you can home in on your child's character type. There is often one standout temperament and underneath it the quieter influence of another one. For example, your child may be primarily a Dominant Type but also quite sensitive. Such a child can often say and do very forceful and challenging things. Yet the pushback reaction they get from a sibling or parent will wound her, expose her vulnerabilities, and cause her to feel picked on. The typical dynamic is one in which the standout temperament acts out while the secondary temperament is often the one to react.

Extroverts

- The Leader/Dominant Type (fire) needs to be spoken to away from friends and siblings and usually after a cooling off period. If challenged in front of a group, he or she will react strongly, so it's best to resist any provocation to have it out publicly. Otherwise, you may be walking right into the kind of firestorm that the child is prone to create. The child seeks to be the agenda setter even though he or she does not yet have the social skills to handle the controls.

  Key phrases: Defer, Deflect Until You Can Be Direct

- The Charming/Hysterical Type (air) needs to be confronted right there and then. If you wait even ten minutes, he or she will charmingly wonder what you are talking about. This child type in particular needs to be lovingly, but firmly, held accountable, even if he or she bursts with theatrical responses.

  Key phrases: Implications of Actions

Introverts

- The Sensitive/Vulnerable Type (earth) should be spoken to with an understanding of the vulnerability he or she often experiences. Use your own stories to show empathy. These children can sense personal sensitivities of others and tend to hit out at them with sarcasm, but they can be extremely sensitive and reactive when the very same kind of mockery is directed at them.

  Key phrases: Safety, Empathy with Quiet Accountability

- The Easygoing/Stubborn Type (water) can become very stubborn if he feels his side of the story has not been heard. It's tricky because this type of inward and quiet child tends to be overlooked or pushed aside. Don't take him by surprise. Let him know, for example, that when you get home and after you both have something to eat (which this type of child loves to do!), you will want to know why he spoke or acted the way he did. This child can take a lot, but don't be fooled. He does not forget. He is very slow to anger, but when he's had enough, a tsunami can hit the family.

  Key phrases: Fairness and Timing

Disapprove—Affirm—Discover—Do Over (DADD)

AN EVERYDAY TOOL FOR WORKING WITH CHILDREN'S ARGUMENTS, PUT-DOWNS, AND DIFFICULT BEHAVIOR

This tool can be used to deal simply and directly with a clash between children or with an individual child when he or she is defiant or stuck. It can be used in the heat of the moment to cool things down or over the space of a day or two when an issue is more complex. It allows you to intervene with quiet confidence when children need help without getting caught in the fray or appearing to be on anybody's side.

FIRST . . . DISAPPROVE

Begin by expressing clear disapproval for the action: "It is hurtful to behave as you did." "We don't speak that way in our family/class." Speak with quiet directness. Mean it.

AND . . . AFFIRM

We know that we are supposed to separate a child's actions from his or her whole being, but it's not always easy. To achieve this, the disapproval needs to be followed immediately by an affirmation: "You hardly ever speak like that." "So often you do helpful things."

(A note on the sequence: Some parents have found that they prefer to reverse the order and affirm before they disapprove. For their particularly sensitive child, this works better, because it establishes a connection right away and calms the type of child who is quick to react and defend himself. This is a helpful strategy that can be applied on a case-by-case basis. All of the tools in this book are meant to be adapted in the way that best fits your family.)

AND NOW A DECISION POINT

- Do I have the time to go further right now?
- Does the child seem ready to tell me a little more?
- Is this a reasonably good place to speak with the child?

If the answer to these questions is a quiet yes, it's usually a good idea to stay in the flow of the situation and move on to the "Discover" and "Do Over" stages. However, if the answer to any of these questions is no, then it is better to defer by saying something like "It looks like we need to give this some space at the moment, but I want to hear what is bothering you, because something must be up. I'll check in with you later today." If the situation is between siblings and has become heated, you may need to do a simple we-direct with both children so that the situation doesn't blow up again.

THEN . . . DISCOVER

Then the adult needs to discover what the subtle issues are. Say something like "What's up?" "Something must be bothering you," or "What do you need?" These types of prompts need to come at the right time to get an honest response.

FINALLY . . . DO OVER

When the issue is clarified, the adult can help the child with a do-over. You might tell the child, "Let's work out a way to say what you need that is more respectful" or "You'll need to make right what happened, and I can help with some ideas if you are a bit stuck."

part three

THE GARDENER AND
THE GUIDE

6

The Tween Years and the Gardener

AROUND 10 TO 13 YEARS OLD

On a breezy spring morning before school, ten-year-old Noah exploded, "Don't you get it? I AM *NOT* A BABY ANY-MORE!" "It had been a fairly regular morning till then," says his father, Mike. "We had tussled a little about Noah cleaning up his room, which I helped him with. What set him off was when I cut him off. We were running late for school, and he was saying that he'd made plans to go to the park that afternoon and join a pickup game of soccer with his friends. I told him it wouldn't work to do that this afternoon because we had other plans already in place. Normally that would have been the end of it, but Noah had been challenging us lately. When he tried to talk to me about it, I told him I had made my decision. That was when he lost it."

"Noah is a good kid but fairly strong too," his mom, Danielle, adds. "We learned early how to stand our ground as parents. Otherwise, he would run the show. He seemed fine with this, but soon after he turned nine, he wanted to have more say in things. We wondered if he was coming into his teens prematurely, but he was still so young."

"Yeah, I am not okay with giving him access to all that teen stuff," Mike interjects. "It's too soon. We don't think he could handle it even though he insists he's not a little child anymore. To be honest, we are at a loss."

The Gardener in Brief

What Mike and Danielle experienced with Noah happens to parents all over the world. And while it may be a common occurrence, it's still confusing and hard, for both parents and kids.

At this phase in a child's life, a parent can see that something has changed. Your kid is not really a teen but is no longer a young child. When you talk to friends or family or seek out reading, there seems to be a lot of information on the earlier parts of childhood, and this is true for the teen stage too, but good sensible information and help for these in-between years is scarce. This is where understanding the Gardener Principle can really make a difference in being able to transition from the Governor stage and signal to your child that you know he or she has changed.

We will look at the Gardener Principle in much more depth in the second half of this chapter, but as you move into reading about what you may likely see at this age, it's good to revisit the big picture.

What kids at this age love to feel is that they are being heard and that what they say is taken seriously. The Gardener role is all about "cultivating" and going with this need. It involves asking your tween what her plan might be for something she wants to do. You should be interested in how they see things. The Parent-Gardener "harvests" these plans and gives the clear message that the child's perspective matters before *the parent* makes a final decision.

Getting Our Parental Bearings

To better understand discipline and support for a "tweenager," it is important to understand what most kids this age go through. What has changed since we were kids? What do we need to better understand about the world our tweens live in today?

So much has been written about teenagers, but this chapter will shed light on this in-between phase to help transition your discipline and guidance so your tween will sense a change while still feeling safe and warmly held. After getting our bearings by examining this developmental stage of our children's lives, we will turn to the practical application of discipline and guidance in the tween years.

The False Dawn

Anyone who is an early riser or has been camping knows about the false dawn. This is a starry light, usually seen in autumn, which appears on the horizon about an hour before sunrise. It looks and feels like dawn has come, and we have the urge to get out of our sleeping bags and start the day, but if we know the truth, we can stay put, warm and cozy, for an extra hour. "Tweenagehood" is a lot like a false dawn. While our kids may start to behave more like teens, it's important to approach their apparent metamorphosis with care for a few reasons.

The term "tween" was popularized by marketers looking to create new buyers for their products. They unwittingly defined an important developmental substage. Although tweens might look and sound like teenagers, their critical thinking is still in its infancy. What's more, long-lasting rebellions are rare, because tweens tend to be conformist. They want to fit in more than stand out as individuals. Our task as parents is to learn more about this stage of our kids' lives and figure out how to *cultivate* it rather than give in or be blindsided by marketing forces and *purchase* for it.

Who Is Influencing a Tween?

The term child development experts use is "norming." It refers to what is normal in a child's life: the daily habits and the people who are involved in his or her life, not the occasional highs and lows—the extremes—of life. What a child *feels* is normal will become the foundation for his or her developing self-esteem and moral and ethical values.

EARLY YEARS

Kids go through three distinct phases of norming. The earliest people to help nurture a young child are parents and other family members. All the little family habits and the social and behavioral boundaries a child lives within give him a sense of who he is in the world.

SCHOOL YEARS

The second phase of influence on a child begins when he comes into more contact with people outside her family, typically when she starts kindergarten, earlier if she attends day care from a young age. The rules and routines of school life merge to some extent with the customs created in the family as the two worlds blend together.

TWEEN YEARS

The third phase—which is when we apply the Gardener Principle—involves the tween years, when kids between the ages of from around nine or ten to thirteen start to feel the influence of the world outside family and school. In spite, however, of the recent explosion of media exposure, it's interesting to note that tweens today are more family oriented than in previous generations. Seventy-seven percent of tweens indicate that family is the most important thing in their lives, followed by friends (47 percent). This is important to remember when we consider that the average tween receives over five thousand marketing messages per week according to the Centers for Disease Control and Prevention (CDC). This data suggests that if we provide a safe haven from the flood of screen-based marketing that inundates children today, our tweens will seek us out now more than ever. The CDC report goes on to say, "Tween self-esteem is in development and fragile, at best. As such, tweens are affected by peers and face pressures and worries that are often focused on how they will fit in and interact with others in society."

TEEN YEARS

In the teen years, where we emphasize our Guide Principle, peer influence on kids becomes even more powerful. We all know this. Norming manifests itself in a peer group, affecting the way a teen dresses, speaks, identifies with music, and even moves. Individual friends may continue to be an influential part of a teen's life, but the peer group, whose members are more narrowly related in terms of things such as clothing styles, exerts a stronger influence. More important for our purposes, though, is that family life continues to serve as the foundation of how a teen norms and navigates the world of possibilities (some good and some quite worrying) that is opening up to him or her.

The Norming Process

No child leaves family values behind when transitioning into a new life stage. Family provides a constant base beat to the rhythm of the tween life. The strength of character that your tweens or teens demonstrate in the peer-group relationships is rooted in the strength and regularity of that beat back at home. That is why it's so critical for us to maintain that steady rhythm on the family front. You will notice that I have listed an age range of five to nine years in the table opposite. When it comes to the Norming Process things get just a little subtler.

Children who are at the "tweening point" are beginning to form unique identities. They think more about who they want to be and what they want out of life. They take on new responsibilities and make small decisions that were previously made for them by their parents. They seek greater independence but also sense that they are not ready to make big decisions on their own. For this reason, they continue to look to parents and older siblings to help them with big choices.

Tweens and Marketing

Marketers have thought a lot about this developmental stage, and parents can benefit from their research. The best way to market to tweens, according to sales experts, is to launch campaigns that promote fun. However, marketers are also quick to point out that fun can be defined in a variety of ways. They advise that campaigns should be sensitive to the fact that tweens are in transition and seeking to exert greater control over their environments. In addition, marketers have found that tweens frequently fantasize about achievement and recognition. They dream about becoming rich, famous, and successful. Researchers also recommend that campaigns appeal to tweens' core psychological needs. For example, tween girls are most likely to be motivated by messages related to beauty, glamour, or the desire to master a particular task. Tween boys are more excited by messages that express power and conquests that pit good against evil and involve acts of bravery.

Perhaps the most defining characteristic of this young generation is that it is the first to grow up in a digitally saturated environment. The greatest dividing factor between how parents grew up and what is influencing their tweens today is the Internet, which has created a more sophisticated language for today's youth, both verbally and visually.

Influences Through the Years

0-5 YEARS	5-9 YEARS	10-13 YEARS	14-19 YEARS
Early Childhood	Middle Childhood	Tween	Teen
Family	Family	Family	Family
	School	School	School
		General Friends	General Friends
			Specific Peer Group

Based on their online experiences, tweens have come to expect quick, easy connections and interactions in every facet of their lives.

What does this mean in terms of direct marketing influence? It is extremely important that the Parent-Gardener "weed out" influences from the *teen and also the adult* worlds as best we can, because if the information available about and the expectations of these later phases are allowed to flood in and influence our kids' lives prematurely, tweens face two basic problems:

1. They are still very much working out who they are. Kids can suffer from overexposure to grown-up stuff. Like delicate forming buds, they are easily susceptible to frost if it gets too cold too soon. This wonderfully sensitive process of discovery needs to come from within them, nurtured by your family values. Marketers' job is to sell stuff, not to care for a child's development. Kids at this age are too young to fully understand this, and that's why we need to protect them from too-adult marketing influences.

2. Marketers know tweens are vulnerable and will strongly associate with brands that give them the sense that they know who they are. In fact, no brand can do this. But images and advertis-

ing can lure kids, distracting them from walking their own developmentally essential, sometimes uncomfortable path to self-discovery.

Tweens and Money

Marketers know that tweens have increased access to money, so they target this age group with a barrage of money-related messages. Tweens vote for their favorite brands, musicians, or toys with their expanding wallets, spending billions of dollars per year. Additionally, tweens' direct influence over household purchases, from orange juice to personal computers to automobiles, is huge, and the marketers know it. And even in today's unsteady economy, tweens' purchasing power continues to expand.

Tweens and Drugs and Alcohol

Many tweens are offered drugs even before they enter junior high. Parents remark exasperatedly and with worry that these choices did not come up for them until their mid to late teens. Well, things have changed.

- In a national study, almost 14 percent of eighth graders reported having at least one drink in the past thirty days, and 11.5 percent had been drunk at least once in the past year.
- Youths who start drinking before the age of fifteen are five times more likely to develop alcohol dependence or abuse in their lifetime than those who begin drinking at age twenty-one or later.
- A 2004 study found that the average age at which kids ages twelve to seventeen began to drink was thirteen years old.
- Younger teens (ages twelve to fifteen) are more likely to say that

they can get prescription drugs than marijuana within an hour, while older teens (sixteen to seventeen) are more likely to be able to get marijuana within a day.

- Students who use marijuana before age fifteen are twice as likely as other students to report frequent truancy and three times as likely to leave school before age sixteen.

Tweens' Future Aims

Tweens fantasize about recognition. They believe achievement, magic, science, or luck will make their dreams of becoming rich, famous, and successful come true. A study conducted by Just Kid Inc. indicates that eleven- to twelve-year-olds value being rich (80 percent), helping others (78 percent), world travel (77 percent), being smart (76 percent), and being popular (74 percent). A majority also value fame (69 percent) and beauty (66 percent).

Tween Boys and Girls: Differences and Discipline

A lot has been written about the differing needs of boys and girls as they enter this phase, and there are key differences to keep in mind when you discipline and support your son or daughter through rocky times. As the Gardener role emphasizes very real listening and observing, it is natural that at this stage in our children's lives we would pay attention to their changing needs as they are reflected in their gender. The danger, of course, in addressing gender at any age is that we can descend into stereotypes very quickly. Yet one can argue that gender issues become even more delicate when we're talking tweens, because they are in such a tender and emergent phase. Because of the delicacy of sexual identity at this age, it is very important to be aware of the changes your son or daughter is going through in your approach to discipline and communication. You need to be conscious and sensitive about how you take your child's gender into account.

HOW TO SPEAK TO TWEEN BOYS WHEN THINGS GET ROUGH

Tween boys tend to be more practical than tween girls, and their emerging gender identity is more closely synchronized to their actions. They can become acutely aware of, and connected to, their burgeoning physical strength and their capacities to make and fix stuff. Like girls, boys are motivated by a desire to succeed or master tasks. But for boys, those urges are rooted more in their psychological need for power, conquests of good over evil, and bravery.

When you speak with your boy about something that is not going well, you do not want to end up cast as the "evil villain" or "threatening monster" in the action movie of his life. If you trip this subconscious wire, your tween son will fight back hard. He may feel he is being courageous and brave, but what you experience is disrespect and rudeness.

With that in mind, here are ten ways to approach your tween son:

1. Keep it short. Three to five minutes is usually the limit.
2. Break it down. Boys need time to process. If there is something you need to put right, think about breaking it down into two or three short discussions over a day or two.
3. Establish an end time. Let your son know when you need to have things cleared up and agreed to. Try something like this: "We need to have this worked out by tomorrow afternoon, so think about what I just said, and let me know at bedtime what your ideas are. If we can do this, no more needs to be said." Boys like clarity and containment.
4. Pay attention to timing. Avoid interrupting him when he is focused on a project or practicing athletic skills. Boys take time to

wind down and refocus, and their reactions might seem like disrespect if you interrupt them when they are on a roll. A good time to talk is when your son is doing a chore. Most boys will not feel bad about spending less time raking the lawn while you explain something to them.

5. Stick to the specifics. Avoid meandering, long-winded, and subtle explanations.

   Unhelpful: "Let's look at the big picture here, because there are some things that I don't think you are seeing . . ." (and on and on).

   Helpful: "We need to work out a time today for you to clean up your room. If that's too hard for you, that's okay. I will set the time."

6. Stay in the now. It is so easy to get drawn back into past situations, and because they are often remembered, this can escalate a situation and divert it away from what you are trying to achieve.

   Unhelpful: "You always ignore our agreements and sneak your brother's stuff. This is the third or fourth time."

   Helpful: "We agreed that you and your brother would ask permission before using each other's sports equipment. I did not see you do that just now. You may have simply forgotten. But how do we put this right?"

7. Keep the primary focus on actions. It's not that boys cannot understand feelings. It's that their doorway into that world is most often via actions. If you point out the cause and effect of what he did in a practical way, your son is more likely to understand the emotions and feelings of those affected.

   Unhelpful: "Do you realize how thoughtless you were, not being on time?" Or: "How do you think it makes your sister feel to have missed her important dental appointment?"

   Helpful: "When you turned up so late after practice and I

had to wait too long, that meant your sister missed her dental appointment. She was going to find out about her braces, and now she has to wait six weeks for another appointment. You might not have meant for that to happen, but it's hard for her."

8. Affirm his actions. Speaking about practical actions is a doorway to boys' emotions and feelings.

   Unhelpful: "You *always* leave stuff lying around for everybody to trip on and try to walk around."

   Helpful: "I really liked it that you helped out by clearing out some space in the garage without even being asked to do it. Your bike fits in much better now. What was not okay was leaving all these boxes in the driveway. I can't get the car out now."

9. Involve him in problem solving. It's important not to "go at" them but to involve them in a search for a solution. Boys like solutions.

   Unhelpful: "Like always, just leave it to me. *I* will ask Joe if I can borrow his pickup truck."

   Helpful: "I need you to help me figure out what to do with all those boxes you cleared out of the garage. Do we know anyone with a pickup truck? Or maybe you have a better idea?"

10. Own it. Tween boys want to feel skillful even though they are just developing practical and life skills. Speaking to a boy in terms of how his actions affect you helps prevent him from feeling accused and incompetent. Otherwise, he will feel the need to defend himself and push back against you.

   Unhelpful: "You don't seem to take seriously the risks of not putting power tools away properly."

   Helpful: "It bothered me that you did not put my power drill back on my workbench. It got rained on, and if I had used it, I would likely have gotten an electric shock."

HOW TO SPEAK TO TWEEN GIRLS WHEN THINGS GET ROUGH

Tween girls tend to be more tuned in to their feelings than tween boys. Their emerging gender identity is more closely related to their growing awareness of subtle emotional currents and how these play into their relationships. They value the ability to express themselves creatively with personalized clothes and accessories. When they were little girls, dress-up clothes, handbags, and jewelry helped them *play* a role. Now as tweens, they are slowly *becoming* that role.

Girls at this age partly define themselves through the relationships they have with family and friends.

I remember once sitting near two playground games of Four Square, a type of ball game played by four players on an eight-by-eight-foot square divided into four equal sections. The players who are not on the court wait in a line and watch. There was a boys' game being played a dozen or so feet away from a girls' game. All the kids were around eleven years old. It's not unusual for boys and girls to decide to play separately at this age. On this day, a dispute arose in each game. I couldn't help but smile at the way each group resolved its dispute.

In the boys' case, the game was stopped. The dominant kid, who was central to the disagreement, tucked the game ball under his arm, like a caveman with his bone. The players argued intensely. Their argument was almost entirely based on the "liner rules" and whether the ball had landed "in" or "out." After no more than a minute, when it became clear that no agreement was likely, the dominant boy stepped in and said, loudly, "Okay, this is getting boring. Let's do a do-over. But from now on, if any part of the ball touches the line, it's out!" All the boys agreed, and they resumed with fervor.

The girls handled their dispute very differently. First, the issue that arose was not about a rule but about the *attitude* of one of the girls. Apparently the girl in question and her best friend had been snickering in line when a mistake was made. This really upset one of the players, who took offense at being laughed at and "whispered about." The accused snickerers fought back. "Do you always have to be so totally sensitive?" they said. "Like, how do you know we were even talking about you?" The offended girl countered with, "Just because I am not completely obsessed with fashion and how I look!" There was a murmur of recognition as some of the other female onlookers acknowledged that something important had been said. Two other girls stepped in valiantly, trying to broker peace. But it was too late. The disputing girls walked off, each with their supporters, as expressions such as "Fine!" and "Whatever!" rang out pointedly. The game dissolved, and the ball rolled down the hill into a bush. The peacemakers shrugged, sat down on the Four Square court, and began to play an intricate hand-clapping game.

While boys generally take a direct and practical route to exploring who they are becoming, girls tend to take more circuitous, winding routes to self-discovery. They ask themselves questions like "Who can I trust?" "What is the truth here?" and "How do I appear?"

When there is a need for discipline and guidance, you do not want your daughter's unregulated, raw emotions to trigger your emotions, as that can be spectacularly unhelpful. She needs help to form an emotional "container" to hold her newly emerging feelings so that they don't spill over in inappropriate ways. You are more likely to be able to model self-control if you have some simple strategies you can use. Otherwise, you may be left wondering, "What am I supposed to do with all this craziness?" Below are some practical ideas that will help your daughter feel she is more in control of her emerging emotions. Using these tools may also help you build a stronger bond with your daughter at a time when she needs you most.

1. Empathize. Let her know you understand that it is not easy. A great way to begin is: "I know this is hard and that you might

not be feeling good about it, and I think there is a way we can work this out. Maybe . . ."

2. Tease out the layers, and choose one issue that is solvable. Tween girls are in the process of becoming aware of relationship subtleties. Their stories can be pretty complex and seemingly mixed up, but what they are often doing is following the intertwining relationship "lines" without much objectivity. Everything feels personal, and it is hard for a tween girl to step back and see the big picture. Remember that this can all seem a bit overwhelming to your daughter. What can calm her down and send her into her day or off to bed in good emotional shape is choosing just *one* of the issues she is concerned about and working to resolve it. It's important to select the one that is most solvable.

      Unhelpful: "There seems to be a lot going on here. Let's see if we can work out how to deal with all this."

      Helpful: "It's great that you can see things from so many sides. How about we figure out a way for you to speak with Sara that does not make it seem like you are just hanging around feeling awkward?"

3. Summarize the patterns you see. Often, a lot of information will pour out. Tween girls feel much better when they feel that their parents are listening, but it's also helpful when you see and clarify the bigger picture.

      Unhelpful: "Chores just have to be done. We all make contributions in this family."

      Helpful: "Okay, I see what you mean. It's hard to be asked to do chores when you feel so pressured about the homework you are getting, and that seems to be a point where things often go wrong. We need to figure out a way to handle this."

4. Restate the issue. Sometimes the issue you need to work through can get lost in a complex bundle of emotions and feel-

ings that your tween daughter needs to express. By quietly re-stating the issue, you provide the conversation with a point of orientation.

Unhelpful: "Honestly, I would expect more maturity from you. This is not making very much sense to me."

Helpful: "Right, but how do you see the amount of freedom your brother gets relating to you tidying your room?"

5. Be careful about your tone of voice and body language. Girls at this age take in a lot more than they appear to. It's important to remember that your daughter is experiencing a kind of second-degree emotional sunburn. Think about how sensitive your skin is to touch when you are sunburned. That is how sensitive your daughter is to your tone and body language. Stay as neutral as you can, keeping in mind that she will inwardly amplify any gesture you make and anything you say.

6. Pay attention to timing. Shouting into a storm is futile. Choose a quiet moment to talk, well after the emotional upset has subsided.

7. Know that she knows she is being "weird." She can't help it and is aware of how out-of-control things feel inside. Sometimes the chaos gets away from her and ends up directed at you. Forgive her, but quietly insist that you both need to work things out when she is not so upset.

8. Know that showing difficult emotions to you is a vote of trust. Girls this age develop crushes on people they can trust *not* to reciprocate their feelings—it's a safe way to feel deeply without having to deal with the practical consequences. In the same vein, they will cut loose emotionally and even appear unhinged only around people they can trust not to get caught up in their emotions: you. Remembering this is vital to helping you keep things in perspective.

9. Know that she is practicing and testing her power. Have you

ever noticed how quickly your daughter can shift from a tornado-like emotional state to behavior that is reasonable and calm and a lot more like the child you know her to be? If she finds that you can stand firm and be warm while she flails, it soothes and settles her. You can become the safe harbor she retreats to after being tossed around by her churning emotional sea.

10. Use humor. It's hard to give an example of this because every child finds different things funny. I remember a time when my mother was having a hard time with my sister. She looked across the dinner table and said in an exasperated tone to my father, "Please speak to the girl!" My father looked around the table at my siblings and grandparents, paused, and, with a twinkle in his eyes, said, "Mmm, yes indeed. Who would like to choose the topic?" Everyone, including my mother, laughed out loud, and the tension was broken. He wasn't being a clown or belittling my mother. He was just being quietly humorous. He did talk to my sister later at bedtime about not speaking so unkindly to her mother.

11. Use ricochet comments. When you have the hunch that your daughter's feelings are too raw but you still need to address something that has gone wrong, try speaking to another person within earshot. You might, for example, mention to a sibling or partner (so your daughter can hear it), "I heard from a few other moms that the seventh-grade party last night got a bit rowdy and that some of the girls left the house and went down to the park because they thought the boys were being gross. I remember how difficult those situations can be, but some parents got really worried because the girls left the party and hung out at the park alone after dark."

12. Know that dads need more time. Many dads have confessed that they can become bewildered by the number of emotive

phrases that fit into a one-minute tween daughter verbal barrage. Up until this phase of their daughters' lives, dads have probably been able to keep up and understand their daughters' needs, but things can shift in the tween years. It's a good idea for a dad (and a mom if need be) to hit the pause button and not feel the need to respond to a daughter's complex emotional demands immediately.

Unhelpful: "It just sounds weird, and it really has to stop."

Helpful: "Okay, give me a few minutes, and I will let you know."

13. Know that you don't need to hammer home the point. It's understandable that we often feel the need to forcefully emphasize a point we are trying to make. Our message seems to get deflected when we are confronted by a daughter's emotional turmoil or sullen withdrawal.

Unhelpful: "You know that it's not okay to speak like that, and you know that it upset everyone, and I will not accept it. Do you understand? I am waiting for an answer!"

Helpful: "Okay. I have talked enough. I think what may be the problem is that you don't see why your bedtime on Sunday night can't be the same as on Saturday because you think Sunday should still count as the weekend. I want you to try and put into your own words how you think I see it." If you get a shrug and no clear response, try, "Yep, sometimes we need time to answer a question like that. I'll ask you again a little later."

14. Recognize your daughter's beauty and intelligence. Girls this age are probably more sensitive to criticism than they are during any other phase in their lives. They can go from calm to "I'm so ugly and stupid!" in a nanosecond. Powerful stuff. Take care when you comment on their appearance *or* on their thinking. Their confidence in both are delicate buds just beginning to unfold, and they are easily damaged.

Pause Point

Among the many ideas detailed on supporting and disciplining your tween girls, which seem especially applicable to you and your daughter?

Perhaps you recall a situation in which you wish you had acted or done things differently. One of these suggestions may go right to the heart of a pattern you have found yourself trapped in when your daughter triggers your reactions.

Rather than feel despondent or even ashamed, try to use this recognition as a springboard for change. Develop a plan so you can shift away from your unwanted reaction. Trust your instincts, and talk to your partner or a friend about how you might build up your capacity to respond more evenhandedly. Remember: Be kind to yourself as you attempt to shift your unwanted response. Not everything a gardener plants will bear fruit, but exploring how the soil could be better prepared is one of the first steps in addressing a problem.

CULTIVATING THE GARDENER
PARENTING PRINCIPLE

I f you were to list the qualities that a successful gardener must possess, what would they be? Hard work, patience, care, and watchfulness. Each of these qualities is also essential to parenting a tween.

A large part of parenting a tween is about staying attuned to your child's changing moods and needs. Tweens have new and interesting things to say. They want to be a part of the decisions that affect their lives. Giving them space and respecting their changing ways of seeing things is natural and healthy. But they are still vulnerable, and their views are often (charmingly) subjective.

A good gardener must contend with the immediate demands of his or her plants but also consider the longer-term needs of the soil. Timing is crucial. When I was a little boy, I watched as my father prepared the soil in his garden. He always had one eye on getting the soil just right and the other scanning the skies. He would *feel* the soil for the right time to plant. I remember the days my grandfather joined us. He would pick up the soil in his arthritic hands, smell it carefully, and even taste it. Then he'd nod in agreement with my father if it was ready for planting. They employed the same sort of care and sensitivity when choosing the ideal time to harvest. As a parent, it's similarly important to proceed with caution and care to make sure to get the timing just right. Here is a brief overview of the Gardener dynamic:

- The Gardener is still responsible for the garden, but listens. When you make time to listen to your child, you reassure him that you are taking him seriously and that what he says counts. He will take a little more care in the way he speaks to you because he realizes he can influence the decisions you make if he shares his viewpoint respectfully.

- The Gardener is still responsible for the garden, but watches. You listen to your child's words but also observe the day-to-day context in which a request is made. Because when your child speaks about what she should be allowed to do, you need to consider this against the backdrop of her recent actions and behavior. For example, a request to go shopping with friends may be fine when your daughter has been showing good judgment, but if she has been out of sorts and you suspect she is learning her disrespectful behavior from one or two of her friends, you will want to notice this and have it play a part in how you respond to the request to hang out with these same girls. Let her know that you have been and will be watching for signs of improvement.

- It's all about perspective. The garden you see in the early morning from the east looks quite different from the one you view from the west at sundown. A good gardener knows this and will consider the different perspectives before making a decision. It's critical for kids to understand that there are several ways to see any situation, not just their own. So when a parent speaks with a tween, the conversation can begin with the statement "Tell me the way you see it." This works much better than "What do you want to do?"

- The taming of the wilderness. Many people know the pleasure and pain of looking at a patch of untended ground and imagining a new garden. We see potential and want to work within the land's natural contours, but it may need to be tamed and shaped before we can get started. A balance must be struck between keeping some of what's lovely and wild and clearing enough space to let sunlight through to nourish the vegetables, flowers, and trees.

  The task of the Parent-Gardener of a tween is similar. Up until now, a child has mostly acted on the basis of his or her own needs and desires. You've done your best to provide healthy boundaries, teach your child good manners, and help squabbling siblings sort things out. But tweens are developmentally ready to be much more conscious of the needs of friends, siblings, teachers, and parents. This growing social awareness can help tame the unruly emotions that can otherwise overshadow the development of good relationships with the key people in their lives.

- Root out invasive species. All kinds of invasive species can overtake a garden. Likewise, as a child enters the middle elementary school years, colorful language and behavior can creep into family life. A parent functions well within his or her "job description" by saying to a son or daughter, "Yes, I understand that you think *everybody* uses the word 'stupid' all the time, *but in our home, we just don't, and you know this.*" Your words and values still have a huge impact.

Asking a Tween "Who Are You Being True To?"

A tween wants to express him- or herself as an individual, although not quite with the full force of a sixteen-year-old. The garden has reached a stage of maturity at which the plants respond well to their environment and have their own ideas about where they want to grow. While things can become a little too tangled, it is good to see how strong and self-sustaining the growth is becoming.

How should you handle your tween's budding individuality? He needs to be true to his emerging self, and his burgeoning individuality should be genuinely welcomed. But he also needs help understanding that it's essential to be true to his family, extended family, friends, school, and community. Like little waves that are created when a pebble is dropped into a still pond, the ripples from his actions move outward from the center (himself) and affect family, friends, school, and community in ever widening circles.

———

Here's an example of the ripple effect of truths:

Thirteen-year-old Lucas emerges from his room. He has on an especially rumpled, smelly T-shirt and a strategically torn pair of jeans that seems to be losing a battle with gravitational forces. There's an atmosphere of excitement in the house because it's time to go to his school baseball game, and Lucas is pitching today. As he enters the living room, Lucas's (low-beam) gaze shifts from mother to father to younger sister. The family dog senses tension and heads for cover under the coffee table. Two or three long seconds pass. No one moves. Finally Lucas looks up and says, with that mixture of nonchalance and exasperation that only a tween or teen can truly master, "Wwwhat?" A long pause follows.

"Are you really going to make me say it, Lucas?" his mother says in a quiet but menacing tone.

Lucas's eyes widen, and his palms turn upward as he appeals to the teenage gods of justice and unfair judgments. Another pause. The dog has now moved to her emergency shelter between the sofa and the wall. Lucas's mom turns to his dad, silently and almost imperceptibly communicating the words "Do something!" The father tries to remember what it is his wife has told him they should do about Lucas.

He senses that this is not the time for levity. Anything other than impeccable fatherly wisdom will not go down well. He decides that deflection is the better part of valor. He needs to buy some time. "Let's talk about this in the car," he says in what he hopes is an appropriately thoughtful tone.

In a tense and potentially explosive situation like this one, it can help to let the tween know that you understand his desire to dress comfortably and be true to himself. But he is also part of a community, and in this situation, he is also representing other people: his family, his school, and his town. So how he presents himself cannot be based solely on *his* truth but also needs to be balanced with *the* truth of the bigger picture.

Back to Lucas's story:

Lucas's parents manage to get Lucas to agree to put his track pants and sweatshirt on in the car, but it is an uncomfortable situation for everybody. Later that evening, when he has showered (of his own volition) and things in the house are noticeably more relaxed, his parents ask to speak with him about the way he dressed to go to an important school event. The father, who has had some time to think, begins, "Lucas, it was hard for everyone today in the car. I understand that it's natural at your age to want to have a say in what you wear and how you wear it. We get that. A lot of things are changing for you at the moment, and you are getting to know what you like and don't like in many different ways."

Lucas's eyes briefly flicker to high beam as he nods faintly. Dad is encouraged because he senses that his son is probably okay, so far.

Mom asks genuinely, "Can you help me understand why you feel it was unfair that we asked you to change out of the clothes you wanted to wear to the game?"

"Because it was, like, no big deal," Lucas shoots back. "I was only going to walk from the parking lot through the school to the locker room and get changed into my uniform. What does it matter what I am wearing?"

The father, a former high school athlete himself, says, "Back in the *olden days* when I represented my school, we all had to wear a school blazer and a shirt and tie into and out of the locker room on game days. I hated it because it was too formal. It felt like the school had way too much control over me." Lucas becomes much more present in the conversation.

"I didn't know you had a sports dress code, Dad, and that you didn't like it!" Lucas says.

Dad continues, "We spoke to the coach, and he set up a meeting with the deputy principal and athletic director. To cut a long story short [a very good idea with a thirteen-year-old male], we came to an agreement that we could wear our letterman team jackets to the game, but for all formal situations, like pep rallies or awards ceremonies, we would still have to wear blazers and ties. You see, Lucas, the way we dress and behave represents ourselves, but it also represents our family and, in school situations, our school. When we played against other towns, the way we dressed and behaved represented our whole community. Do you see what I mean?"

Lucas nods. He gets it.

Mom senses it's time to wrap things up. "We are going to get plenty of practice at this, Lucas, because we get dressed every day," she says. "And I want us to be able to work together without feeling like we are enemies. If we have to remind you that, while you are being true to yourself, you also have to be true to our family values, I want you to know now that we are not criticizing you. We are trying to keep the other things you need to be true to in mind because, as parents, that's our job."

Teaching Tweens to Adapt How They Act According to Where They Are

When a twelve-year-old's traditional grandparents visit, her parents tell her to wait until everyone has finished eating before leaving the dinner table. She slumps down and says, "This sucks," under her breath. Deeply embarrassed by his daughter's rudeness, the father takes her into the living room and says, "Look. I know you have spent a lot of time at the skate park this summer. That might be how people speak there, but you absolutely must not speak like that in front of your grandparents."

What the father clarified for his daughter was that there are unspoken rules of civil behavior. We must take into account the people who are around us and modify our behavior accordingly. The father was clear and straight with his daughter. Kids this age have a growing capacity to tune in to their surroundings and self-regulate.

When you help your tween moderate her behavior, you are teaching an essential life skill. No one wants his child to end up at a college or job interview speaking the way she would at a pickup game in the park. Sound far-fetched? It happens all the time when essential social skills have not been learned. The tween phase is the perfect time to step up your insistence that the quality of both spoken and unspoken communication is important.

Body language is just as important as the spoken word. Some researchers have estimated that over 90 percent of all our communication is conducted nonverbally through body language. So it's important to pay close attention to facial expressions and postures, to eye rolls and slumps, in situations in which such expressions are inappropriate.

"Can You Help Me Understand Why . . . ?"

When something slips in your child's behavior, it's most effective to provide a subtle reminder. Your tween will respond well if it seems like no big deal. Open the conversation with "Can you help me understand why . . . ?" which gives your child a chance to explain how he sees it without feeling he is being judged. Tweens can explain a situation in an astonishingly honest and open way. They are much more likely to relax and communicate clearly if they feel you are genuinely interested. There are a lot of changes going on for a child of this age, so tweens can be understandably unsure of their place in the family, especially if something has happened which they think you might not approve of. By framing your question as "Can you help me understand why so much food did not get put back in the refrigerator?" you are asking your child to be a "friend to the court" rather than cross-examining him or her as a hostile witness.

The "Plan Sandwich": An Everyday Way to Improve Communication and Build Your Tween's Social Capacities

As tweens grow up, the Parent-Gardener involves them in family decision making in a different and expanded way. Here is a basic framework you can use and reuse when you are figuring things out with your tweenager. It's called the Plan Sandwich: There is a soft layer at each end of the conversation, and the "meat" is in the middle.

THE TOP LAYER: "WHAT'S YOUR PLAN?"

When you ask a tween, "What's your plan?" you immediately signal that you want to hear his take. Use this question when he asks permission to do something or even when things have gone sideways and need to be set right. If he seems unsure, you can help him along. But for you to have a productive conversation, he needs to be respectful in three ways:

1. **Time:** "Tell me at a good time." At this age, a child's brain centers are maturing, and he or she can better understand appropriate timing. Asking tweens to wait for a good time to tell you something helps them shift from an early childhood tendency

to want to do everything *right now* to a growing sense that there are good and bad times to ask for something.

2. **Team:** "Take others in the family into account." Tweens can develop the capacity to be team players and to understand that there are other needs in the family. It's okay if an early tween (a 10-year-old, for example) does not find this easy. He or she can be prompted if you ask questions like "That all sounds pretty good, but how do we get Josh to his soccer game on time if I drive you to the park?"

3. **Tone:** "Speak respectfully." It's also important to teach a tween to moderate his or her tone. Prior to this developmental phase, children often need to be told use their "inside voice." If your child gets frustrated and shows signs of becoming disrespectful, give him or her a chance to cool down. The brain-based reality is that a tween's ability to self-monitor emotions and calibrate tone of voice is in its infancy. It's still a "delayed response." A tween may be rude or awkward in what she says and how she says it, but she may not realize it fully in the moment. If you give her a little time to revise her response, she will often do much better. One of the best ways to provide the space and feedback needed is to stay as centered as possible and say something like "You have been doing really well so far, telling me about your plan. And you probably don't mean to be disrespectful. Do we need to come back to this later, or are you okay?"

THE MIDDLE LAYER: "I'LL THINK ABOUT IT."

Your tween must understand that you (or you and your partner) will be the one to review and decide on the plan. A good Family Gardener will take time to reflect. Just because your child told you what *he* wants, that does not mean the plan will be implemented exactly in that way. It's very important for your tween to understand this. You may decide that the overall plan is fine, but the specifics often need modifying. If at all possible, try to make some of the plan happen even if it's not possible within the time frame your child has in mind. The important thing here is that you give yourself some time to reflect and, in doing so, model good impulse control. This also serves to let the discussion cool down a little.

THE BOTTOM LAYER: "HERE IS MY DECISION."

When you are feeling solid in your decision, speak to your tween. Remember that now you also have to abide by what you asked your son or daughter to do by choosing a good time and explaining that you took the others in the family or friends into account when you were thinking about the proposed plan. You have a very good chance of being able to communicate calmly, largely because you have given yourself the time needed to feel centered.

You might say to your son who explained his plan respectfully, "You did a great job telling us about your plan, Miguel. I really like the way you are learning to wait while I think about it. I was going to say it was not possible, but because of how considerate you have been, we are going to try to set up the playdate with Aaron. It can't be tomorrow because we have a lot already happening, but I will ring Aaron's mother and do my best to help make it happen soon."

WHEN PLANS DON'T WORK OUT

Sometimes the plans you and your tween have made do not work out. If this happens, let her know that you will not forget and involve her in figuring out how you can still make it work. Your tween must practice adapting to what life brings her way. Parents who have introduced their tweens to the Plan Sandwich say that the tweens adapt much more easily because they have practiced planning and how to work things out together. One parent described her kids as having "grooved into the way we plan things." And if you use the Plan Sandwich well, all those furious or sullen meltdowns that used to occur when an anticipated activity did not take place will become a thing of the past. There will be letdowns, but when a parent and tween can share the feeling of disappointment and rework the plan together, a forward momentum can be maintained rather than the tween feeling that nothing worked out and it's never going to happen.

LIFE SKILLS FOR NOW AND THE FUTURE

The Plan Sandwich strategy helps develop and strengthen the following:

- The ability to get and hold on to an overview of the big picture.
- An understanding of cause and effect: The way things are done now will affect the way things turn out in the future.
- A sense of when to hold back and when to go for it.
- A grasp of how to speak at a time and in a way that assures you will be heard.
- The knowledge that your perspective, while important, is only one of many.
- The ability to adapt quickly when plans need to change.
- The ability to make plans with a team of others.
- The ability to accept feedback and the fact that your plan can be improved.

These are all good qualities, but what elevates them to must-haves is the fact that our kids are moving toward an adult work world where jobs with salaries and good benefits are few and self-employment, contract-based jobs, and freelance work are much more common. Reread the list above. Doesn't it read like the very best tool kit for making it in the job market, that they will soon have to navigate?

From Little Things, Big Things Grow

Short daily bursts of exercise keep our bodies healthy. The same is true of tweens' social abilities. As you've probably noticed, the strategies we have looked at in this chapter are the kind that you can use again and again in the daily conversations and brief interactions you have with your tweens. The constant repetition and reinforcement of family aims and values develop a strong, healthy social reflex in a tween. And your family, friends, and teachers will notice that your son or daughter is respectful and courteous as a result. It's not an oppressive discipline. It's an inclusive one. Your tweens will be respectful but also grow as individuals and know how to take initiative. They will sense when it's the right time to go for it and stay with it. They will have fun and make good friends because they have learned from you that relationships are all about valuing the little things and respecting others.

Responding to Differing Abilities

Although we have been talking about the tween years in general, we all know that every kid is different. Some kids need extra help making plans. Maybe they are at the younger end of the phase. A ten-year-old's social interests and abilities are quite different from a thirteen-year-old's. And a girl's facility for understanding the subtle emotional currents that flow within a family is often more acute than a boy's. Paying attention to these differences is a core part of the Gardener Principle because it cultivates slow and deep observation before deciding on a course of action. Whatever the reason for them, it is vital to operate within the limits of your son's or daughter's capacity to make plans. If you sense that your child is getting frustrated or not doing very well, these three suggestions should help:

- First, slow it down. Spread your planning over several brief discussions.
- Second, move in close, and be positive about the ideas your tween hatches, even if they are unrealistic and disjointed at first. It's your job to help make them possible.
- Last, be a planning jigsaw master: Place your kid's ideas in the right spot because you understand the bigger picture. Know that if you do this quietly and warmly your son or daughter will soon get the hang of it.

In Conclusion

THE GOVERNOR PREPARED FOR THE GARDENER

In Chapter Two, we delved into the themes of healthy boundaries. As you read the current chapter, you saw that tween-focused discipline and guidance practices work effectively because of the three foundations that were framed, poured, and formed during the Governor phase: (1) impulse control, (2) acceptance of loving authority, and (3) healthy boundaries.

THE GARDENER NOW PREPARES FOR THE GUIDE

This chapter has been about adapting our parenting to help our kids build social skills and become family team players. We build upon and expand these capacities in the teen years so that the critical life choices our teenagers face can be made with increasing social understanding and empathy. For a teen, the ability to take others into consideration when making choices serves as a counterbalance to the self-exploration so common during those years, which can tip over into self-absorption. It helps prevent a teen from moving toward entitlement and selfishness.

7

The Teen Years and the Guide

14 TO 19 YEARS OLD

A light rain was falling as I walked home from school after football practice. A group of my friends, also sixteen, pulled up beside me in a bright red, tricked-out Camaro they had borrowed from one of their dads. One of my teammates, who'd been MIA at practice, was at the wheel.

The driver's window slid down. Smoke billowed out, along with a strong smell of pot and booze. Two of my buddies shouted for me to get in. They were animated, and, yes, there were two cute girls with them. As I took this in, three thoughts struck me in rapid succession. First: "This looks like a lot of fun." Then: "Coach would tell me this is definitely not a good idea." But most of all, I heard my father telling me, "This is a mistake. You all are better than this. Be strong. Be yourself."

I took too long to process all this, because my friends yelled out, "See you round, sucker," and peeled off. As I walked home, I felt conflicted, but when I sat down to dinner with my family, I knew I had made the right decision. I didn't even bring it up, not because I wanted to keep it secret; it just didn't seem necessary. Being with my family settled my doubts, and I got into the home groove. I helped wash the dishes and began my homework. My decision that evening seemed like no big deal. But it may have saved my life.

The next morning I went over to a friend's house to hang out. The second I saw him, I knew something was very wrong. The red Camaro had slid off a winding road at high speed and crashed into a tree. My teammate was dead, and his girlfriend was fighting for her life. The others had been released from the hospital but were all banged up.

Word spread quickly through our small town, and when I got to the football field for practice later that day, I saw my dad and coach talking together. I walked over but couldn't find the words to tell them that it was because of them that I hadn't joined the tragic ride. They had been there with me on that curb when I made the decision not to get in. I wanted to thank them, but the words just wouldn't come out.

In the locker room, my coach asked me if I would like to speak with the team. As captain, I was supposed to step up. I nodded but didn't know what to say. There didn't seem to be any point to talking because nothing could bring our friend back. Then a strange thing happened. All the words I had wanted to say to my dad and coach poured out. I thanked them and told my teammates we needed to come together as a team to support our friend's family, our families, and the others who had survived. The room went quiet. Then we dedicated our season to our teammate.

The Guide

So here we are, the parents of a teenager. It's been said so many times that it must be true: "Those years passed *so* quickly." On an intuitive level, we can sense that our kid is now living differently in the world. He or she seems to be more awake to the contradictions and challenges of society and also of family life. Something needs to change in our approach, particularly when the inevitable tensions arise between a teen and a parent.

This is where the Guide Principle comes in and can help transform these potentially strained years into a time of ever deepening connection. We are sold the portrayal of the fresh, eye-rolling, posturing, and dismissive teen by many popular television shows, but simply put, the teen years absolutely do not have to involve lurching from one frustrating and disconnecting exchange to another. The Guide shifts further from the Governor, who gives instructions and direction, and the Gardener, who listens to a tween plan and then makes a parental decision. Now the Guide spends time in conversation with a teen and gets a good sense of what a son or daughter wants to achieve both in the short term and into the future. When it starts to feel like a teen is straying from the direction he really wants life to go in, his parents will already have the base for a conversation on how to refocus and get back on track. This is the best chance for teens to lean forward and engage, because it is *their* life and *their* hopes and dreams that are being honored.

In this chapter, we are going to explore the qualities, strains, and stresses that define the teen years in order to set the foundation for addressing this new dynamic with the Guide Principle.

Getting Our Parental Bearings

As my own story above demonstrates, parents have a huge influence on the choices their teens make. They may not admit to us that we play a role in their decision making, but they get their bearings from us, and this is at the core of the Guide's work. If our parenting feet rest on solid ground, our sons and daughters will tread upon firm, supportive moral ground themselves. One seemingly small decision can save a friendship, or even a life.

Let's turn our attention to the topics of discipline and guidance before we move on to practical parenting strategies.

Second Birth

Teenagers are strong yet vulnerable. In many ways, they are like newborn babies. Thinking about them in this way can help us understand some of their befuddling behavior.

For example, infants are prone to picking up viruses. They get sick easily because they lack well-developed immune systems. Teenagers suffer from similar vulnerabilities, albeit on an emotional level. As their self-awareness emerges, teenagers develop and nurture a delicate but strengthening emotional resiliency. Sensitivities that were in gestation during the tween years burst forth and make themselves felt, resoundingly, in family life. Just as the arrival of a newborn baby changes everything at home, the birth of a full-blown teen rattles the walls of family life to their very foundations. Babies cannot regulate their crying without being held and reassured by their parents. Teens also cannot temper their new hyperemotions without a calming parental presence.

Craniosacral professionals, who specialize in infant skull and vertebrae health, maintain that it is essential for a baby to cry in order for the pressure to build up in its cranium so its head can develop a healthy shape. In a similar way, it is developmentally necessary for a teenager to get emotional; it is an essential part of how she develops her self-image and begins to know herself. It is normal for infants to cry and teenagers to emote, but both need soothing so that they don't end up in more serious distress.

And yet, just as it is often frustrating to figure out how to soothe a crying baby, it can be quite difficult to understand why a teen is behaving erratically. We do all we can to keep from lashing out at a crying baby, no matter how challenging this may be. We should likewise do our very best not to react negatively to stormy teens, as they are easily wounded and emotionally defenseless.

Babies build up their immune systems when they feverishly burn off viral or bacterial infections. Emotionally fevered teens burn off life situations that they can't handle. In either case, we must stay close as parents and make sure things don't escalate to a dangerous point. But we can stay centered if we understand that fevers, emotional or physical, are a normal part of development.

We've all seen a mom or dad "spot" his or her toddler. The parent may try to hold the child's hand, but at some point he will push the parent's hand away and wobble forward on his own. Like a gymnastics coach, the Parent-Guide stands close by, ready to soften a fall and prevent serious injury.

Parenting a teenager is quite similar. In the early teen years (thirteen and fourteen), a lot of emotional hand-holding is needed. But at fifteen or sixteen, as they take their first unassisted steps into the world, teenagers often push the supportive hand away. It is critical that we not walk away at this juncture, even though we may feel our children are ready. Just as the toddlers needed us to stay close by and maintain a watchful presence, our teens need us nearby too. Just as toddlers learn to walk by trial and error, our teens are exploring who they are and might become in the same way. And we are there, not to catch them, but to sympathize, perhaps bandage a "life wound," and from time to time, step in firmly if we see that serious and lasting emotional injury is likely. Our teens may storm and rage, but if we know in our hearts just how vulnerable they are, we will persist in guiding and disciplining them with loving firmness.

Family Still Matters

In the previous chapter, we looked at norming, the process by which a child, tween, or teen is taught what boundaries and expectations are in place. We also looked at the three phases of norming, beginning in family life, moving outward into school life, and finally shifting to predominantly peer-influenced socializing.

We all know what a strong influence peer groups exert in the teen years. And how, in some extreme cases, in the absence of steady, caring parents or guardians, teens can become completely attached to their peers, at times with painful consequences. But thankfully, for the vast majority of teens, family influence remains the strongest guiding force in their lives, even more so when a parent works as a Guide who is sensitive to the teen's direction in life and can step in if needed.

Amplification

At a birthing class I attended with my wife, a midwife spoke about what husbands should do when their wives are in labor and emotionally vulnerable. Her advice applies perfectly to parents dealing with volatile teens. She asked the expectant fathers to pay close attention. "When your wife or partner is in labor, she may not be able to speak to you like she normally would," she said. "You do not have to repeat your words or shout if they don't respond. Even though they are concentrating on giving birth, they hear every word you say. They need you in a very big way during this wonderful, scary time." One expectant father raised his hand and asked if that meant he should whisper. "No, not really," the midwife responded. "Just try to be as centered and calm as you can, because your wife is going to need you more than she ever has before. Just be you." The men looked focused and serious and grateful that they now knew the role they had to play. As parents of teens, our role is similar. We need to remain centered and calm as we pilot our kids through life's intense experiences.

Though our teens often appear only vaguely interested in what we say, they amplify our words inwardly, especially if we are talking about something that directly affects their lives. This is particularly true when they are upset and the doors to their feelings are flung wide open. We need to take special care with what we say and do in these moments, because that is when our teens are at their most vulnerable. Not an easy task, of course, because our parental buttons are most likely to be pushed in such charged moments. Keep this amplification gauge in mind: The impact of what we say in normal conversation is often doubled in a teen's mind and tripled in volatile situations. Because of this, a Guide often needs to speak quietly knowing what he or she is saying is being heard even though it sure does not look like it.

Self-Centered or Centering the Self

What can appear to be selfish and self-centered in a teen often reflects a need to focus on the pivotal inner changes he or she is undergoing. Whether your teen pushes back or retreats into sullenness at new ideas or parental requests, remember that she doesn't necessarily do this to disobey you and be difficult. More often, she is reacting negatively and lashing out because she is already struggling to absorb what's coming her way and can't cope with more.

We all filter our surroundings through a lens of "how this will affect me." In teens, this tendency is considerably intensified. We may think we are being objective and talking about the big picture, but our teens tend to extract and enlarge the bits of conversation that relate specifically to their own lives. This frustrates parents, who feel their words are being manipulated or misunderstood. But the developmental reality is that teens are self-absorbed because they need to be. However, the work you did to cultivate your child's social skills in the early childhood and tween years should help keep your teen's healthy tendency toward self-focus from devolving into actual selfishness.

It's best to accept a teen's tendency to self-focus as developmentally necessary rather than fight it. As a Guide, you can remind him that it is your job to see the big picture and make it clear that, while you will always listen to his needs and requests, you also have to consider his siblings and the family as a whole. He may be self-absorbed, but when you do this as his parent, you model the self-sacrifice and consideration for others you hope will become a part of his social fabric as he matures.

Sleep

Two mothers compared notes on teen sleep issues during a break at a high school parent evening. "Scottie stays up late on his computer, and then, in the morning, he is utterly impossible," said one. "Yes! It's the same with Sarah," said the other. "She looks drained and exhausted but insists on staying up way past midnight. Then she's incredibly touchy and on a super short fuse all day." Both moms complained that their teens' tiredness affected the mood of the entire household.

Sleep experts say that ten- and eleven-year-olds can function well all day on ten to eleven hours of sleep. Teenagers also need around ten hours to stay alert and effectively regulate their emotions throughout a long day. But at this critical developmental juncture, many pressures on their time, such as very large amounts of homework, socializing, and screen use, can cause them to stay up late and wake up exhausted. "The average teenager gets about six hours' sleep, so he's sleep-depriving himself completely," says Dr. Richard D. Simon, Jr., medical director of the Kathryn Severyns Dement Sleep Disorders Center. "This is a much bigger problem than people think," Dr. Simon argues. "They underestimate the problems of being sleepy in the daytime and how it impairs mood and affects performance."

When we don't sleep well, that deficiency follows us into the next day, making it hard to handle the slings and arrows that come our way. As Charles Czeisler, chairman of the National Sleep Foundation, puts it, "The exhaustion associated with [lack of sleep] places a physiologic burden on us, and we actually are much less resilient."

Teens tend to feel more comfortable going to sleep later. Their circadian rhythms—the patterns in the times of the day when the body feels it needs to rest or sleep—kick in around ten or eleven at night. But they often go to bed much later, and wake-up times cannot be adjusted on busy weekday mornings to compensate. There is still homework to complete, early sports practice, and the pressure to get to school on time.

Because sleep deprivation makes a teen more emotionally raw and reactive than he or she already is, it can lead to challenging behavior, disciplinary issues, and strained family relationships.

The good news is that circadian rhythms can be managed. As a first step, engage your teenager in a conversation about sleep patterns and the effects of sleep deprivation. Choose the right time to talk, perhaps on a Saturday afternoon after your teen has slept in and is feeling refreshed. Here is some advice you can give:

- Try to go to bed at the same time each night, give or take fifteen to thirty minutes.
- "Front-load" any screen use (TV, computer, phone) so that it happens earlier in the evening. Declare "screen-free time" ninety minutes before bedtime. This is important because:
    - Multiple studies have shown that the light emitted from LCD screens interferes with the body's ability to register that it is tired. This kind of light exposure also suppresses the release of the melatonin hormone, which promotes sleep.
    - Teens often use screens before bedtime for social-networking purposes. It may be fun to connect with friends, but it is also stimulating at a time when body and mind should be unwinding and relaxing.
- Reduce the intake of sugar and caffeine throughout the day and especially in the evenings.

- For teens, deep, refreshing sleep occurs between ten at night and three in the morning. After that, they tend to go into more restless and dream-filled sleep. So it is better to go to bed earlier to get more rejuvenating sleep time. As one father told his basketball-playing son, the first phase of a night's sleep is "the time when you make three-point shots." The second phase of the night, he said, "is two-pointer time."

- Get up earlier. In a group conversation about teen sleep, one mother commented, "Late nights and late mornings are just not possible on the weekdays for our son. When we agreed to a ten P.M. bedtime and he got into the swing of that, he started getting up earlier naturally and was able to finish his homework and prepare for the day. Not only was he thinking more clearly in the morning; he also said he really liked having everyone out of his way. When we came down, he actually would look up and say a cheerful 'morning' rather than his trademark sleep-deprived grunt."

- Exam cramming by listening to audio CDs and MP3s during sleep is not effective. The body shuts down during sleep and will not absorb this kind of sound and translate it into learning or memory. It mainly serves as an irritant.

- Sleep consolidates learning. Matthew Walker, director of the Sleep and Neuroimaging Lab at Beth Israel Deaconess Medical Center, suggests following a three-step process in order to prepare in an optimal way for exams:

  1. Get a full night of sleep before a day of cramming. This will allow your brain to be as receptive as possible to laying down new information (a dry sponge is a good analogy here, and if you don't sleep, it will still be waterlogged with learning from the prior day).

  2. During the following day, learn the material deeply (i.e., think about what you are learning, and understand it, rather than use simple rote memorization).

3. Get a full night of sleep afterward to cement and consolidate that information into the architecture of the brain. Indeed, a recent study of our own demonstrated that, following learning, sleep not only enhances individual pieces of new information but also builds associative links between them, allowing you to "see the bigger picture."

- Establish other rhythms, such as meal and shower times. The body's inner clock is strengthened by these rituals, establishing sleep as one of several healthy daily rhythms.

- Avoid big talks before bedtime. Set them up for a specific time the following day or on the weekend. Doing this helps ease a teen's anxiety about whether or when certain issues will be discussed.

- Darken the bedroom. Good curtains are important. Make sure all lights from electronic devices are either covered or out of sight.

- Establish a relaxing bedtime routine. It can be very helpful for a teen to use this time to reflect on the day that has just passed. During this time, you can ask your teen what worked well and what was challenging. That way he or she gets a chance to let the day's burdens go, and you get a glimpse into your child's world. Refrain from talking a lot. Just listen and prompt gently.

- Some natural sleep aids, such as chamomile or valerian tea, can be helpful. Some teens have found that taking a natural aid called Rescue Sleep, a Bach Flower product, makes a difference.

- You should also model relaxing behavior yourself by avoiding phone calls, screen viewing, and general busyness and bustle late in the evening. If you wind down, your teen is much more likely to sense that the home is shifting gears to bedtime mode.

Friendship Circles

"But they're my friends! And they've finally accepted me. You can't keep me from hanging out with them!" fifteen-year-old Jenny yelled furiously at her dad. He was concerned that the group of girls his daughter had just begun to connect with were unreliable and could easily reject her. It didn't seem right for her to drift away from her two longtime friends—girls who had stuck together and supported each other through all the challenges and changes of their tween and early teen years. And he remembered all too vividly how gaggles of popular, fashion-conscious girls dominated the social scene when he was in high school. But the extreme efforts his daughter was making to talk, walk, and dress like this particular *it* group worried him. It seemed like Jenny was not being true to herself.

When we talk to teens about their friendships, we are stepping onto hallowed emotional ground. Rather than tiptoe around them, we can frame these conversations in a simple, sensible way. Remember, a good Guide knows the terrain his or her teen is walking through and can speak from experience in a way that communicates empathy without seeming to know it all.

First, explain that all friendships are not the same: "While you can be friendly with most people, there are a select few who are loyal and trustworthy. Other friends are fun to be around, but you would not turn to them if something serious happened." Teens are usually quick to acknowledge that some friendships are superficial and others run very deep.

But it helps them to hear this from you. Extroverted teens can be so keen on being accepted and socially successful that they try to make everyone a close friend. This can lead to repeated disappointments and anxiety. It may also signal to other kids that these outgoing teens are needy or socially manipulable. Introverted teens, on the other hand, may withdraw from social life altogether or have only one friend and reject any other kids who may want to get to know them. While these behaviors are, to some degree, normal, we can help our teens calibrate their friendships without being critical or intrusive. If we help them figure out where they stand, they will feel safe rather than lost in the confusing world of social interaction.

Balancing Single-Peer-Group Influence

When we help our teens differentiate their friendships, they are less likely to invest too much in a single peer group or be swayed by people who may try to push them to do something they are uncomfortable with. They are also less likely to fear rejection and engage in risky behavior in order to fit in with the crowd, because we have helped them understand the many layers of friendships. It is much easier to walk *away* from a group of people who are doing things you don't like if you have someone else to walk *toward*. This is what a good Guide can offer. It establishes a "family base camp" for the teen to come back to when things get hard with friends.

The Table and Friendship Circles

A very effective way to explain differences in friendships to your teen is to use the metaphor of tables and the various places we find them. As Jaimen McMillan, the founding director of the Spacial Dynamics Institute, said to me, "You cannot control what comes at you in life, but you can control where you meet it."

We often gather around a table for both mundane and important moments with family and friends. The people we sit with and the kind of table we choose says a lot about our relationships. Some tables are a part of everyday life, and others we only sit at occasionally. When you give advice about the level of a friendship, it is so good to see the lights of recognition come on behind a teen's eyes when you are using the table metaphor. You have had this kind of conversation with your child many times before, and your kid has benefited from your figuring things out with you. In this situation, you might say, "You know, I get the feeling that Sadie would like to be closer. You know, at the kitchen table. She has been more of a casual friend—at the picnic table in the park—for a while now. How do you feel about that?" Because your son has gotten used to this way of talking that keeps thing calm and clear, he might respond with something like "Yeah, I know. The guys have been telling me about it. I think she is nice, but maybe the garden table is good for now as she tends to dump people a lot."

DISTANT FRIENDSHIP CIRCLE

This kind of table is in the local park's picnic area. You only really go here once or twice a year to attend community events. You come across people whom you see around and are happy to see but don't know so well. These are people you are polite to, and the conversation is friendly but light. You'd certainly never share secrets or anything sensitive about yourself here. At the end of the event, you say goodbye and go home. If you see any of these people around town, you wave and say hi. But the connection is superficial.

OUTSIDE/OCCASIONAL FRIENDSHIP CIRCLE

You might gather at a table in your garden with family or school friends. They don't just walk into your yard; you choose to invite them. You may share similar interests. They might be teammates from your sports club or fellow thespians in your drama group. You have a good time with them, but they only visit occasionally. While you enjoy their company, you don't expect much more than a friendly connection.

CLOSE FRIENDSHIP CIRCLE

Now let's extend the table metaphor and imagine a small porch table with three or four comfortable chairs around it. This is where people often sit with good friends. More meaningful conversations take place here about things that are happening at school and in town. It's in this kind of place that more relaxed relationships develop. It's with porch-table friends that topics come up easily, because you have some shared interests and circles of friends in common. These are the kind of friends that you can laugh with. It seems natural to talk with them about things like how to support a friend in common who is having a hard time.

INNER CIRCLE

And finally, there is the kitchen table at the "heart" of your home. Here you eat meals, play games, and drink hot chocolate. You have quiet talks about hopes and worries, shed tears in trying times, and squabble and laugh. Only a few friends whom you trust deeply and whom you will probably be in touch with for many years join you here. With them, you can be yourself and share your fears, as well as your hopes for the future.

What your son or daughter will realize is that not everyone can fit around the kitchen table, or even the porch table for that matter. As we get farther from home, there are fewer intimate friends and profound relationships and more pleasant acquaintances. We may really like someone and wish that we could be better friends with her, but the reality may be that she has little time or lives too far away.

———

This table metaphor is a good way to explain things to your teen if he invites someone to the kitchen table who is not so reliable or trustworthy, and he discloses private things that should not be shared.

You can also use the metaphor when reassuring a cautious or with-drawn teen that it is normal and okay to have distant friends as well as close ones.

How would this way of differentiating friendships help the dad we heard about above when he talks to his fifteen-year-old daughter Jenny? If he approached the conversation this way, she'd be less likely to feel that her dad simply disapproved of her cool new friends. The conversation would be based on her level of closeness to the other girls rather than pegged to parental judgments and teen defensiveness. The father would probably place fashionable friends at the garden table, while his daughter might argue that they are porch friends. Either way both of them would be likely to agree that these new friends were definitely not kitchen-table people. At least not yet. And having deepened her perspective, Jenny might also pause and place a little more value on her long-standing friendships.

Stages

Adolescence is such a broad, clinical term. It does little to describe a time of tremendous inner tumult and critical self-discovery for young people. We'd do better to break the teen years into three very different key stages, as described below. Not all kids will go through these stages in order, but getting a sense of the architecture of these teen phases can help us better understand why our kids act the way they do and help us stay steady in our guidance.

Below I will paraphrase the three stages outlined in Betty Staley's wonderful book *Between Form and Freedom*.

NEGATION: AGES 13–14, THE "NO" YEARS—CLOSED FOR RENOVATION

In this stage, teens shut down a lot of outer emotional activity to focus on their inner "emotional re-modeling."

Embarrassment

Your son or daughter may sometimes suffer from a severe emotional sunburn. He or she becomes acutely sensitive to any criticism or praise and is readily and regularly deeply embarrassed.

Time Alone

Because of an acute sensitivity to the world and the people around them, young teens like to spend a lot of time alone, whether walking in nature or holed up in their rooms.

Role Identities

Teens also take cover by developing a role identity. They become skaters, music fanatics, or avid sports fans. As they role-play, they'll dress, talk, and walk in a manner that puts a little distance between them and the world around them. The guardian of a troubled young teen who dived headfirst into an aggressive music genre told me, "The harder the world came at the kid, the more he got wrapped up in all that violent music stuff. It was like he was putting on some kind of soul armor."

When Roles Go Too Far

It's normal to experiment with various roles. But if life is overwhelming, a kid at this age can take role identity too far. If you have a gut feeling that your daughter is losing herself in an image that is not really who she is, figure out what she may be struggling to cope with and see what you can do to dial back the pressure she feels. However, be careful not to challenge your teen head-on about the way she looks, acts, or speaks. Too direct an approach may cause her to feel even more misunderstood and drive her deeper into hiding. When a parent calms things down in his teen's life (decreases the number of activities she is engaged in or the pressure she is under), his child can reclaim her true identity. This can be a very emotional moment for parents, who feel as if their child has just been returned to them.

TURNING POINT: AGES 15–16, THE "MAYBE" YEARS—OPENING SOON

Many parents notice a shift in the way their teen relates to family, friends, and community at this age. Dark emotional clouds are still present, but the sun breaks through more often. An OPENING SOON sign is posted at around the age of fifteen. It can even be replaced as the teen heads toward sixteen or seventeen with an OPEN FOR LIMITED HOURS sign, which signals greater self-regulation and an ability to share her feelings with her parents.

Standing in the Doorway

The teen stands with one foot in "no" and the other in "yes." A parent can be dealing with sullenness and flare-ups one day and the next day (or hour) feel a mixture of bewilderment and pride as his or her teen behaves thoughtfully, maturely, and considerately. You'll hear statements like "Don't treat me like a baby!" and, hours later, after some questionable antic, "What do you expect? I am just a kid!" We can accept the confusion, conflict, and frustration a little more readily if we understand that our teen is standing on a developmental threshold, and her behavior will swing from one side of the maturity spectrum to the other as she feels her way through to the next stage.

Dualities

Behavioral swings and dualities are characteristic of this age. Here are some examples:

1. You may look out the window and catch a glimpse of your son in the driveway, drenched in sweat, playing an intense game of one-on-one basketball with a friend. Later that day, you'll see him sprawled out on his bed overwhelmed by a slothlike lethargy. This mysterious lethargy becomes incapacitating, especially if the lawn needs mowing.

2. Your daughter shows genuine compassion for the plight of refugees in one of the world's underserved regions. Moments later she lashes out cruelly at her sister for being "such a total loser."

3. Your teen posts signs on his door that read, ENTER AT YOUR OWN RISK or POSTED: TRESPASSERS WILL BE PROSECUTED. These postings tell you—not very subtly—that he needs to be alone. He may even create a big scene and refuse to go on the family camping holiday. Yet he desperately needs to feel he's included and is deeply wounded if an ice cream was not brought back for him, even though he was at a friend's house when the family went to the store.

4. Your daughter may spend hours in the backyard practicing one soccer skill with an intensity that you marvel at. She is similarly passionate in her never-ending phone conversations with friends. Yet she lets homework assignments pile up and often seems distracted and unfocused.

Establishing a Counterbalance

A key to parenting a teen at this stage is understanding that he will be subjective and single-issue focused. We need to counterbalance that by focusing on the big picture and guiding him when he gets lost. The mistake we often make is insisting that our teens get the big picture. They are not yet equipped to do that. That's why *we* are here, and that's exactly what the Guide can do.

Here is an exchange between a parent and teen that many of us will recognize.

Mother: You are often asking me to see your point of view and the big picture. But aren't you being subjective now? It gets us nowhere.

Daughter: What does "subjective" mean?

Mother (embarrassed by the cliché she is about to use): It means that you might not notice the forest because you can only see individual trees.

Daughter: You mean I learn about the forest one tree at a time?

Mother (hopes rising): Yes, exactly.

Daughter (sincerely): I am fifteen. Isn't that my job?

Mother (smiling in agreement): You know, you are right. But it's also my job to know where we are in the forest so we can find our way out.

If we accept that teens have limited big-picture capabilities, a lot of frustration can be avoided. It's pointless to expect that a young teen will be great at something he or she is not yet able to do. The teen may partially grasp an issue, but a high level of objectivity is at least a few years away.

We tend to see the teen years as a time of nonconformity in which our kids challenge the status quo and value their rights to express themselves as individuals. This is true, of course, but there are two other dynamics at play that form a counterbalance. First, our sons and daughters still need to conform, and they do. It's just that they generally conform to the unspoken dress and speech codes of teen life. Second, just when our teens seem to want to live by their own values and ethics, they lean heavily on the moral underpinnings that we helped develop in all our years of parenting them. As one mother told me, "I didn't mean to eavesdrop on my daughter's conversation with a friend. But it was such a relief to hear her express strong disapproval about the way another friend had been treated. She spoke clearly and with conviction. But what almost made me cry was that the values she expressed were so clearly based on what my husband and I had tried so hard to instill in her."

Friends, Soul Mates, and Crushes

At this age, relationships become more and more important to your teen. There are two things to look out for. If your kid is outgoing (an extrovert), he can overcommit socially. There is an understandable exhilaration about all the things he can do and places he can go. But a parent's job is to step in and help his or her teen prioritize. One tip: Don't ask your son or daughter to dump a plan. Instead, defer it to a later time. That way the teen is less likely to feel he or she is letting friends down. And the plan's urgency may even fade as it gets displaced by other fun possibilities.

However, if your teen is quieter and more taciturn (an introvert), she may begin searching in earnest for one special friend—a soul mate. She may stop hanging out with big groups as she cultivates this close friendship. Our task here is to help keep our teen engaged with other kids as well. One parent kept these social connections alive for her daughter by taking her to a horse stable each week for riding and horse-care lessons. This brought her daughter into contact with a whole other set of young people. And as it turned out, the horse-stable friends proved to be an invaluable social safety net when her "soul mate" suddenly moved to another state.

As teens grow up, they also *grow out,* into their community and the world beyond family and school. It is not uncommon for teens traveling through this exciting new landscape to be attracted to someone who awakens in them a desire to be different. They'll love the way this person moves, talks, and dresses. But on a deeper level, the person a teen has a crush on represents hope in general.

The subject of a teen crush is usually unavailable. It might be a sports or music star. But it can also be someone close by—a teacher, coach, or family friend. The teen's daydreams will include all sorts of scenarios in which the object of his deep feelings notices and values him. But it's important to remember two things. First, the teen is simply exploring an awakening capacity to love someone in a more conscious way. In this sense, teens are practicing. They have shifted from role-modeling (which they did in the first phase of their teenage years) to seeking a deeper connection with another human being. And second, the crush can become crushing if the object of a teen's devotion reciprocates in any way. A teen seldom develops a crush on someone he or she feels might respond. And if the person does respond, the teen might feel that person is creepy.

It's important not to undervalue this new capacity for loving from afar, because it is real. And when a parent is dismissive or derisive, it can be very wounding. Think of a crush as a wonderful, newly developing capacity for devotion. Don't make light of it by teasing your teen. A good Guide is respectful and keeps a watchful eye.

AFFIRMATION: AGES 17–18, THE "YES" YEARS—OPEN FOR BUSINESS

Two seventeen-year-old boys were talking on the bus on the way to a basketball game. "I'm glad that my parents are smarter now," one said. "Yes, my parents lost the plot there for a while, but it's better now," responded the second. It may well be that each set of parents had made small improvements in their parenting abilities. But it's much more likely that these teens were beginning to see their parents and others in a more balanced way.

In this last stage of the teen years, our sons and daughters come to realize that they are not the sun around which the family orbits. The sun is actually the shared core values their parents have cultivated and the moral direction that those provide in their own lives.

Something special can open up during these years. Most of the emotional remodeling is finished, and the teen is now "open for business." As one father said of his eighteen-year-old, "When my daughter was growing up, we had such an affectionate relationship. That all faded away when she hit her teens. But now that she is older, it's back again, only now it's not just affection. There's mutual respect too." Another parent responded, "I know what you mean. That closeness went underground when my son hit his teens. Now that he's older, it's bubbled back up like some underground spring. My advice to parents of a younger teen is to remember that healthy water still flows, it's just belowground. What comes up in the final teenage years has, in a way, gone through a purifying process and is better, even more clear."

Let's take a look at some specific changes that often occur at this age.

New Powers of Thinking and Perspective

These young men or women are much more likely to be able to see issues from a variety of angles. Previously they may have taken a single position and argued it to the end. But now they are beginning to understand the complexities of life. They look to literature and science for metaphor and meaning. And many start to take more of an interest in community and world events.

Idealism and Disappointment

As teens wake up to the world around them, they take in all its beauty *and* its strife. And they can become disappointed in local and world leaders. It makes sense that teens should be incensed or saddened at the suffering of others. But it's important that they not fall into a cycle of cynicism. A sensitive Guide empathizes but also offers other ways of seeing an issue, reminds the teen that there is still goodness in the world and people who care, and offers proactive solutions.

To keep your teen from feeling ineffectual and bitter, build a bridge between her interests and her actions. For example, if she is outraged by reports of deforestation in the Amazon and the effects it is having on indigenous populations, engage her in a conversation about the practical things she can do to help. Whether she fund-raises, develops a school research project, or gets involved in tree plantings closer to home, she is much better off feeling actively connected to the issue.

One teenager, whose mom volunteered at a shelter for domestic-violence victims, became distraught when she heard that the shelter might have to close due to lack of funding. She riled up her soccer teammates, and they dedicated their off-season to raising awareness and funds. The interest and the efforts of the teenage girls caught the attention of several local and regional media outlets. The ensuing spotlight helped attract enough funding to keep the shelter open.

Establishing the Counterbalance

We enjoy hearing our sons or daughters share thoughtful insights at this age. But just as we must serve as the objective counterbalance to our younger teens' subjectivity, we must counter our older teens' idealistic tendencies by making sure that they are also grounded. When your seventeen- or eighteen-year-old is being philosophical and theoretical, share with him or her what those ideas mean to you on a practical level. For example, one father who was a farmer was listening to his eighteen-year-old son, Diego, speak knowledgeably about the need for less-polluting electric vehicles. The father asked how that works when a large pickup is needed to haul stock trailers and do general maintenance. Together they discussed alternative fuels and how they could restrict the use of the pickup to only farm use and look at getting a very fuel-efficient car for family trips. Diego went further by suggesting they use all-electric golf carts for transportation around the farm. The father pointed out that this would require some serious upgrading to the tracks and that they would need to do some figures to see if it could work.

Likewise, when you hear your teen render an opinion that is detached and dispassionate, talk about how that makes you feel. This is critical to helping your teen stay connected to the world.

Criticism vs. Critical Thinking

It's wonderful to hear teens at this age penetrate a subject critically. They may read a newspaper report and take it to task for its bias. They may witness the self-destructive behavior of a sports star and ask whether the athlete had ever considered the effect he has on his family or team. Teens at this age need help to prevent their growing capacity for critical thinking from spilling over into negativity and put-downs. The best way to steer clear of disrespectful and toxic comments is to explore other people's perspectives. For example, rather than deny that what happened to a friend was wrong, ask your annoyed teen how his other classmates saw the situation. How would the teachers view it? How would his friend's parents see it? Some might be even more outraged than your son, while others might not see the situation as unfair. By taking a 360-degree walk around the situation and considering differing perspectives, you move from one-sided criticism to multifaceted points of view. When you do this with your teen, you help him develop critical thinking.

Sexual Relationships and the Parental Response

Particularly at this stage of a teen's life, questions about sexual relationships surface. You have only to thumb through a magazine in a doctor's waiting room to see highly suggestive, sexualized photographs of teenagers. Teens constantly see and hear the message that to be sexual is to be desired and accepted. It's hard to counter this message, but not impossible. I have spoken to countless young people—individually, in small groups, and as entire high school bodies—about the dilemma of whether or not to become sexually active with a partner. The key to helping a teen navigate this issue is to pivot away from the question of sexual activity and toward striving for loving relationships.

The average age of first sexual intercourse for an American is seventeen, and the question on many young people's minds is "Should we do it?" When you shift the discussion from sex to an exploration of different types of love, you are not avoiding the issue (sexuality) but giving it context. In his book *The Four Loves,* C. S. Lewis provides helpful insights for teens navigating the crosscurrents of sexuality. In the section below, I have framed these four layers in terms of their meaning in the lives of teens.

Four Kinds of Love

When you speak with your children about complex and confusing topics like sexuality and sexual relationships, let them know that there are some important layers to consider, that thinking about them has helped you, and that there is a way to figure it all out. Choose a moment when there is time to share points of view. They need to know from the get-go that you do not expect them to agree with everything you say, nor do you claim to be right. There are many ways up the mountain, and a good Guide knows it. Let them know that these issues are important to you and that you want to know what they think.

When you guide the conversation, you will almost certainly need to adapt what is laid out here and put it into your own words and your own voice. Because your teen is now older, you will be able to share a little more of your own biographical relationship history without embarrassing her. Take care not to overdisclose. Your aim is to help your teen better understand what her relationship with another person is based on. With a broader perspective, she can make informed decisions and avoid unnecessary pain and confusion.

Eros

This is the first and most earthly kind of love. As is the case with all four types, this description is based on the wisdom of the ancient Greek thinkers and philosophers. Eros was one of four gods who gave shape to the world. The other three were Chaos, Darkness, and Abyss. Eros was a child of the night and came to embody sensual desire, fertility, and ecstasy. In Roman times, he was called Cupid and carried a bow and arrow. Once you were shot by his arrow, you became blinded by love for another person.

When you talk to your teen about this kind of love, point out that

Eros is the root of the word "erotic." In erotic love, you have a strong physical attraction to another person that can't be easily explained. Something within you is deeply moved. You may feel personal boundaries fall away and your normal relationship limits shift. Tell your teen that while it's normal to have such intense feelings, becoming involved in a sexual relationship based solely on erotic attraction (because the other person is "hot") is problematic.

First, erotic love is blind. Once "stung," you might overlook important aspects of a person's character. The object of your love may be kind and good, but he or she may also be cruel, manipulative, and uncaring. When you are consumed by this kind of love, your personal defenses evaporate, and you expose your most intimate self, both physically and emotionally. It's dangerous to do this if you know little about the other person and what motivates him or her. You may also be disrespecting yourself. Being true to yourself involves finding out who the other person really is and what he or she will bring to your life, in more than only a physical way. It's extremely hard to hold back when erotic feelings and desires motivate you. Your teen may wonder, "Can this kind of love be wrong when it is so intense?" The answer is no. The experience is completely natural, but if a teen bases a serious relationship on Eros *alone,* he or she is likely to end up deeply disappointed when the initial high wears off.

Philia

The second level of love is based on friendship. Aristotle defined it two ways: first, as a friendship based on mutual benefit ("a cobbler and the person who buys from him") and, second, as a connection based on shared interests or hobbies.

Teens have no problem understanding this type of relationship since it is such a big part of their daily lives. They may become convinced that, if they've found someone who is *into* the same things they are (music, sports, clothes) and to whom they have a strong physical attraction, it's okay to plunge into sexual relations. Your teen may feel that he knows the person he is attracted to and that he is not just jumping into bed with someone because that person is "hot." If your teen expresses this, let him know that you respect his perspective and are glad he is so familiar with two of the four levels of love.

However, a teen should not see being in love on two levels as a green light for a sexual relationship. Here are three reasons why:

1. What happens when a teen's tastes change? People jump into long-term relationships and even marriages based on great sex and mutual interests. The dilemma? As one partner grows and matures, his or her interests can change. When that happens, that person may either break away (and hurt his or her partner) or stay in the relationship but feel restricted or imprisoned. The chances that two such people could grow together from such a young age are very slim.

2. It can get boring. No matter how much two people like the same couple of bands or sports team or movies, a relationship based on common interests is two-dimensional and can quickly become unsatisfying. For example, if you are speaking with your seventeen-year-old daughter who is about to go away for the weekend with a best friend whom you can see might be becoming more, you might say, "It's great that you and Anna are so totally into the same music, and I think the festival is going to be a lot of fun, but you spoke last week about how being with her can feel a bit restrictive since the only thing you seem to have in common is the one band. Can you help me understand what you meant?"

3. Relationships can get rocky, and that's normal. However, relationships based solely on Eros (sexual attraction) and Philia

(common interests) often don't survive the rough patches because the bond that holds the couple together is not robust enough to handle emotional turmoil.

Here's what often happens: Two teens get involved with each other because they share a strong physical attraction and have mutual interests. Sooner or later one person gets bored and feels constrained or criticized. He or she breaks it off and looks for someone who is a better match as a lover and friend. But without a greater context on which to base a relationship, history is likely to repeat itself. This dynamic leads to a lot of hurt and disillusionment. And it's certainly *not* how any teen wants to live his or her life.

But what if you are wondering, "Why is this inevitable? And even if it is, why is this such a terrible pattern? I certainly had a high school boyfriend with whom I broke up, and while it was horrible at the time, I now look back on him only with fondness. Isn't that also part of normal development?" The answer for this that many teens will be open to is that you are not suggesting your teen live life avoiding being uncomfortable, as being uncomfortable can often be an essential part of learning. The important thing here is to not keep repeating the same pattern over and over and being hurt in the same way. The main lesson injury and pain teaches us on a physical or emotional level is that we need to do something different and approach things in a different way.

Friends with Benefits *"But hang on. . . . What about friends with benefits?"* your teen asks. In this kind of relationship, friends seek sexual pleasure with "no strings attached." For teens, this is often limited to oral sex but can involve intercourse as well. It may not be easy for a parent to talk to a teen about this topic, but "friends with benefits" is a widespread social phenomenon and needs to be addressed with care. In a mixed-gender relationship, it is often the girl who gives out most of the "benefits." And while it may sound like no one can get hurt going into sex with this attitude, both parties have to keep their emotional barriers up and their expectations low. When discussing this sensitively with your teen, point out that sex and love are not supposed to be detached. A friends-with-benefits relationship is like having sex with both partners in body armor. A clumsy undertaking, no doubt, and certainly a bizarre image. Yet teens engage in such relationships often.

What happens if a teen enters into this type of dissociated sexual relationship and then finds he or she wants a more genuinely affectionate connection? The person the teen wants to connect with may not emerge from behind his or her barrier and reciprocate.

It's critical for teens to realize that beginnings are important. They set the tone and direction of a relationship. So if a teen suspects he might like to take a friendship deeper, putting on his friends-with-benefits armor and having sex is not the best approach to building a healthy relationship.

Sure, teens have deep waves of sensual awakening, but something to remember when we speak to our kids about this delicate subject is that more and more teens are also becoming savvy to personal boundaries and not allowing themselves to be drawn into this kind of relationship. Take care to give your kid credit for being at least somewhat aware of this issue, and give him or her space to express it.

Caritas

The word "charity" comes from the Greek term Caritas. Giving to someone freely without expecting anything in return is a very telling act as well as a sign of emotional connection. In the First Epistle to the Corinthians (chapter 13, KJV), Paul speaks of "hope, faith, charity, these three" and adds, "But the greatest of these is charity." Selfless giving is a high form of love.

Maria asked her teenage son Scott, who was on the brink of "taking it to another level" with Cara, his girlfriend of a couple of months, "Would you give Cara your most valued possession and expect nothing back? Would she do the same for you? I think this needs to be clear, Scott, before any couple considers having sex, because this is the level you are heading toward." Here, Maria defined the implications of the "level" her son was referring to, putting it into clear perspective. Scott and Cara did eventually sleep together, but not until after they'd finished high school a year later. Maria became close to Cara, who confided to her that she "fell totally in love" with Scott when he spoke to her about not having sex until they were very sure where they were going to be with each other in life.

Like many parents, Maria had to come to terms with the fact that her belief that sex should be a part of marriage only does not hold as much sway with younger generations. But she was relieved and grateful that Cara and Scott deepened their relationship before committing to each other on a more intimate physical and emotional level.

It takes time to develop a profound relationship with a partner. It takes even more time to be certain that your potential sexual partner reciprocates your feelings and level of commitment. When teens have been in a relationship for some time and the question of having sex arises, it usually springs from a strong feeling of mutual commitment. At this stage, parents can speak with their teenagers about the future prospects of the relationship. When sex is delayed, a broader base of mutual respect can be built. And the stronger the foundation, the more likely a relationship will last. If your teen wants a relationship to succeed and you recommend that she wait, you are guiding her toward *her* goal rather than simply giving her well-meaning moral advice, which she is likely to react to negatively.

Agape

The Greek term Agape is often translated as "unconditional love." It is considered the highest of all forms of love, and—in the relationship context—it extends beyond charity to the love of another person's treasured dreams. In Agape, you are so connected to your partner that you sense his purpose in life and will do all you can to help him achieve it. When this kind of love exists, a couple can expose their deepest fears and hopes to each other knowing each will understand and not betray these vulnerabilities when the relationship hits a rough patch.

Agape looks past appearances. We have all seen this kind of love if we have seen a person become terminally ill, physically or mentally disabled, or disfigured and watched his partner find a way to deal with the enormous challenge with grace. She looks past the outer realities to who her partner is on the *inside*. This kind of love is free from emotional infatuation and highs and lows. It is often called holy love because it weaves the other three forms into a unified "whole."

Young people in the last phase of their teen years intuitively understand this kind of love. They long for it and aim for it as an ideal. When you speak to your son or daughter about transcendent love for another person and your hope that it will be present before he or she enters into a sexual relationship, your teen isn't likely to roll his or her eyes. At this age, idealism is strong, and setting a goal like this does not seem unrealistic.

One of Shakespeare's most quoted sonnets goes right to the heart of Agape. It is often heard in marriage ceremonies and at other times when people are trying to find the words to express their love and to commit to doing all they can to help their partner's dreams become reality:

Love is not love
Which alters when it alteration finds,
Or bends with the remover to remove:
Oh, no! it is an ever-fixèd mark,
That looks on the tempests and is never shaken.
Shakespeare, Sonnet 116

THE GUIDE PARENTING
PRINCIPLE

∽∽∽∽

As you know by now, a skilled guide provides you with the information you need to make choices and gives you the freedom to do so. He listens to what you want to do and see and helps you find the best path. He doesn't simply send you on a well-beaten track because it's the safest, best-known route. He draws from a rich store of personal experience to help you without imposing his own preferences. A good guide will not hesitate to step in and tell you clearly and directly if you are wandering into dangerous terrain.

Parenting a teen is much like guiding a hiker. We know that ultimately a teenager will develop her own picture of what she wants to do with her life—she will want to find her own way. But *how* she comes to that picture and *the landscape she hikes through* can be strongly influenced by thoughtful parental guidance.

Our parents helped us set forth into the world. Sometimes we welcomed their support. Sometimes we rejected it. But how and when our parents approached us had a resounding impact on how much we understood and accepted. They were most effective when they listened and respected our changing needs without caving in and letting us do whatever we wanted. However, some of us had parents who clung to a restrictive and authoritarian parenting style, rather than making a healthy transition from Governor to Gardener and then finally, in our teen years, to Guide. We don't want that for our children.

WHAT IS MY TEEN'S DIRECTION IN LIFE?

A teenager needs help developing a picture of what he wants to do with his life. He will make mistakes, ranging from minor to stunning, which can be tough for a parent to accept. The key to being a good Guide is helping your child find his or her direction. This does not happen overnight, but rather through a series of conversations and experiences. Teens' hopes and dreams may range from lofty and unrealistic to cautious and unambitious. They can be about college and career or just about what to do in the weeks and months ahead. They may be about righting the wrongs a teen sees in the world or about helping a friend in need. Understanding these goals, big or small, long- or short-term, helps you build a picture of what your teen wants. Engaging in this process with a deep and genuine interest will bring you and your teen closer together.

THE CROSSTOWN BUS TALK

So how does this rich store of hopes help you when things get tough? Teenagers can seem spectacularly disinterested in our opinions. And we feel deeply disrespected when they slouch and drop their gaze as we try to share our views on a tense matter. One father wrote to me, "It makes my blood boil when I try to talk to my seventeen-year-old daughter about my concerns. But the more I insist she be respectful, the more preoccupied she becomes about her nails or hair."

The best way to interest a teen in a talk when things are getting wobbly or have already gone off the rails is to ask her whether a choice she is about to make (or has made) will move her toward *her* goal or distract and derail her.

When your conversation is focused on your teen's directions, hopes, and dreams—the big picture of his life (or even his coming week)—you are much more likely to connect. Go *with* his self-exploration and interests rather than *against* them. If something gets weird or troubling, we can kick-start a talk with our teens about what they envision by saying things like "You know, was that a crosstown bus? Did that help move you toward what you want to do, or did that take you away from where you want to go? Is that group of friends really helping you, or are they distracting you?" In this sense, the metaphor of a crosstown bus signifies something that is not taking you forward in the direction you want to go, for instance, downtown, but instead across town and, as a result, getting you no closer to your goal.

The father of a fifteen-year-old shared the following story with me:

"My daughter is pretty typical for her age. She is fairly balanced but can also go through tricky times. Friendships are very important to her, and there was one kid in her group she really clicked with. The two were motivated about schoolwork but also about being active, instead of just hanging out. They'd get on their mountain bikes and ride challenging trails. But there were two or three other friends who started 'going super girlie,' as my daughter described it. She didn't seem that interested herself, but I was concerned that these girls might lead her down a path that wasn't good for her. But the minute I criticized them in any way she'd vehemently defend them.

"One evening, while we were driving to the ice cream parlor, she started telling me about the stuff these girls were getting into. I tried to make a snap comment, but my daughter cut me off. 'Can you just listen, Dad?' she said. I was silenced and humbled. She told me they were 'doing demeaning things to fit in with the in crowd and keep boys interested.' She told me she still liked them and they were fun to be around but it wasn't the same anymore. I was bursting with curiosity, but I contained myself . . . barely. She felt that, while they could still be friends, they were 'going in a different direction,' and—of her own volition—she started to distance herself from them. Pretty soon their influence waned, and their names stopped popping up in conversation.

"I learned so much from that moment by being silent and listening rather than being accusatory and meddlesome. She is now a lot more confident about talking to me about her difficulties. She knows I won't be too judgmental. And if I talk, I make sure it's about what her direction is and what she can do to keep heading that way. I am so proud that my daughter can find her way like this. Our conversations are 'no big deal,' as she would put it, but to me they are a beautiful bridge that connects us."

SUPPORTING CHOICES AND ANTICIPATING CONSEQUENCES

As the frontal lobes—or "executive" region—of the brain develops, the teen becomes better able to anticipate the consequences of different actions. But the area is still forming, and teens benefit greatly from adult guidance. Here are three steps you can take to help your teenager:

1. Ask your teen what the two or three main choices are that he or she has to make about a given situation. If necessary, help him or her tease them out. A teen often needs to do more research before all the options are clear. Discuss how he or she can find the necessary information.

2. Anticipate what the outcome might be for each choice should your son or daughter choose this path. For example, you could summarize what your teen laid out by saying something like "Okay, you have come up with three options. If you choose to work over the summer, you will be able to pay for your driver's education classes and be on the road sooner. If you choose to go

with your friend to his grandfather's place, you will have time to relax after a pretty stressful year, and you will be better prepared for a demanding new school year. You could also take some summer classes. That would give you an academic head start but no time to unwind." You'll have laid out the pros and cons of each choice in a simple, straightforward way.

3. Help your teen feel confident about her choice. Tell her you are impressed by her mature selection. But don't make her promise that she will stick with that choice no matter what. You don't want your teen to feel locked in, even if you want her to understand the importance of commitment. Things can change. Let your teen know ahead of time that you are there to help regroup and replan if necessary. This kind of assurance is especially helpful to teens who get stressed out, overplan, procrastinate, and get stuck in a cycle of anxiety.

THE PATH LESS TRAVELED

"When my Alexis announced that she was not going to college because she planned to work with a landscaper, I was shocked," one father told me. "She was a gifted artist and really good at science. She could have gotten into a top college and gone on to a great career." Our kids never stop surprising us. Alexis's decision to take an unexpected path really tested her father.

She was lucky to have an open-minded father who allowed her the space to explore her options. "I could see that this was something she had a real connection to," he said, "but I could also see that it sprouted from a mix of her artistic nature and a keen interest in botany. It was actually quite intuitive of her." He suggested that she spend a year gathering landscaping work experience but also take a college course in a field related to her work. After working for a year, Alexis got a degree in ecology and now works in the developing world.

Parents who are willing to listen carefully and nonjudgmentally to their teens' plans can help them clarify what they really want. A teen may choose a well-established path that fits his or her needs and desires perfectly. But when parents are unconditionally supportive, they give their teen the confidence to explore the unconventional as well, which may also end up being deeply satisfying.

YOUR GUIDING WISDOM AND EXPERIENCE COUNTS

Our kids have been raised on the stories we tell. They particularly like the ones in which we misbehaved or pushed the envelope and got into some sort of trouble. It's helpful to keep these stories flowing when your teen needs guidance. You can send him or her a clear, strong message— *and* avoid being perceived as too judgmental or emphatic—by quietly communicating helpful lessons and values through stories. You don't want to appear as if you think you know it all and hear "Yeah, I know, Dad, but that does not mean you know how I feel!" in response. But a well-placed story that parallels your teen's experience can open the door to a hearty conversation. You can frame your story like this: "I think I get what you mean, because when I was about your age . . ."

STEPPING IN—STEPPING BACK

Even though your teen is competent and manages so much in his or her life, the Guide needs to step in quickly and firmly if something dangerous is about to happen. Let's say your teen is involved in a car accident and shaken up. She calls you in tears, and when you get to the scene, you find the other driver shouting at your daughter. Although she is eighteen and capable of defending herself, you must step in to calm things down. She called you because she knew you would provide that kind of unconditional support and tell her it would be okay.

When Daisy heard from her seventeen-year-old son John that he intended to travel in Central America with a friend during summer vacation, she invited a friend of her own, who was from that part of the world, to have supper with her and the two boys and discuss their strategy. It quickly became clear that John's plans were vague (typical for kids at this age) and based on romantic notions of what traveling in this region would be like. After listening carefully and thinking about what she'd heard that evening, Daisy told John she would support his plans only if he spoke further with her friend and "got a lot more practical about the whole thing." Daisy asked to see a travel budget, with a provisory emergency fund in case either traveler needed to fly back home. She told John she would help out financially only if he worked to earn a majority of the funds needed himself. She wanted to know about the possible risks and what his plans would be to handle them. She really liked his idea of going "someplace where [he] could help." Over the next few months, they researched possible work-experience placements in Ecuador.

John got into a couple tricky situations on this trip. When he got home, rather than avoiding speaking about the dangers he had faced, he was able to tell his mother about them. Because she had engaged with him and been willing to help achieve his goals, a deeper bond had been forged between them, one that allowed for honesty and openness.

Stepping in and stepping back becomes more nuanced when you have to balance heading off trouble before it happens with letting a teen suffer the consequences of his or her own poor decisions. One father bridged these two dynamics. When he saw trouble looming, he would tell his two teenage kids about his concern. He would say, "You can probably handle whatever might happen if you don't set aside specific times to study before your exams, but I would stop worrying and nagging and sleep a lot better if you ran your plan by me so I'd know you are on it." This is a respectful way of reaching out to teens. It does not presume they are blind to the danger they might encounter. The teens' father is merely signaling that he will back off and give them space if they are honest, direct, and share their plans with him.

Being a Guide can move us into the polarities of parenting. It is challenging and exasperating and yet also profoundly satisfying. It takes us into deep places that not only help us bond in a new way with our son or daughter but ask a great deal of us in terms of our own willingness to grow and stretch. It offers us the precious opportunity to look through the eyes of our children and to see the world in a fresh and new way when we stand with them on the relational hilltops and look out over the fields and valleys of their future lives. Soon they will be walking alone forging their own paths, but for now, we get to be beside them for a little while longer.

∽∾∽∾∽

part four

THE RESCUE PACKAGE:
TAKING THE PULSE

8

The Rescue Package

We do our level best to guide our kids. Some days work out fine, but on others, we wonder why it has to be so hard, and it feels like our family sails are in tatters and we are taking on water after a storm. You have heard a lot about how the Governor-Gardener-Guide principle can help you parent your child, tween, and teen effectively. But some of you may ask, "Is it too late? My kid is fifteen, and I've done everything wrong. Have I totally messed things up?" The answer is an emphatic no. It's never too late. The Soul of Discipline approach can be applied at any age or stage. Even a volatile fifteen-year-old can be turned around.

Here's how you can begin today. Find the level of discipline and support your child's needs from among the three G's of the Governor-Gardener-Guide principle by asking yourself a basic question: "Who does my kid need me to be right now?" As you read this chapter, explore how we, as parents, can free ourselves from focusing too much on the kind of discipline we think our kids need based on age and turn our attention instead to the kinds of boundaries we have to set to help them properly orient themselves.

Why Parents Resist Boundaries

A parent must first understand and accept that boundaries are important and need to be clearly set. Ideally, the limits you set for your young child will shift and expand in the tween years and then grow outward again in the teen years. However, many parents find it difficult to develop firm boundaries for their children. Let's take a look at why parents worry about setting limits before we explore strategies for correcting situations that have already spun out of control.

GLOBAL TYRANNY

One subconscious concern we all share is steeped in recent history. We worry about the terrible havoc that blind obedience to a dictator can wreak in society. When people become "sheep" who unquestioningly cede to a tyrant's demands, they give up personal responsibility. This drains them of empathy and can lead to all manner of inhumane actions. No parent wants his or her child to become a passive sycophant. We prefer to raise strong-willed kids who will question authority and not be afraid to stand apart from the pack when they are pressured to do something that is contrary to their beliefs. Some parents feel that when they set boundaries they are hampering their children's individual freedom and not giving them the space to develop and strengthen their sense of individuality.

RECOGNIZING FAMILY TYRANNY

Some parents do not want to set boundaries for their kids because they recall how uncomfortable it was to be raised in a home where their

Pause Point

If you experienced an oppressive upbringing, ask yourself,

"How old was I when I had intense exchanges with my parent?"

parents demanded unquestioning obedience. If an adult is still recovering and struggling to move on from his own oppressive childhood regime, it is easy to understand why he might struggle with and even strongly resist setting boundaries for his *own* children.

For most people, things spiraled downward in the tween and teen years. Whereas a little child can be told directly what to do and how to do it, teenagers are a completely different story. Yet so many parents make the mistake of addressing both age groups in exactly the same manner. It's an approach that can lead to much heartache and sow the seeds of family discord, which can last a lifetime and unconsciously color our adult lives and the parenting styles we use to raise our own children.

Lambs and Wolves

The Governor-Gardener-Guide principle provides us with a template that we can follow as we tailor our disciplinary approach according to our kids' personal growth and needs. We are in no danger of creating submissive, "sheeplike" kids if we build healthy boundaries when our children are young, especially under the age of eight or nine. Think of children at this age not as sheep who follow us blindly but as lambs who need the security of *fences,* or *boundaries,* to keep them from wandering into dangerous territory where the wolflike influences of modern marketing and pop culture can attack their innocent and un-protected presence.

The key point is that, as long as parents consciously adapt the boundaries they set according to their child's changing needs, there is no danger that they will either suppress or overwhelm him or her. In fact, the opposite is true. Having well-defined, age-and-behavior-appropriate boundaries helps children, tweens, and teens feel cared for and secure and therefore strengthens your family bonds. What matters most here is not whether or not to set limits but when, where, and how you set these boundaries.

Putting the Genie Back in the Bottle

Too many little kids are given an overabundance of choices at too early an age, as well as more power than they can handle responsibly. As we have discussed in earlier chapters, such children unconsciously seek safety by stepping into the unintended leadership vacuum created by the well-meaning parents who provide them with too many options and too much sway over family matters. Then, when they hit their teen years, things get complicated and messy because these kids have been given too few boundaries and have been prematurely exposed to a great deal of freedom—alluring possibilities normally associated with the teen years. Parents panic at this stage because, as one tween's dad said, "Some of the stuff I've allowed my kid to have access to is just plain nasty. It's really got me worried." As soon as we realize how quickly and dramatically things can go wrong if we allow our tweens and teens the same leeway we gave them as younger kids, we try to compensate by putting restrictive boundaries in place.

Is a parent's reflex to impose limits on a troubled teen wrong? No, not at all. In fact, this reflexive response is powerful and correct. Every parent's primal impulse is to protect and provide for his or her kids, and we should not second-guess or suppress this instinct. What we need to do is shape and channel this drive so that it achieves maximum effect while triggering minimal resistance from our kids. We want them to sense that a firm hand is on the tiller.

———

Here is a story from a few years back that illustrates this dynamic: There was a big thump out in the waiting room of my family counseling practice one day, and the normally unflappable receptionist popped her head around the corner and said, "I think you better see these people *now*." Through the door came an irate auburn-haired fourteen-year-old girl. Her father followed, looking embarrassed and also angry. She said, "When I was like four years old, Dad, do you remember calling me 'little buddy'? Do you remember how I was your little buddy? That was my name, right? That is what you called me all the time. Do you remember how you and your little buddy would go to, like, ball games? Do you remember I got to go to parties?"

A dam of frustration had clearly burst. She continued, "Do you remember you were always saying, 'You choose, little buddy. What would you like to do?' Now I'm fourteen, and you treat me like I'm a baby. You want to know where I'm going all the time. You want to pick me up at times that *you* set. And you even try to ground me. *Ground* me! Like, what is *that*!"

The dad hadn't even uttered a word yet. Clearly he was of the adult male species that requires a pause of more than two or three seconds in order to formulate a thought and get the words out in joined-up syllables. I had never met these people before, but I must confess that at that moment I was both concerned at the level of the girl's anger and morbidly fascinated by the interaction.

She was not done. "You don't trust me!" she shouted. "You give me no space anymore. Why don't you trust me?" Dad's face turned a deeper shade of scarlet. "Well, there *is* an answer," he said. "Then what is it?" she shot back. "Why don't you trust me?" "Because you could get pregnant," he stammered, the words bursting forth from deep within. At that point, I jumped off my seat and joined them. "Wrong answer," I said to him quietly. "Wrong answer," I told the girl. "He didn't really mean that this was his only problem." In her surprise, she replied much more quietly, "He did mean it." The father concurred: "Yes, I did mean it."

When she was little, the dad had given this child many choices and a wide range of liberties. And he'd treated his daughter as if she were his buddy. As a result, there were few clearly delineated boundaries between his adult world and her child's world. She had seen and heard a lot. She had witnessed her father shouting at ball games, drinking with his friends, and dissing all kinds of authority figures. Therefore, she had little respect for either her father or authority in general. The dad had behaved this way with his daughter because he had wanted to be close to her. Little had he known that it would backfire when she got older and he instinctively began to tighten the reins to keep her out of serious trouble.

She was a lovely girl, and a number of older boys were quite interested in her. The potential for risky behavior was there—as it often is in the teen years. The problem was that the dad, having undercut his own authority in her childhood and tween years, had very limited influence on her now. As a result, their relationship was becoming very strained. Essentially, the dad was trying to put the genie back in the bottle, and the genie was not happy.

Over a few months, the dad and daughter did manage to work things out. The daughter eventually accepted the fact that she had to tell her father where she was going and what time she would be home. That may sound basic, but it was a breakthrough for them. The dad made very good use of the Gardener Principle, and their relationship found more solid footing. Anxiety affects us in various ways. The dad reported that, for the first time in more than a year, his stomach pain was gone. He was now laying the supportive foundation that had been lacking in their relationship during the Governor years and that would help him to become an effective Guide as his daughter grew into womanhood.

What to Do When Things Go Wrong: The Easy-to-Install Guide

THE GUIDE BECOMES THE GARDENER

If your teenager is not making good choices and not respecting your efforts to be his or her Guide, you may become incredibly frustrated. Instead of realizing that you are witnessing a brief though difficult phase, you may get a sinking feeling that this is a long-term state that will be ingrained in all your interactions. Here are some teen tendencies that can become troubling habits:

- They seem aimless and have no clue about even a general direction they might pursue in life.
- They seem to be content to just drift with the crowd, even if the actions of their peers are problematic and unhealthy.
- They have little response to your interest in hearing about their plans for the future.
- They deflect or close down conversations in general, even when your timing is good.
- They push back against you when you quietly point out the possible pitfalls of their plans.
- They insist on freedom but are resistant to responsibility.

In general, you may be doing your best to treat them like the young men or women you see them physically becoming, but emotionally they are very often behaving like ten-year-olds. Once you realize that this is your major clue, you can tune in to the emotional development and type of behavior of a ten-year-old rather than your child's chronological age.

The Guide Principle is based on you being able to *guide*. You need to be able to enter into a conversation with your kid. Not all the time and not in an adult way, but there does need to be a baseline of acceptance that you can work through things together. The whole dynamic of a healthy parent-child relationship is built around being able to have a good sense of the emerging direction your son or daughter is taking. If you keep insisting on having discussions about the future and get frustrated when your kid cannot manage it, you have probably sent her the message that she is failing to live up to your expectations. The main option she has when this unhealthy cycle takes over is to fall back and away from you and sink deeper into a peer culture where she feels she is being accepted for who she is. At that point, the peers, rather than you, are raising your kid, which is exactly what you were trying to avoid in the first place.

If your teen's interests are vague, that's okay. But it does give you a clear message that he needs an approach that holds him a little closer and addresses his disorientation with a structure to help him orient himself. You need to dial back your expectations of his capacity to communicate with you. And this is where the Gardener Principle is best. It is very likely your child needs the structure and safety that being a part of the family ecology brings. Some redigging, replanting, and possibly even some pruning is needed. Having read Chapter Six, you know how to be a good and steady Family Gardener.

When you feel more structure is necessary, consider switching gears and speaking to your teen less about the future and more about the present. Remember the key dynamic of the Gardener Principle: "Tell me your plans." You want to be sure that your son or daughter understands the needs of others in the family and the fact that his or her words and actions affect everyone.

Some parents ask, "Do I tell my kid that things are not working and that we are going to do things differently for a while?" On the one hand, it's perfectly fine to quietly let this new dynamic filter into the family on a day-by-day basis—especially if you feel that by verbalizing it you will stir up a lot of resistance. On the other hand, if you do feel it would be fruitful to talk things over, make your discussion brief, and avoid either asking a lot of questions or justifying your decision. Otherwise, you may be expecting too much from a kid who really needs less talk and more form and shape to his or her life.

THE GARDENER BECOMES THE GOVERNOR

If your tween or teen is not responding to your shift to the Gardener role by becoming a helpful part of the family team, he or she may need to be refamiliarized with the much more restrictive boundaries that you can apply lovingly but firmly as Governor. Let's say you feel your kid is bad or antisocial, and out of anger, desperation, or guilt, you are not becoming more strict. You simply need to tell your child with clarity that he or she must respect your authority and family leadership.

Are you convinced that your teen's misbehavior is not a passing phase (of a couple weeks' duration) but a habit that is becoming entrenched? Here are the telltale signs that this is the case:

- Your teen does not understand that his or her actions and words affect others in the family.
- She demands that her needs be met and is surprised when she is told that this is not the way the world works.
- He shows poor timing by insisting that you respond to his demand whenever it is made, no matter what else is going on.
- Your teen does not accept your decision even after you have listened to his or her request in a genuine and respectful manner.

If your son or daughter consistently exhibits these behaviors, does not attempt to become part of the family gardening team, and continues to live as if he or she is the sole occupant of the planet, you can—with utter conviction—introduce or reintroduce your child to the Governor and explain what this is going to mean in his or her life. As mentioned above, you can either briefly explain the characteristics of the new regime or begin to implement the new rules with no discussion.

Some parents ask, "What if my child doesn't accept boundaries and the Governor Principle?" The answer is that it simply does not really matter whether a teen *accepts* the boundaries, because you are not *asking*. If you act with authority, parental conviction, and love for your child, something quite primal within your kid will sense the strength of your resolve, even though it means a temporary curtailment of his or her freedoms. What the Governor dynamic provides your child with is closeness, safety, and parental involvement. He or she will sense this pretty quickly because it is what kids value. Deep down children know this is what family is all about.

Long Days and Small Solutions

For most of this book, we have applied each one of the parenting approaches—Governor, Gardener, or Guide—to a developmental phase. However, in this "Rescue Package," we have freed ourselves from age parameters, and I have instead recommended the application of the approach most appropriate to an individual parent-child dynamic.

There is one more basic way parents can use the three G's. There are many times during a single day when a parent needs to come up with the right disciplinary approach or response to keep everything on track. The Governor-Gardener-Guide principle can also be used during such daily struggles. Let's imagine your defiant twelve-year-old says, "I don't care if I make everyone late for the concert. I am not wearing that dress!" and continues to act out (as she did when she was years younger) even after you've reminded her that her younger brother is nervous about the song he is about to perform and has worked so hard to prepare.

Rather than shout at your tween in this kind of situation, the mother can revert to the Governor Principle for the amount of time it takes to work through the Five Essentials of Healthy Compliance (see Chapter Three), which every Governor relies on. First, you hit the *Pause and Picture button*. Next you *start small* by letting your daughter know that she can cover up the frilly shoulders she doesn't like with her favorite cardigan. Then you *stay close* by going with her to the closet to fetch the cardigan. You *insist* by calmly repeating what *is* going to happen and making certain that you are not drawn into negotiation, and finally you *follow through* by staying focused (by not answering the phone if it rings, for example) and getting everyone into the car. Within fifteen minutes into the journey to the concert, your sunny daughter may re-emerge as her own personal thunderstorm passes. She is back to her normal, goofy self, and you can remove your Governor's hat and put your Gardener's cap back on.

Different Ages Under the Same Roof?

One mother asked me, "How can a parent be a Governor to one young child and a Gardener to another without developing some kind of mental health issue?" It's a question that comes up a lot. When a squabble breaks out between your seven-year-old and your twelve-year-old, and your fifteen-year-old will not get off the computer when you tell her to, what do you do? Kids have sensors that signal them when their parents are grounded or balanced. If you deal with disciplinary issues in the ways I have advised in this book, you are very likely to be calm and firm at such moments.

In any case, you'll want to avoid disciplinary multitasking. It accomplishes nothing and will frustrate you no end. Choose one child to focus on, and let the others know they will hear from you shortly. Remove the child you've chosen from the hubbub, and work through the issue with him or her in as firm and supportive a manner as you can manage. Use the Disapprove—Affirm—Discover—Do Over tool discussed in Chapter Five. It works well in such situations and signals everyone that you are not taking sides. When kids believe you are being objective, they won't interrupt all the time to argue their case. A mother of four told me that when she employs "single-tasking" discipline, "the whole climate of the house changes." The other kids sense that she is grounded and relax. When she loses her cool and shouts, the children pick up on this energy and behave worse. When she focuses calmly on one child, the situation both with the child she is speaking to and with the rest of the kids improves, since all the children now feel safe.

We Are Always Holding Our Kids

I remember getting lost on the way to a conference while I was sharing a car with a dear friend and colleague. He had been an elementary school teacher for more than thirty years, and we had time to talk about our work with children while I found my way back to the right road. He told me that early on he had tried a *stepped-back* approach, hoping that the content of his teaching would be enough for the children to be mostly respectful with each other. Then he decided to try the opposite: He became more involved and *stepped in* to regulate the children's exchanges. Both *stepping in* and *stepping back* have their place in the developmental lives of children. We discussed how parents and teachers can learn to support their children more effectively. Sometimes kids need to be held close—they are reassured by our proximity. However, we should, at times, relax our hold, if we sense that they need room to grow and explore. In later years, our hold on our kids will be much lighter because they'll need the freedom and space to move out into the world. But even while they are taking these steps toward independence, we are still holding them, whether they know it or not.

A Story That Sums It Up Perfectly

Connor was slumped in the chair, one leg dangled over the armrest and the other on the edge of the coffee table. His parents, David and Liza, frowned at him and asked him to sit up. He adjusted his posture into a semi-slump and continued to look down. Connor was fourteen and had grown up in a caring, socially active family. His parents were kind, respectful people who treated him and his younger brother as equal members of the family. The children were consulted when big decisions needed to be made. Recently Connor had been given the final say in his high school selection process. His parents believed that raising him this way would ensure that he would become socially sensitive, caring, and a good decision-maker.

Instead, Connor was "critical and dismissive" toward his parents and constantly put his younger brother down. What troubled David and Liza the most was that Connor was "making poor choices" at school and spending a lot of time with questionable friends. They had tried hard to reason with him and "talk it all through in a calm and respectful way," but they had not been able to get through to him.

The following week, David, Liza, and I decided on a course of action. We would cut back on the number of choices we gave Connor. We hoped that would help motivate him to become more of a team player. David and Liza agreed to focus on two things. First, they would insist that Connor treat his brother more kindly and be more respectful toward them. Second, they would require him to tell his parents where he was going and what time he would be home.

After a couple of weeks, David and Liza felt their new efforts had "brought them closer together" as a couple and helped their younger son feel safer and more relaxed. But Connor was not responding well, and his parents felt they had failed to get through to him.

We decided to backtrack further and discussed the need for basic disciplinary foundations. It took some time to help David work through his concerns about not setting boundaries that would be too restrictive. He genuinely wanted Connor to "be free to be himself," but as Liza put it, what they were experiencing right then "was not at all the real Connor." She felt that Connor was "getting lost" and thought they needed to "step it up."

We discussed the Five Essentials of Healthy Compliance. David wanted to "start small" by having his son help him build a new fence in the yard for the dog they had recently decided to bring home from the shelter. David had only agreed to adopt it on the condition that the boys promised to pitch in with building the fence and caring for the dog. His younger son was helping, but Connor wasn't. Liza wanted to work with Connor to clean up the "pigsty" that his room had become. So with clear pictures in mind and good intentions, they embarked on their "missions." We all laughed when Liza said with grim humor as she was leaving, "Okay, I am going in. I may be some time."

The following week, Connor's parents reported that they had made some progress. Apparently Connor thought they were "being all weird" and that "this would all blow over soon." This made David all the more determined to follow through. Liza said that, in the spirit of "keeping it small and doable," she and Connor had done some "light tidying up" together every evening and made the bed every morning. The simple act of doing something together with Connor again had brought her to the brink of tears. She'd been surprised and relieved that Connor had not put up a huge fight. Both parents felt that this approach was beginning to work because Connor sensed that they were both serious.

Over the next month, Liza and David established their authority and set boundaries in other areas of Connor's life, including specific times when he needed to be home after school and on weekends. "I learned a lot about this process," David acknowledged. "Not getting drawn into negotiation and justifications with Connor was one of the hardest things I have ever done, but I could see that the whole thing would implode if I did, and we would end up back in the horrible place we had started."

When they both felt that they were "in a strong place," we talked about giving Connor a bit more freedom. David was confident that he could "lighten up a little." He decided to tell Connor that, *if* he was willing to be respectful and run his plans by them *and* accept it when the times had to be adjusted, he would have more say in what he did on weekends and after school. Liza wanted to focus on helping Connor become more genuinely respectful of his brother (and her and David). She planned to tell him that, if he could act more respectfully and mean it, he would be on the fast track to more choices and freedoms. Liza had been raised in a family community in which being "well-mannered" was often "fake." She said that, provided you said the words "bless her heart" after any cutting comment, it was considered fine. She made us all laugh when she slipped into her hometown accent and said, with a pure and innocent look on her face, "Oh my, would you look at her hair? Bless her heart."

Connor was slowly allowed more choices, and family life improved. The process also helped David become a much more effective parent. "I feel like we got our boy back," he said. "He is much more on board with the family. And when he gets sassy and starts in with his dissing— like any teenager can—all I have to do is give him 'the look.'" David was sending Connor a clear message: "If you go there, there will be consequences." He was not doing this in a threatening way, just with calm authority. Liza was also upbeat about Connor's behavioral shift. "What I like is that we can now do things without having to go into long, utterly exhausting explanations that end up in some endless power struggle," she said. "We have way more time and energy to do the things that are fun and bring us closer together."

These parents had the courage to face a difficult disciplinary situation and accept that something fundamental needed to change. But figuring out exactly what to change can be confusing and complicated. Liza and David came to understand and accept that, although they had raised their son in the best way they could, he had missed two key developmental disciplinary stages, which were critical to his learning to navigate the life situations that teenagers encounter. His parents had been Connor's Guides but seldom his Gardeners and hardly ever his Governors. Their son had not learned that parents have ultimate authority and define their children's boundaries. Connor had become self-centered because he had not learned to control his impulses. He had become willful but not genuinely will filled. He had not learned the art of making plans that take into account the needs and feelings of other family members. He had become headstrong but not thoughtful.

In Conclusion

When you calibrate your disciplinary approach according to your individual child's physical and emotional needs, things become much simpler. From time to time, you may find it necessary to dial back into Gardener or Governor mode for several weeks or months. Or the shift may take just a few hours or even minutes. What matters most is that you are adjusting this kind but firm strategy to your child's current needs, instead of superimposing a fashionable disciplinary regimen that sounds effective but may not take your child's ever-changing physical and emotional states into account. What is particularly heartening is that the Governor-Gardener-Guide approach can help you build a stronger, more secure relationship with your child and shift the entire family dynamic so that more focus and energy is spent building strong and enduring family connections.

part five

A DEEPER DIVE

9

Avoiding Discipline Fads

When you speak with older folks, you get the sense that, in their day, raising kids just got "done," that parenting had more to do with intuition and action than conscious thinking and planning. Parents didn't do a lot of research or second-guessing, because their confidence was buttressed by tradition. They raised their kids the way their parents had, for better or worse.

For most parents, those days are gone. We may mourn the loss of tradition, but we also feel liberated. Unfettered by the weight of expectations, we can now parent our children as we see fit. When we gaze with deep love and apprehension at the extraordinary infant we have brought into our lives, we quickly realize that we may well need guidance to navigate this momentous responsibility.

In this chapter, we will take a look at parenting practices over the last three generations and offer strategies for making our way through today's discipline landscape. Parenting has changed dramatically over the years, swinging from one polarity (or fad) to another. Each pendulum swing is a reaction to its predecessor, a tightly controlled, conservative way of disciplining kids at one extreme and an unrestricted, liberal approach at the other.

Blind Obedience: Pre-1940s

Many of the seniors I spoke with in the eighties and nineties had lived through the effects of the First World War and become parents during the Great Depression of the thirties or the Second World War. They told me stories of hardship. Back then, discipline was synonymous with hard work. In fact, discipline *wasn't* really an issue, as immediate survival was more pressing. Everyone in the family "did their bit." A child either did his or her work properly and contributed to the family's livelihood or didn't. And if the effort was not good enough, the focus was on getting it right. Discipline was practical, tangible, and left little room for negotiation.

I recently saw a report card from over a century ago: 1911. Today's report cards update parents on how a child is doing academically and behaviorally, but in 1911, teachers gave children a card to take home in which they were tasked with assignments such as baking pies, sweeping floors, and washing dishes. *Home*work was literally work to be done in and around the home. It was very specific and nonintellectual. Kids learned that discipline was intricately related to the work they did to support their families. Parents were certainly not there to serve the many needs of their children. When physical chores helped place a child firmly in the material world, discipline was a lot simpler. Similarly, when children participate in meaningful tasks at home, the kids become integral to the creative flow of family life, and discipline is less complicated.

The Transitional Years: 1940–1960

After the postwar economic recovery and into the fifties, discipline began to change. But it wasn't until the sixties and early seventies, when people began to think and write much more about how best to parent, that a new style surfaced. A newly stable and prosperous society was shaking itself free of the old ways.

That pendulum was set in motion, swinging from tight and strict to loose and freewheeling and relaxed. Every ten to twelve years since then, it has swung from one polarity to the other. The freewheeling years would gradually give birth to a collective worry that "we're not giving our kids enough guidance" or "our kids are getting out of control." After years of restriction, there would inevitably be widespread concern that parents were being "too uptight" and that their "kids were being suppressed."

The Freedom Years: 1970s

In the seventies, young people pushed back hard against the "Do as I say, not as I do" approach. Parents who worried that accepted disciplinary conventions were too cold and punitive started allowing new freedom. Mandatory chores began to disappear from the home. Parents talked about wanting their kids to be experimental and creative, rather than chained to the home. They were largely reacting to the blind obedience under which they had been brought up and moved toward a more lenient approach. For them, a child's "no" did not represent intolerable defiance. It was seen as healthy self-expression. Kids were now allowed to discuss, negotiate, and even debate with their parents.

However, by the mid to late seventies, some parents began to worry that there was such a thing as too much free expression. One dad told me, "When my two boys started getting in trouble at school, I had to rethink all this great freedom I had been giving them." One day, as he was picking up his kids to go to a sports game, he witnessed an exchange between his elder son and a teacher that was "unmistakably disrespectful and cocky." He said, "I realized this was getting out of control. I've got to get these kids back in line."

The Gold-Star Years: 1980s

Behavior modification (or "B-Mod") was introduced to parenting in the late seventies and became popularized throughout the eighties, largely due to Dr. B. F. Skinner's concept "radical behaviorism," which lauded a gold-star system that involved the giving and taking away of privileges. Here was a way to haul your kids back in line. It worked! . . . for a little while.

What concerned parents about behavior modification—with its rewards and punishments—was the underlying motivation for compliance. Children did not understand and accept a parent's true authority: They complied because of what they "could get" out of the exchange (the star, the reward). Behavior modification works for about three to six months. If you are dealing with an out-of-control kid, it can seem like magic. But the trouble is that kids start to build up behavior-modification *calluses*.

Kids say the darndest things, particularly when they are figuring out how to beat a system. Things that I have heard over the years as a school and family counselor have made me both smile and flinch. Kids see right through a technique and figure out straightforward ways of working it to their advantage. In the section below, I discuss some children's comments that I have read, overheard, or been told about.

BEATING THE B-MOD SYSTEM

Bargaining Chips

I overheard a young child in a supermarket line say, "Well, I'll do it for three cookies and a soda." I expected her mother to say, "This is not up for discussion," but instead she said, "No. You may only have *one* cookie and a soda." Intense bargaining followed. I just wished she was wearing an earpiece that I could use to communicate with her secretly, the way a producer prompts a TV anchor, so I could whisper, "Just say no quietly but firmly."

Cost-Benefit Analysis

A parent says, "If you don't stop [whatever you are doing], young man, you will not be having any lasagna tonight." A child runs a cost-benefit analysis and says, "Well, I don't like your lasagna anyway, so I'm not going to stop." A parent says, "Jonathan, if you don't stop, I'm afraid we will not be going to Sophie's house." The child's mental wheels turn, and he says, "I don't like Sophie. It's you who likes Sophie's mother. So I don't care if we go anyway." In both scenarios, the parent ends up momentarily powerless.

The Expert Negotiator

The child takes on the role of tiny attorney. A child told her mom, "You didn't see anything, so there can be no consequences. You have to prove it first!" The frustrated mom told me, "Every small point is up for negotiation, and it's utterly exhausting and humiliating to be spoken to in that way by a five-year-old."

Upping the Ante

You remember privileges, right? You were given privileges (the reward), which could be withdrawn (the punishment) if you did something wrong. But when a child said to his father, "No, the privilege needs to be better," he was upping the ante. He was basically saying, "Sorry, Dad. I'm not going to do what you tell me to do because the reward you propose is not good enough." Allowing this undermines the authority of a parent and reinforces the message to the child that he can "get more" for himself in any bargaining process.

Leverage Removal

A couple of grown-up brothers visiting their dad had a laugh remembering an attempt at behavior modification by their parents. They recalled their defense against this disciplinary tactic: "No. I don't want it because you'll just take it away anyway," they'd say. Their answer was both ingenious and, sadly, quite common. They refused to accept any "privileges." They even boycotted Christmas for two years. They just said, "We don't want any presents," because they realized that, if they didn't accept presents, then the parents couldn't use taking them away as leverage against them.

Hostage Taking

Behavior modification often results in hostage taking. Children refuse to do what you ask and bargain constantly. "I'll only go to sleep if you lie down next to me," they say. Hostage taking is a blend of two or more of the other behaviors described in this list.

———

As far back as 1971, American cognitive scientist and philosopher Noam Chomsky expressed serious concerns with Dr. Skinner's emerging brand of behaviorism. He criticized Skinner's methods, saying that he "had no science of behavior" and was irresponsibly applying results from experiments on animals directly to human behavior.

And the truth is that even dogs seem to respond better to warmth and clarity of direction than to simple punishments and rewards. Last year, I found my neighbor looking frantically for his pit bull. "Whenever I run out of dog biscuits," he told me, "he just ignores me and runs away." Hmmm.

For the most part, parents have moved away from using behavior modification as their principal disciplinary method, although some of us may regress or fall back into it on occasion. What's more concerning is that it seems to have leaked into our schools like a semi-permanent stain. All around the world, chalkboards list students' names. Some names have gold stars or check marks, others a multitude of negative X's. These chalkboards could easily be called "The Walls of Fame and Shame." The problem with this technique is that kids who are incentivized in this way don't follow an instruction because of the teacher's (or parent's) authoritative direction; they do it because of what's in it for them. It becomes all about what they will get in return rather than the relationship they have with their teacher, and it ultimately undermines the teacher's authority.

Parents Become "the Management": 1990s

Parents started moving away from behavior modification because they didn't like being prison wardens and because they saw that their kids responded by working the system to their own advantage.

So back we swung on the pendulum to inaugurate the era of behavior management. In this system, the parent was the *manager,* and the kids were the *team.* Family discussions were no longer led by a parent. Instead, team meetings made up of stakeholders were facilitated by a manager. Parents may not have used these exact terms, but the books that promoted this system sure did.

Parents were staying in the workforce longer and having children a little later in life. So they brought what at the time appeared to be successful team-oriented practices from the office to home. As managers of a workforce, parents wanted to give their team (the kids) a lot of choices.

An important part of behavior management is called "natural consequences." The team, or individual team member, chooses a course of action—even if the manager knows it is probably not a wise choice. The team member experiences the struggle and success or failure. The idea is that the team will learn and grow more naturally than if you stepped in and steered it in the right direction. In this sense, emphasis was put on the learning of the team and not on the implications of its actions. Now it has been widely argued that largely autonomous work teams with little regulation can make self-benefiting decisions that do enormous harm to the economy and society.

This practice can work well with adults in the workplace. After all, don't we deserve a certain level of autonomy? But in a family, we are *not* all adults. Children simply do not have the capacity to flourish under these circumstances. The frontal lobes of their brains have not yet developed enough to facilitate big-picture thinking. They are only equipped to make shorter-term and more self-oriented decisions. So it is not at all effective to stand back and let them make a series of bad decisions in the name of natural consequences and then, after they have made a mess of things, ask them (as some very influential parenting books suggest) whether or not the choice they made was good or bad.

Imagine this scene:

Your four-year-old son, Max, is climbing up the bookshelf with a serrated knife in his mouth and a homemade patch covering his left eye. You look over the top of your *Raising Feral Kids* parenting book, thinking, "Oh no. I forgot to screw that darn bookshelf to the wall." And then a millisecond later: "Is that really the bread knife in his mouth?" A fleeting thought about your health insurance coverage follows, along with a mental image of the emergency room. Fortunately, you are reading the chapter that gives you tons of information about— you guessed it—natural consequences and allowing and then reviewing children's choices.

So you steel your nerves and decide to let the scene play itself out. Your resolve is sorely tested when Max's younger brother ambles by the same swaying bookshelf your ascending pirate is clinging to. Glancing to the left and then to the right to ensure that no one sees you breaking the "choices and natural consequences code," you swoop in and remove your little one from the danger zone. Just as you do, the bookshelf falls. Max, while not completely impaled, is hurt and sob-screaming as only a four-year-old can as you dig him out from under the bookshelf debris. You catch yourself wondering about genetic links to the maniacal risk taking ingrained in your partner's side of the family but quickly cast the thought aside because you know what to do. You say to yourself, "Okay, I have a plan. I am going in."

You pick Max up off the floor and kneel down low because, according to the book, you must have "eye contact while you *review the choices*." You are thinking, "I am almost six feet tall, and he is barely three feet. There's got to be a reason for that." Nevertheless, you set aside your height and developmental differences, because this is the main event, for which you were willing to sacrifice life, limb, and an IKEA bookshelf.

Slowly and calmly you say, "Max, I feel we need to have some eye contact. Okay, you can keep your eye patch on. Shall we review your choices? Well, I'll ask anyway. Was that the *best* choice, a *good* choice, or a *very poor choice,* Max?" Now, Max has been around the block before, and even though he is upset, he knows what to say to cut this "reviewing the choices" thing short. He shouts, *"Poor choice!"* You should be delighted that he got it right, because as the book states, he has now "internalized and taken responsibility for his actions." But he screamed the words while glaring at you and burrowed under the books and refused to come out. This does not seem like the ideal outcome. You start to wonder, "Am I a bad parent? Or is this really bad advice I am reading?"

BEATING THE MANAGERS

Behavior management is a system. And as we have discussed, children and teens can become strongly motivated to beat any *system*. Here is a list of pitfalls that make behavior management a problematic disciplinary approach:

Unionizing

If you set yourself up as "the management" and have two or three kids, they *will* unionize. I've heard kids say, "Well, we all don't want to do it" and look at each other and heartily agree while Mom or Dad is thinking, "This is not the way it's supposed to go. They are meant to be *'invested* in the process.'"

Leadership and Department Confusion

If we try to manage our children rather than act as authoritative parents, we can inadvertently set the family up for all kinds of confusion. We find ourselves chasing after our kids as they take decision making into their own hands. We start reacting to them rather than guiding them, and in the ensuing chaos, we end up losing our tempers and shouting, "Enough! Just do what I told you!" When we manage our kids, we give them choices and options, but no clear directions. When things go wrong, we angrily demand they do what they were told, though we never actually told them what that was.

Immunity

The parent asks, "Was that a good choice?" and the child responds, "I don't care if it was a good choice. I don't care." It's almost like kids have become immune to reason, and it feels like they are impervious to our suggestions.

The Hostile Takeover

A younger child might say, "You're not the boss of me" or "You can't make me." In this frustrating and unsafe situation, the child takes over the agenda and dictates what he or she will or will not do.

The Strike

The child or teen crosses his or her arms and refuses to engage no matter what the parent says. It's like a union strike: The kids just walk off the job.

Sneakiness

A child says to a friend, "Well, I wait until she's talking on the phone, and then I get all the food that I want." Behavior management can encourage your child to do things behind your back, when you are hoping for cooperation and an open and trusting relationship.

Denial

The kid looks right at the management and says, "Yeah right. It wasn't me." We all hear that from time to time, but it becomes a big problem when a child denies pretty much everything. It can turn into an emotional reflex, and this is frustrating to the parent who is trying to point out that something should have happened differently.

The Reversal or Boomerang

A very grown-up seven-year-old told her mother, "You need to say you're sorry to me now." A ten-year-old said, "That hurt my feelings. Do you want to think about an apology, Mum?" These little girls had heard this kind of thing so many times that they were now parroting it right back to their mothers. Needless to say, their mothers were not impressed. I once heard about a twelve-year-old daughter who said with absolute composure, to an increasingly irritated father, "Yes, I can see this must be frustrating for you." The father later commented that the daughter even used his tone of voice.

Ignoring

When a child simply shuts down and ignores you, it can be infuriating. At least when he or she was denying things, there was some kind of communication. The child says, "I won't listen" and pretends that his or her shirt sleeve is much more interesting than anything the parent could possibly say.

Deflection

The child simply does not allow what the manager is saying to enter into his or her world. The comments "whatever," "yeah, maybe," and "uh-huh" are uttered in a well-cultivated distracted or bored tone. It can feel as if your children are practicing parental aikido on you, whereby they simply deflect the forces that come at them. This leaves the parent feeling brushed off and disrespected.

Intimidation

This response from a child or teen is troubling. He or she will say, "I can get very angry, you know" and even subtly threaten you with aggression. Some teens will stand intimidatingly close and glare.

———

When relations break down between an actual workforce and management, a process of negotiation and bargaining begins. If there is still no resolution, an arbitrator is appointed who has authority to develop a binding agreement that both parties have to abide by or face legal action. In other words, there is a process, and someone always maintains ultimate authority.

In a family, there is no such process or safety net. There is no higher power or arbitrator. The parent, then, *must* assume that authoritative role. The bottom line is that it's just plain silly for parents to try to be managers, because we cannot resign (nor can we fire our kids).

OPEN CHOICES VS. APPROVED OPTIONS

Behavior management promotes choice-based discipline, and there's nothing wrong with giving kids choices. But choice must be introduced at the right developmental stage, when the child has the brain capacity to weigh consequences. Otherwise the child is given too much power too early in his or her development. Up until the age of nine, children have a barely developed understanding of socially oriented cause and effect. When kids are given too many choices at an age when they are not able to process them, they become confused and feel unsafe. They get the sense that no one is in charge, which makes them uncomfortable and scared. Kids can even develop a sense of failure when given choices they are not able to process. The bottom line: A repetitive cycle of Choice—Review—Poor Choice Was Made—Sense of Failure discourages children.

The behavior-management style can have negative behavioral consequences. One parent told me, "I tried to raise a responsible child by giving him lots of choices, but I've ended up with an entitled child, whom I hardly recognize sometimes." This was a very tough admission for a caring, well-intentioned parent to make.

Rather than giving kids *open-ended* choices, give them *limited options*. For example, a parent might say to a child, "You may have any one of the three cereals I put on the counter for breakfast. Whichever one you decide on is fine with me." By doing this, you give the child the feeling that he or she has freedom, without relinquishing your authority. And the child likes the fact that, whatever cereal he or she picks, there is no chance that it will be reviewed and possibly found to be a "poor choice."

"Good Job!" Behavior Affirmation: 2000s–

Ever since the late nineties, following the excesses of parent-managers, there has been a swing back to control and command parenting. Let's call it behavior affirmation. It's subtle and seems on the surface to be liberal, positive, and encouraging of a child or teen. However, while it is normal and natural to affirm children and let them know how much you appreciate their help, behavior affirmation takes praise to a whole other level—almost maniacal in its intensity and frequency. In fact, it's like a sugarcoated version of behavior modification, only the emphasis is placed on *praise* rather than *punishment*.

Behavior affirmation means everything is a "good job." Like behavior modification, it manipulates a young child's hunger for attention in order to control him or her through the parent either approving and rewarding or disapproving and punishing.

Here is a situation I witnessed that sums up some of the problems with overpraising:

A dad got out of his van with lots of kids on a Saturday morning. It was a large family, or perhaps some of the kids were friends, as there were six or seven children of similar ages. He had a backpack full of art supplies and went to the picnic table and set things up. He got all the drawing materials out. The mother helped set up too but then walked away with a noticeable spring in her step, as this was her long-anticipated Daddy morning, her morning off. Once he had set all the kids up, he circled around as they drew, saying, "Good job, Amanda. That is so beautiful. Oh, Sophie, that is such a masterpiece. When we get home, we can send a photo to Grandma. Actually, let me just take a picture, and I'll send it to Grandma right now. Oh, Jonathan, that's a beautiful horse. Good job." He was so sweet, but he had gone into verbal-affirmation overdrive.

Then he went into a store to get some snacks. Everyone seemed

relieved that the incessant chatter—all the praise—had stopped. Jonathan, the older boy, who must have been ten or eleven, looked down
and said of his much affirmed drawing of a "horse," "Yeah, right. This
is meant to be a cow." He crumpled up the page and sat sullenly.

Your heart goes out to that dad because he was doing the best he
could and overaffirmation is nothing unusual for many parents today.
We all want our kids to be self-confident and to feel they are successful,
but in our attempts to achieve this, we risk being inauthentic.

HOW HYPERPRAISE CAN LEAD TO BIG DISCIPLINE PROBLEMS

It's not a good idea to exploit a child's need for attention in order to
control his or her behavior. If we indulge in hyperpraise or reward-
disapproval discipline, we risk something precious—our real connection with our son or daughter.

When you overaffirm kids, the following can happen:

Cynicism

Kids can become cynical because they know that not *everything* they do
can be a good job. The parent who overreaches with praise risks shut-
ting down some of the precious trust in her relationship with her child.

Fakers

Kids don't bracket things very well. A child will sense that his or her
parent is being "fake" and may assume that he is not being "true" in
other family situations either. This can be a serious problem when you
are disciplining your child. She pushes back hard because she thinks
you are sometimes inauthentic and doesn't realize that you really mean
what you are saying. Such defiance is actually an attempt to ascertain
what is "real." Overpraise is at the root of this unhealthy, habitual family dynamic.

Guilt-Praise Cycle

The Guilt-Praise Cycle is an unhealthy, self-perpetuating family dynamic:

1. Overaffirming causes a child to feel unsafe or unseen.
2. The child provokes the parent in an effort to be seen and feel safe.
3. The parent becomes frustrated or angry and speaks harshly.
4. The parent then feels guilty about the angry words he or she spoke.
5. The parent compensates by heaping more praise on his or her child.
6. The cycle begins again.

Ten Ways Overpraise Hampers Our Kids

1. **Self-centeredness in the family:** Kids who are overpraised often become self-centered and struggle to develop empathy. If a child, tween, or teen does not have an emerging sense of the effects his actions and behavior have on his siblings and parents, family life can get very difficult. And when parents try to point out what is happening, the self-absorbed child will likely be either clueless or defensive. When you ask a child whom you've overpraised, "Don't you see how mean you are being to your little brother?" you'll be met with a shrug from your former golden child.

2. **Self-centeredness in friendships:** The same problems can arise in friendships. The most enduring bonds are based on much more than what one person can get out of a relationship. As we discussed in Chapter Seven, C. S. Lewis describes four layers of love and caring in order of value:
   - Eros is all about instinctual attraction and desire, or what I want and can get.

- Philia—or conditional friendship—has to do with common interests: "We are into the same things."
- Caritas, or charity, is when I give to another with no coercion or expectation that I'll receive anything in return.
- The last and highest form of love or caring is Agape. In this form of love, I will selflessly help the person I love become who he or she truly wants to be.

Children raised to float on a sea of overpraise will find it very difficult to move beyond what a relationship can either "get" for them or "share" with them. Having friends who are "there for you" (Philia) is wonderful. We all want this for our children. But our children have to be raised to be there for others as well (Caritas) and not expect to be served and praised when they have done nothing to merit it.

3. **Self-centeredness and school achievement:** Overpraise makes our kids want to "*look* smarter rather than *get* smarter," says Stanford psychology professor Carol S. Dweck. Kids who are praised endlessly while growing up—right through their teens—will only take classes that cover material they know well and can ace so that they will be praised, rather than challenge themselves in classes where they'll struggle and maybe get a B or a B–. They can develop an acute fear of failure. Ironically, through behavior affirmation, we inadvertently encourage kids to take fewer risks and therefore limit their learning opportunities.

4. **Self-centeredness in future marriages/partnerships:** Future partnerships end up harvesting some of the wayward seeds planted in a childhood overfertilized with "Good jobs." What wife turns to her husband and tells him *everything* he does is a job well-done? Certainly in a close relationship, your partner, who is dear to you, will tell you on occasion that something you did was less than wonderful. If you haven't been raised to accept criticism, you may not deal with it well. You will feel be-

trayed and bereft and go through a whole range of low-order emotional responses, because you've been brought up thinking that you *always* do a good job.

5. **Self-centeredness in the workplace:** The same is true in the workplace. One of the key markers of success is the ability to seek out, receive, and act on both positive and negative feedback on your work performance. You succeed when you are engaged in a continual process of self-improvement and are able to adjust as a result of the information you have digested. People who have been raised on an overdose of praise will be much less likely to seek genuine feedback if there is a possibility that it will include criticisms or negative assessments of their performance. These young adults will tend to seek out only the coworkers who agree with and praise them. They may stagnate and hit "ceilings" at work without understanding why, because they are convinced that "*everybody* says I am doing great."

In his book *Punished by Rewards,* Alfie Kohn discusses the widespread use of overpraising, which has troubled family counselors for some time in their work to help parents control the inauthentic "Good job!" reflex. Kohn highlights some key overpraising dangers, including manipulation, stealing a child's pleasure, and creating praise junkies and watch-me dependencies, which we've added to our list.

6. **Manipulating children:** Suppose you offer a verbal reward to reinforce the behavior of a two-year-old who eats without spilling or a five-year-old who cleans up all his or her art supplies. Who benefits from this? Is it possible that telling kids they've done a good job has less to do with their emotional needs than with our convenience?

The reason praise can work in the short run is that young children are hungry for our approval. But we have a responsibility not to exploit that dependence for our own convenience. A "Good job!" to reinforce something that makes our lives a little easier can take advantage of children's dependence. Kids may also come to feel manipulated even if they can't quite explain why.

7. **Stealing a child's pleasure or creativity:** If we're continually hovering over a child, talking while he or she is working on a project and offering constant praise, it doesn't allow that child to sink down into a deep creative space. Those of you familiar with the Simplicity Parenting practices will know how important creative play is for a child: It helps him or her digest the world. If we're always praising children, they never get to quietly process all the myriad experiences and associated images they have absorbed. This can lead a child to feel overwhelmed, making the difficulties associated with fight back or fall back we discussed in Chapter One very possible.

8. **Creating praise junkies:** "Good job!" doesn't reassure children; ultimately, it makes them feel less secure. It may even create a vicious circle: The more we slather on the praise, the more kids seem to need it. Some of these kids will grow into adults who need someone to pat them on the head and tell them that whatever they did was okay. Surely this is not what we want for our daughters and sons.

9. **Watch-me dependency:** One mom told me, "When I stopped good-jobbing, I got a life back, because I didn't have to watch everything and praise everything." She added, "It's worth doing just for that." Refraining from overpraise forces children to be goofy or outrageous in order to capture your attention and receive deserved praise.

10. **The charm offensive:** As with criticism, kids can boomerang praise back at you and each other, and they will "good job" other kids, becoming charmingly manipulative.

An exchange involving a three-year-old named Suzy who gave great praise raised a red flag. Suzy came from a home with serial good-jobbing parents. She tried to take a doll away from her friend Bree, but Bree wouldn't give it up. So Suzy heaped praise on another doll that she did not want. She crowed about how beautiful and good it was. She even said the magic words "Good job" when this doll drank imaginary milk from a bottle. It worked. They traded dolls. Suzy had tricked Bree to get the doll she wanted. It makes you wonder how learning to manipulate at such a young age will affect Suzy's future friendships.

HERE ARE SOME SIMPLE ALTERNATIVES TO BEHAVIOR AFFIRMATION

Slow-Soft-Say: The Art of Being Present

A quiet, loving presence is deeply affirming to a child. Anything else can be distraction and verbal clutter.

Let's take the example of a child painting or working on a construction project. If you walk by, slow your pace and pause. Many parents say that learning to pause is not as easy as it sounds because we are always busy or on the move. We have bought into the belief that perpetual activity is equivalent to being effective and successful. Instead, we need to learn how to pause and notice our children quietly.

The Slow-Soft-Say practice is a way to consciously interrupt over-praising.

Slow your pace and pause.

Soft eyes see your child.

Say little.

Parallel Parking

Rather than repeated verbal affirmation, try parallel parking. Take your work with you, and sit next to a child who is engaged in an activity, and just be with her. Let her see that you are also capable of focusing on a project, even if it is only for fifteen minutes. Write a card to a friend, fix a hinge, knit, or peel carrots into a bowl next to her. Many parents discover a child will also parallel park beside them when they are doing a project in the workshop.

When you sit with a child or teen who is in that creative space, a connection opens up. Maybe an occasional word is exchanged, but essentially you are just there. It's as if you and your child are in a boat floating down a gently flowing river on a sunny day, gazing at your surroundings. No words are needed. The quieter you are, the deeper your experience.

ESTABLISHING AN AFFIRMATION BUDGET

Many parents have said, "Not talking is really hard." If you are a serial affirmer, talking and good-jobbing less often takes getting used to. But the economical use of meaningful affirmations helps build stronger family ties. Here are eight beneficial ways to use affirmation:

1. **Semi-verbal affirmation:** Why not just look at a child's painting and say, "Well, well." That's it. Nothing more. Just a little affirmative "Hmm!" or "Gosh!" Such benign comments don't distract a child. They keep him or her on track and communicate genuine encouragement.
2. **Praise the process:** When you praise the process, you encourage your child or teen to keep on task and affirm the process rather than just the outcome. You might say, "That's coming along well" or "You've *really* moved that along."
3. **Be specific:** Young children learn mainly through doing. When we are specific, we help them orient themselves in practical achievement. Say things like "Thank you for setting the table without even being asked." Tweens and teens appreciate when parents remain in this matter-of-fact or non-weird zone.

4. **Affirm the timing:** Letting children know when they exhibit good timing helps strengthen connections with siblings and parents. Tell your child, "That was a really good time to help your little sister. That big log was way too heavy for her to lift on her own." This can also help in disciplinary situations. A parent can say, "Sarah, you had such good timing when you helped your sister build her fort yesterday, but today was not so good because she told you she didn't want any help. That's why she got upset."

5. **Affirm the difficulty or mistake:** Just noticing that a child or teen has worked hard on something difficult is one of the best ways to affirm his or her efforts. You might say, "That basketball drill I saw you doing with the team was not easy for you, and you really kept at it." This encourages stick-to-itiveness and signals to the child that difficulty and mistakes are an essential part of learning.

6. **Say what you see:** "You put your shoes on by yourself" or "You used a lot of red in your drawing today." This helps a parent avoid forming a judgment. It often leads to a child describing his process and feeling good about telling you how he did it. This is an especially useful tool in speaking with tweens and teens because a judgment will often close them down and make them retreat even further into themselves, while an observation, on the other hand, will open up communication.

7. **Ask a related question:** "What was the hardest part to draw?" or "How did you figure out how to get the feet like that?" A child might respond with, "Yeah, well, it was hard, but you know how Brendan's feet are really wide, and they're just like ducks' flippers, only he doesn't like us saying that, and . . ." And a big story materializes. Again, you see the child's world emerge and are present to her enthusiasm. She knows whether she's gotten this just right or it's not quite right yet. No parent

wants to close his or her child down by judging her performance like some pseudo–art critic.

8. **Recall and review previous successes:** "You know, even though
you're frustrated with your drawing now, I have often seen you
work these things out by yourself." Children live in the now,
and this kind of affirmation does two things. It lets a kid know
that you understand his frustration and that it's okay to feel
that way. It also clarifies that, while you empathize with his
emotional state, you see the big picture and remember his past
successes. This is much better than flooding him with suggestions, which you may be tempted to do, but which will likely be
rejected because they make him feel inadequate.

How to Get Off the Swinging Pendulum

We want to avoid a situation where our kids are aware that we have
been reading another parenting book based on the latest fad and they
roll their eyes as if to say, "Look out, she has been reading another one
of those books." Children understand when Mom or Dad isn't really
being her- or himself. What our kids need is for us to stand on our own
ground. If we understand recent trends and the pitfalls of overuse of
affirmations and hear ourselves drifting into a style that has all kinds
of downsides, we can catch ourselves, pause, and get back to speaking
in our own voice.

10

Discipline and the Four Pillars of Simplicity

How to Dial Back the Outside Pressures

If your child exhibits the "flooded" response we discussed in Chapter One, you should now have a good sense of what is triggering that erratic or unpleasant behavior: too much pressure coming from outside and not enough rest or downtime to allow him or her to develop better resiliency. There are four key ways you can immediately reduce these pressures and prevent pushback and a flooded response. If you've read my book *Simplicity Parenting,* some of these concepts will be familiar to you, but it's important to revisit them in the context of discipline:

1. Balance and simplify the amount of stuff your child or teen has (such as books, toys, and clothes).
2. Strengthen rhythm and predictability.

3. Balance and simplify the number of scheduled activities.

4. Filter out adult conversation.

In Chapter Eleven, we will take this one step further by looking at the huge behavioral benefits of filtering out the adult world by going low screen or no screen.

1. SIMPLIFYING THE AMOUNT OF STUFF

A great starting point for dialing it down is clearing out the clutter. Reduce the number of books, toys, clothes, gadgets, and other extraneous items in a kid's room and around the house in general. Countless parents have reported that, when they reduce physical clutter, their child's or teen's behavior improves. This makes sense if you consider what happens in the mental and emotional life of a child when he or she has less. When children have fewer things, what they do have becomes precious. And if they are playing with other kids, they learn how to share what little they have. The more a child's imagination becomes fired up by one little object—that blanket he's putting over a frame, those two cars she drives along the living room rug, that plank of wood that becomes a roof, whatever it is—the more likely it is that he or she will find multiple uses for it, since there aren't that many other options. When this happens, the limbic system and the frontal lobes of your child's brain, which stimulate collaboration and cooperation, are encouraged to develop. The limbic system is critical for emotional processing and behavior and has also been connected to the development of emotional health, social cooperation, and *empathy*.

Parents who have adopted the Simplicity approach say things like "When I've got less stuff around, my three kids actually fight *less*. Isn't that strange?" It may seem counterintuitive, but in fact, when there are fewer things to play with, kids have to collaborate more. They can't dart about from one toy or digital device to another, a behavior pattern that stimulates the amygdala, which in turn triggers the primal fight-or-flight response. A child with too many toys and gadgets is likely to develop unhealthy play rather than good, creative interaction. As I mentioned above, the area of the brain that develops as a child learns to find multiple uses for a single toy is also related to the building up of social cooperation. The positive changes in behavior and cooperation you see when you simplify your child's or teen's home environment may appear magical, but they are grounded in developmental fact.

Encouraging your children to play in a cooperative way means a parent needs to arbitrate much less to sort out conflicts. Why wait until there is fighting over toys to be forced to intervene and remove them? Intervene proactively, and enjoy the giggles and long moments of quiet play with the few simple toys you thoughtfully provide.

2. RHYTHM AND PREDICTABILITY

The best way to handle behavioral flash points—the times each day when your child is especially difficult—is to establish rhythm and predictability. Classic flash point moments are getting out to the car in the morning, sitting down to do homework after school, and bedtime with its attendant bathing and teeth brushing rituals. If you pay close attention, you can actually feel or see these rough patches coming and prepare for them. Recognition is a first step toward building rhythm and a different (positive) kind of predictability into the day.

We often brace for impact as those challenging times of the day approach. We strap on our defenses and say, "Wish me luck, I'm going in" as we open the door, make a suggestion, or pull up to the curb to interact with the child we know will be out of sorts. It's hard to feel centered when we are anticipating trouble. We may come on too strong, "shouty," or overly stern. "I am serious now. There will be consequences for any misbehavior!" you say when your daughter is splashing away merrily in the bathtub. In such a situation, you've preemptively disciplined—and perhaps even scared—your child (who may or may not have been about to do that naughty thing she did in the bath last time). Or we may go the opposite route and become tentative and unsure of ourselves: "Let's see if we can, um . . . Who would like to get into the bath now?" The positive, middle-road approach is rhythm. Turning these times of day into smooth, repetitive rituals not only helps center a child but also shores up the foundations of parental calmness.

To establish a rhythm, mix the big- and small-picture strategies. The "big" is about trying as best we can to have the event happen at the same time each day. That might mean that you have a specific time for it on weekdays and you relax a bit on weekends. But the key is to have times that are only semi-flexible and stick to them. The "small" way to build rhythm is to zero in on all the little details. It's about having the soap in the same exact place, the toothbrush and toothpaste laid out in the same manner, the towel folded just so. For older kids, it could work like this: If your son or daughter makes his or her school lunch in the morning, adding rhythm would mean making the sandwiches in the same place on the counter, on the same cutting board, with the food laid out pretty much exactly the same way each morning.

You might think that all this emphasis on rhythm seems a bit too boring and routine. Don't we want creative and spontaneous homes (subtext: chaotic)? One mom once told me that she came from a home where everything was "locked into tedious routine." She was understandably wary of re-creating this dynamic with her own kids. But there is an important distinction to be made between routine and rhythm. A routine is a cold, repeated series of actions. It often involves sending a child away from you to do a chore. It separates a child from the flow of family life. Rhythm, on the other hand, is warm, often fun, and it connects a child with siblings and parents. Tasks that are rhythmic are often done with a parent taking a quiet interest in how the child is getting on. The same exact task can be either routine or rhythmic. The way in which you approach and implement your strategy makes all the difference. The task becomes rhythmic when a parent performs it *with* the child or teen. You are moving through the day together, chatting and laughing as you connect. The task itself becomes secondary to the connection that develops as you work together.

One mother of a "squirrely" young daughter told me this shift in perspective made all the difference for her family: "Everything used to be hard and 'wrestly.' Now we look forward to the exact same times of the day I used to dread. Who would have guessed?"

When you've built rhythm into the fabric of your child's day, you actually free up the possibility for the kind of spontaneity that used to keep everyone on edge. Living a rhythm-filled life allows us to launch (or lurch) into the unexpected or be just plain goofy. Here's one dad's story:

"We were sitting at dinner one evening when I burst out with, 'Who wants to go and see the UConn women's basketball game?' My two daughters, then ten and twelve, shouted, 'We do!' My wife looked surprised. She knows well that the college basketball environment is high velocity, super-loud, and raucous. And we are supposed to be the 'simplicity rhythm family,' right? She then asked, 'When is the game?' 'It starts in thirty minutes,' I said sheepishly. Without missing a beat (well, maybe one or two), she announced, 'Come on. Let's go! Let's just pack up supper and eat it in the car.'

"Thirty minutes later, we were walking into that modern-day pleasure dome known as a basketball arena. My girls stood wide-eyed, mouths agape: There were jumbotron video screens flashing, cheerleaders launched into the air and caught by muscular young men, and T-shirt cannons firing T-shirts high into the crowd of many thousands.

"We got home at ten-fifteen (on a school night) and moved into rhythmical autopilot. The dinner 'debris' was cleared away, baths were taken, and teeth and hair brushed. I turned out the light at 10:40 P.M. but was amazed at how everyone just knew what to do and got on with it. The next day, the girls slid right back into the rhythms and grooves of the day and were fine. There were no signs of grumpiness or out-of-whack behavior. I am certainly no superstar parent, but I now know from experience that the strong and simple rhythms that run through our family life help keep us calm and open up the possibility for spontaneous fun."

If you are doing your best to make life rhythmic but still feel things are a bit too hectic, you will want to work on rhythm's sibling strategy: predictability. While it may not have quite the power of rhythm, predictability can still bring a vital sense of security to a child.

Predictability also deals with big and small picture realities. The "big" approach to predictability is to help your child create a mental road map of the coming day. Some parents will sit with their child or teen at night and do a quick next-day run-through. You have to be careful not to overdescribe. Leave as much as possible to the kid's imagination. Some parents join the child in visualizing various major points in the coming day at bedtime. Others simply ask what their child's "rose and thorn" were in the day that has just ended and what "thorn and rose" he or she might foresee for the coming day. A "rose" is a happy event, and a "thorn" is something that was or will be challenging.

If you decide to adopt the practice of previewing the day ahead, pay some attention to the flash point moments in which your child or teen typically struggles. If the mood is right, you can even make a simple plan about how to deal with any problems that come up. But it's often enough just to picture and recognize that these are sometimes hard moments. This helps these difficult experiences become more like shared conundrums.

The "small" approach to predictability and previewing is to break down what the next few steps will be for your child: "Toby, we'll be going upstairs and getting ready for bed soon. I'm just going to finish off the dishes first." You are giving a child a preview of what is about to happen rather than just scooping him up and whooshing him up the stairs. Having a predictable, rhythmic life is critical to experiencing far fewer difficult disciplinary moments in your family.

3. AVOIDING OVERSCHEDULING

Kids need time to process and digest what happens around them. In Chapter One, we explored how a child's inner world strengthens largely through storytelling, reading, and play. Many parents and educators are worried about the erosion of playtime at school, in day care, and even at home due to overscheduling. Play for a young child and downtime for a tween or teenager are critical to healthy emotional and social development. Rather than stuff our children's lives with back-to-back activities, we need to embrace the gift of boredom, because boredom is the precursor to creativity.

When a child is bored, we do not have to immediately scramble to set up activities. In fact, when we introduce new activities to help our children alleviate their boredom, we increase their pushback. This might sound counterintuitive given the fact that parents worry that their children will misbehave if they allow them to be idle. Such parents think busy schedules are the best way to avoid discipline problems. A mother of three wrote the following in a letter she sent me a few months after a discipline workshop: "When I had my first child, I was quite unsure about a lot of things. But most of all I didn't know what to do about discipline. I thought the best way to avoid discipline problems was to keep him busy. I enrolled him in classes and sports, and he seemed to go along with it, but he would become fresh and difficult at home. So I enrolled him in more activities. His behavior did not improve. If anything, he got more disrespectful. He would ignore me. . . . To be honest, I was setting up a situation where we would not spend all that much time together as nothing much enjoyable seemed to come about during these times. While all this was developing, I had my second child, and I pretty much followed the same pattern for her, and the same difficult behavior happened.

"Having a new baby brought me to your workshop, as I knew something had to change. I thought I had messed up twice, and I was not going to do it again. . . . I came away with ideas for my older two kids and not just for my baby. I have cut way back on their activities, and it was surprising that neither of them seemed to mind all that much. Now they love it. . . . What seemed to be most important was that I was around and available without having to do much in terms of playing with them. I took a deep breath and let them be bored, and it worked just like we talked about. They started [playing] all manner of funny little games that they would invent. My eldest boy particularly got into building forts in our yard. . . . We are now closer as a family, and there is less fighting and explosions. I still have to resist putting them back in a bunch of activities because everybody else seems to be doing it, which makes me feel guilty. But all I have to do is remember how it was last year, and I am fine with the way things are now."

What is most touching about this mom's experience is that she discovered for herself something powerful: The more she had tried to withdraw from her kids' lives (by scheduling them to spend time in activities with others), the more they had tried to draw her back in, the best way they knew how, by acting out and challenging her. She realized that they were doing this not to be bad but to bond with her. And she mustered up the courage to stand apart from the "new normal" in which so many parents super-schedule their kids and allow her own crew downtime and even boredom.

What should you do when your children next moan about being bored? Resist the urge to find them something to do, and instead, out-bore the boredom! You have to become really boring and leave them alone to solve the puzzle of what to do with their newfound alone time. One tip: If you're dealing with more than one child at a time, try separating them. Maybe hold one close and send one to do a chore, or just give them space—but not together, because they might relieve their boredom by fighting with each other. Keep them separate for fifteen to thirty minutes, and you'll be amazed at the creativity that breaks out. Their inner world and creative juices start flowing.

Children digest all the busyness of the outside world through play. That's how they process what they encounter. Believe it or not, if you provide the space for children to play and have lots and lots of downtime, you will deal with many fewer disciplinary issues. A child can be self-orienting if he or she is provided with rhythm, time to digest, plenty of downtime, and time to play. Then the child will call much less often for adult attention through bad behavior. As parents, we want to build up our child's inner being so that there isn't the need for so much discipline at home. The more we slow down our children's lives and bring rhythm and predictability into each day, the more inner strength and self-esteem they will develop, and the less often we will need to discipline them.

4. FILTERING OUT ADULT CONVERSATION AND INFORMATION

The fourth principle of simplicity and balance involves the filtering of adult conversation and adult-oriented information out of our children's lives.

The proper degree of separation between the adult world and a child's world is crucial to that child's well-being. Yet it's a delicate balance. Too much separation can mean a child does not attach to the parent, and the parent does not bond with his or her child. If there is too little separation, the child has access to all sorts of adult information and comes to believe that she is her parent's equal. That is not a healthy dynamic either.

If children hear information about world events such as wars, bombings, global warming, rape, and famine, they will almost certainly feel that the world is an unsafe place and full of violence. Children know they are vulnerable; they do not have cars to flee in or weapons to fight with. So when we, as a society, allow them access to adult information, we erode their sense of safety. We unintentionally provide them with the unconscious message of their utter vulnerability with every news cycle we allow them to see or hear or adult discussion they overhear because we didn't filter it out.

There is so much adult information that our children should not hear—for example, our conversations about Aunt Annie's struggle with cancer, Daddy's trouble at work with his boss, or their teacher's weaknesses. When we discuss these adult issues in front of our children, we essentially raise them to our level and lose our authoritativeness. If we pull all the veils away from the adult world and show ourselves with all our glaring weaknesses, our children inevitably feel unsafe. Many wonderful, egalitarian-minded parents want to share too much with their child too early because they believe their child has a right to know things and will be better off with the truth. But what these parents fail to recognize is that they are exposing their kids to information that children are not developmentally able to process, and this erodes their sense of safety. The sad irony of this is that, rather than producing a globally minded young citizen of the world, it can lead to a nervous, anxious, and stressed child.

The chrysalis or protective sheath in which childhood unfolds can be thinned or even stripped away. We can apply what is happening to our planet as a whole to our children's feelings of safety in their world. Just as we must not dissolve the protective layers around the earth by polluting the atmosphere with elements that the planet cannot handle, we must not strip away our children's sheaths by flooding our family atmosphere with information that they cannot handle. As it stands, many of our children suffer from severe emotional sunburns because they've been exposed to too much too soon. Before we say anything in front of our children, we need to ask ourselves four key questions: Is it kind, is it necessary, is it true, and will it help my child feel safe? Unless you can answer yes to all four of those questions, don't say it.

In Conclusion

Balancing and simplifying your kid's life is the vessel in which all the strategies of the Governor, the Gardener, and the Guide can be held. Without this kind of container, much of what you do to support the behavior of your child or teen will be like trying to put new content into a glass already full to the brim and spilling over. This overflow is caused by the too much, too soon, too sexy, too young dynamic that has become the norm of modern living. By dialing back the pace of family life, you provide the time for your child to be nourished by absorbing what has already flowed into his or her cup due to day-to-day life. Balancing your children's lives makes space for new experiences and, in particular, for the boundaries you are setting to be kept. As one mother of two children put it, "Before simplifying our family life, whatever I said to my kids seemed to set them off and make them goofy or defiant. After calming down the pace of our days and giving more downtime, everything became easier. What I especially noticed was that when I had to give a direction or make a transition my kids would come along in a much better way." She later added, "I thought this was just something small that only I could see, but my friends noticed the change and said how much more fun we all seemed to be having. Up until I heard that, I didn't realize how much better I felt as a parent, but most of all I could just be *me* again."

11

Discipline in the Digital Age

How a parent handles the influence of screens (televisions, computers, phones, and other devices) used to be a part of a general discussion about filtering the adult world from our kids' lives. In recent years, however, it has become a major stand-alone concern as alarm has spiked among parents and educators about how children of all ages cope with the tsunami of information and distraction digital devices offer. Because of this, I have included a more in-depth look at discipline in the digital age in this book. It's a sensitive issue for some who feel that technology has significantly improved education and entertainment, as well as for those who believe screen exposure is the *new normal* and do not want to question the status quo. It is clear to me, as a parenting adviser, that we have to approach this issue with consciousness and courage and accept the fact that—as in many other areas of our kids' lives (such as when they are fighting or arguing over a favorite toy)—there will be times when we have to step in firmly and take careful control.

To be clear, I am not antiscreen, but I am passionately pro–human relationships and pro–family connections. I am just as committed to the reality that children develop in phases and at each stage they need the right environment in order to flourish. Frankly, I would be relieved if the evidence supported screen use for kids being okay. It would make Katharine's and my life as parents a whole lot easier if we just went with the popular tide and got our kids smartphones and tablets and opened the door to social networking. However, both the balance of research and my plain old gut instinct tell me that something is seriously wrong with the way in which perhaps the most powerful tool humankind has ever known is being placed literally in the hands of children. As you will see in this chapter, the evidence is mounting that this twenty-year unregulated mass social experiment is not going so well, especially for kids and families.

Strong family bonds take time to build and nurture. The increasing demands of work life, with its invisible digital arm reaching right into our homelife, means our time with our kids has become more precious and limited than ever before. Therefore, it makes sense that we should live every moment with our kids to its fullest and not allow ourselves to be displaced by the allure of digital distractions.

During a morning break in a workshop in British Columbia, a couple with three children, ages four to fifteen, spoke about their experiences with screen media. But it was their bold decision to dial back their kids' screen use dramatically that caught my attention. The mother was nuanced and insightful about the positive changes cutting back had brought about in their family life. But the dad put it bluntly: "The screens used to be in charge. Now Barbara and I are. It's that simple." They'd noticed that their kids got along better now. But the biggest change involved discipline. "To be honest, I only went along with this because Barbara was so determined that we try to limit computer, phone, and TV use, and I was so tired of everything becoming a fight with my kids," the dad continued. "They talked to me like characters from movies in which kids took control. When we cut down on screens, they stopped challenging us at every turn. It's weird that we've all bought into the media so much when it makes it so much harder to be a good parent."

We may only just be beginning to understand how so much screen exposure affects our kids. In this chapter, we will examine the effects of screen exposure as they pertain to parental guidance and disciplinary issues.

Screens have certainly become ubiquitous. Our kids encounter them at school, in shops, at gas stations and airports, and in libraries and restaurants. But they are also in their backpacks, pockets, and hands. Only a decade or two ago, you had to go somewhere to view a screen or be at home. At that time, we talked about the effects "television" had on our children. But today the term "screen," which encompasses the multiple media-delivery methods available, is much more appropriate. And screens go wherever we go. There is no geographical or locational separation. It's a new world. And it's a big deal in terms of what it means to our families.

The debate about screen use for kids has been raging for years, and it often gets heated and polarized. I am not without my own bias, of course, but I am also an avid reader of studies that portray every facet of the issue. I was sitting at my desk putting the finishing touches on this final chapter when a new research report caught my attention. Many studies make subtle claims. Some are not that well designed. Others are funded by questionable sources. But this report was thorough and, well, simply put, a game changer. I don't say this to be sensational. Nor do I use these words lightly. I have read hundreds of papers on this topic. But every now and then a research study is published that is exceptionally solid, and its findings so encapsulate the topic that it deserves serious, careful attention.

The Learning Habit Studies was the largest survey of family routines ever conducted, with forty-six thousand participants. Researchers from Brown University School of Medicine, Brandeis University, the Children's National Medical Center, and the New England Center for Pediatric Psychology conducted a three-year study and worked with WebMD, The National PTA, the *Huffington Post,* and *Parents Magazine* to enhance national outreach.

Here is an overview of some of their key findings:

Effects on Learning and Grades

They found that after just thirty minutes of screen time a day, children's grades began a steady drop. After two hours, researchers observed a dramatic decline in grades, and after four screen hours a day, a student's average GPA fell an entire grade.

Since so many kids use computers and other devices to help them complete homework assignments, the team also took this into account. They found that even when more screen time led to more time spent on homework, children's grades still dropped.

Effects on Sleep

Children and teens who spent four hours on screen time a day took an average of twenty minutes longer to fall asleep than children who had more limited screen time.

Emotional Effects

More time on devices also led to increased social and emotional volatility in kids and disconnectedness from family. The hours spent on screens have to come from somewhere in the day, and researchers found that this had a clear impact on the amount of time spent with family, which is critical to healthy child development.

Conversely, they found that the more time children spent interacting with family (doing things like simply talking, playing games, or just hanging out), the less time they spent on their devices. Kids who spent more time with family had better socialization skills and were better able to handle their emotions.

Focus and "Grit"

It's easy to overlook the value of your kids' ability to work through a challenge. That is, until it becomes a discipline problem that parents are compelled to deal with. The research team found that grit, which is defined in the study as the ability to perform a strenuous or difficult task without giving up, *decreased* as children's screen time *increased*. On the other hand, when children in the study had limited screen time and were given chores to do, they performed better socially, academically, and emotionally, and they had better control over their focus and attention. Contributing to simple household tasks, such as setting the table, cooking, or helping with laundry, gave children a better sense of self-esteem and responsibility.

In an interview with the *Huffington Post* on January 6, 2015, Rebecca Jackson, coauthor of the book *The Learning Habit,* spoke about parents having an inklings of these effects. However, she said there seems to be a "disconnect" between this generalized intuition and parents' thinking about their own children. "There's a difference between knowing something and suspecting something," Jackson said. "We are aware that the average American child spends eight hours in front of a screen, but we often don't associate those numbers with our own children. Those numbers tend to be about somebody else's child."

To recap, we have one of the largest studies ever conducted in the field by researchers from very respected institutions concluding that screen use can have serious negative effects on our kids, specifically:

- on their learning and academic abilities
- on their social and emotional lives
- on their sleep
- on their ability to pay attention
- on their ability to overcome challenges
- on their connection to their families

And all of these effects were present when the kids were consuming four hours or less a day of screen time, which is half the national average! What a wake-up call. Particularly when we consider why screens are first introduced to children. The most common reason parents give for providing infants and toddlers with screen time is that they believe that it is beneficial to their children's brain development. The American Academy of Pediatrics states that there is no credible evidence that any type of screen time is beneficial to babies and toddlers and some evidence that it may be harmful. How can an activity like screen use be good for the brain if such relatively small amounts of time using these devices can compromise such a long list of crucial developmental abilities?

It's not just the Learning Habits Studies team who have pointed out the serious dangers of screen overexposure. In older children and adolescents, excessive screen time is linked to increased psychological difficulties that include hyperactivity, emotional and behavioral problems, difficulties with peers, and poor school performance. Dr. Jane Healy points out that too many fast-paced images from screen time prevents the brain from learning how to pay attention and leads to problems focusing. And the instant stimulus of screens can cause children to become impatient in complex situations. Dr. Daniel Siegel describes computer screens and the trancelike state they bring about as "the quick and dirty route" of visual processing "where the mind becomes filled with deeply ingrained and inflexible patterns of response."

This is just a sampling of the research findings that make it crystal clear that even seemingly small amounts of screen media can harm our kids and our connection to them as parents. Many parks and schools will not allow children to climb trees because they might fall and get hurt. But should we not be more concerned that sitting right under those trees are kids playing on screen-based devices that can really harm them? And not only do we allow it; many adults strongly encourage it.

One of the most commonly expressed counterpoints from parents who consider going low or no screen is that all this is a real part of our lives now; screen exposure is widespread. This attitude or belief should give us pause, because what it suggests is that a life dominated by screens is a normal and healthy existence. Instead of accepting it, we should be shocked into asking ourselves if we can think of any other situation in life in which we, as a culture, allow, support, and even encourage an activity in the face of such overwhelming evidence of the potential harm it inflicts on children.

Fitting In

We all want our kids to fit in. This is a big concern for any parent and is often the reason for letting the digital deluge into family life. But the question is "Fit into what?" Do we really want our kids to fit in with a group of kids who are so overexposed to and influenced by screen content? Such kids are likely to experience difficulties with attention, academic learning, speech, separating reality from fantasy, self-generated creativity, social and communication skills, and impulse control.

I have watched the friendship patterns of my own children and the children of many hundreds of other low- or no-screen families. After twenty years of careful observation, I can do the "friendship math" on this one with confidence. Here's how it looks:

GROUP ONE: THE SUPER VIRTUALLY CONNECTED KID (SVCK)

Out of every ten possible friends, at least four will be heavily into screens and spend around the national average of seven and a half hours a day on a screen. Most parents are appalled by this data, but clearly, some kids are spending this amount of time on screens and others even more, because the seven and a half hour figure is an *average*.

GROUP TWO: THE SWING VOTERS

For every four kids who are truly in the steely grip of the digital dragon, three or four are moderate users. If these kids are given the opportunity, they will spend time away from screens and enjoy themselves thoroughly. The trouble is they don't get many chances to play or hang out with friends away from screens.

GROUP THREE: JUST REGULAR CHILDREN

Now we are down to just two or three kids from very low-screen—a carefully monitored couple of hours a week—or no-screen homes. These kids tend to be creative, innovative, adaptable. That makes them the alternative CIA. They don't sit and stare at or interact with someone else's creation. They themselves create, because they have to. They have been given the gift of boredom and have had to figure out ways to engage and entertain themselves.

Back to the Friendship Math

Let's say you are considering dialing it back and going low or no screen. What does this mean for your kid's possible friendships?

1. It's probably true: There is no denying that the SVCK group will likely not be interested in playing or hanging out with your

child or teen. Your child will miss out on the wonders of "acro-speak" such as OMG, OMF*****G WTF***, FF***S, SOB, LOL, LMAO, and my two favorites, rich in irony considering the communication medium, TMI (too much information) and IRL (in real life).

2. Super virtually connected cool kids and intermittent popular-ity: Emerging research challenges the belief that a kid has to be physically attractive and aggressive to be popular. The key: There is a difference between "perceived popularity," which relates to attractiveness, aggression, and the ability to socially manipulate via a cycle of acceptance and rejection, and being truly well liked. This is the difference between high-visibility, intermittent popularity and low-key, enduring popularity. In other words, looks and intimidation seem to work for tweens and teens, but only in the short term and only on the surface.

A study in the *British Journal of Developmental Psychology* found that well-liked kids have a good "theory of mind," which is the ability to be empathetic and see things from another child's point of view. In addition to this, research shows that kids who can regulate their emotions and impulses have a bet-ter social life. When kids do better socially, they suffer less fre-quently from anxiety, have fewer worries, and experience little difficulty joining in with a group.

So when parents struggle with the issue of limiting screen exposure because they don't want their kids to become social pariahs, they should consider that significant screen exposure contributes to:

1. Making kids aggressive. Does aggressiveness lead to long-term popularity? Not really. Who wants a long-term friend who could lash out at you, put you down, or reject you at any moment?

2. Poor empathy and lower social skills. These are not at all the ingredients for popularity. Who wants a friend who is only interested in him- or herself?

3. Poor impulse control, impatience, and inattentiveness. Do these qualities result in popularity that lasts? No. Who wants a friend who walks away?

It is the well-liked kids who have a happy social life at school, in the neighborhood, and at home with siblings. Their friendships are not based on manipulation and fear or the latest digital gadgets and fashions. These kids have the strength of character not to buy into all the *stuff*. Sure, they may dress nicely and occasionally watch a movie, but that is not what defines them or how they define themselves. As these kids grow up, they are able to use their moral compass in both small daily encounters and big life events. They do not rely on *outer* confirmation to know who they are. They have not watched thousands of hours of someone else's creativity on screens. They have found and nurtured their inner source of creativity.

3. No big sacrifice: A growing number of parents have begun to shield their children from playmates who consume a heavy diet of screen entertainment. It may be heart wrenching to see kids whose precious beings are buried under a landfill of toxic pop culture, but as parents, we should have *no problem at all* knowing that these media-dazed kids will not be that interested in hanging out with our kids. Or that our kids will not want to hang out so much with such *high visibility* or temporarily popular kids. Do we want our kids to be part of the jostling crowd competing for acceptance with the *in group*? Of course not! We hope our kids have the inner strength to make social adjustments along the way, because such social dynamics are part of life. We do not want them to sacrifice their precious sense of self in order to become the cool kids of the moment.

After all, when push comes to *love* and things get tough, whom do you want as a friend? Someone who will respond to your pain with an OMG text then instantly shift to the next possible "twit . . . er-er" or someone who will sit with you and listen to your story? We sense, deep down, whom we can connect with. They are our true friends.

Manipulation: The Story of Sara's Heartbreak

Sara was excited. She'd just received a text from Hailey, the coolest girl in the class. Sara was being invited to join "The Mix" to see a movie. The Mix was a powerful sixth-grade girls' clique. After Sara quickly accepted, Hailey and The Mix were super friendly toward her. They even included her in some group-texting banter and skillful put-downs of other kids in the class.

Sara's mother was surprised and admittedly pleased but also wary. She would later say, "Something was a bit off about the whole thing, but I could not put my finger on it." Nevertheless, she gave in to Sara's pleading and allowed her to go along.

On movie night, the girls met up at the local multiplex cinema. Sara found herself at the front of the ticket line and bought her ticket. The Mix girls were texting each other furiously as they waited to buy their own tickets. As they all approached the crowded entrance to the various theaters, The Mix hung back deliberately and let Sara go ahead into the theater she had a ticket for. They then very casually walked into a different theater, which they had tickets for. At first, Sara looked around, wondering where the other girls were, and presumed they'd had to sit somewhere else in the crowded cinema, and that she would meet up with them at the end of the movie for ice cream. But when everyone filed out, Sara looked and looked for the girls without success. The theater emptied out, and she got nervous, because Hailey's mom was supposed to pick them all up. She checked her phone and saw a four-word text message from Hailey: "i dont think so."

Sara teared up. The whole thing had been planned, from Sara's placement at the front of the line to the girls hanging back in the lobby and the earlier pickup for The Mix. And the worst was yet to come. The Mix had taken plenty of shots of Sara going into the theater alone and posted them online captioned with disparaging comments.

Hailey and her friends had manipulated Sara by using the powerful twin tools of acceptance and rejection. The Mix was expert at drawing people in and then pushing them away in a socially crippling way. They'd sent Sara—and the whole class for that matter—a strong message of dominance. Sara would have never told anyone what had happened. She would have bottled it up, preferring to face the humiliation alone. But once the photos were posted, the whole embarrassing story came out.

"I should have trusted my instinct," Sara's mom said. "I should have insisted on talking personally to Hailey's mother rather than leaving it all to texts between the kids. I will *never* make that mistake again. I just could not imagine that the girls could do something so nasty and so planned out." Sara's mother was kind and clear when she said, "These girls are not 'bad kids.' They just need us [the parents] to be much more involved."

Aloneness vs. Loneliness

What's great about kids living a life in which they are not constantly connected to myriad social-networking options is that they will not confuse "alone time" with loneliness. They will not be driven by the need to be connected but will be more content in their own company or together with a few close friends. They will not be drawn into "friending" and judge themselves by the numbers of "followers" they can drum up. Most of us know that true friendship is not about friending and being followed at all. It's about the quality of individual relationships. Kids who are okay with being by themselves will and do attract other kids. And we all want kids who can stand on their own ground—who can be themselves. So many of our life-altering, breakthrough moments come when we are alone with our thoughts and feelings.

There's a deep irony as well as a deep concern regarding superconnected kids, because in fact, they struggle mightily with alone time. If a child or teen does not know how to be alone, then he or she will feel lonely. This sets up a truly troubling cycle, because a lonely kid will try to bypass the feeling of loneliness by seeking out more and more virtual friends. Does this pattern remind you of anything? Longtime addiction counselor Felicitas Vogt and I, together with some high school students, developed a definition for addiction as being "an increasing and compulsive tendency to avoid pain, boredom, loneliness, silence and self-development by displacing it with outer stimulation."

We risk unleashing the beast of addiction upon our kids by supporting their frenzied friending, tweeting, and follower urges. Believe it or not, the social-networking giants refer to their clients as "users," which is the same term we have for people who use drugs. Coincidence? Of course! But it's worth our while to pause and wonder. If we want our kids to be okay with *being alone* and not get caught up in such a potentially addictive cycle, we must provide them with digitally unplugged time.

Parental Authority as a Barrier to "Cool"

Screens often promote idealized or "beautiful people" images and products that are worrying to parents. Not only do a lot of the clothes and products promoted so seductively cost more than many families can afford; the ads subtly and not so subtly suggest over and over to a child that "you are not good enough unless you look like this."

In a 2006 interview with Salon.com, then Abercrombie & Fitch chief executive Michael Jeffries was surprisingly unapologetic about Abercrombie's brand strategy: "In every school there are the cool and popular kids, and then there are the not-so-cool kids. Candidly, we go after the cool kids. We go after the attractive all-American kid with a great attitude and a lot of friends. A lot of people don't belong [in our clothes], and they can't belong. Are we exclusionary? Absolutely."

Marketers know full well that by using multilayered screen and social-networking strategies they can infiltrate friendships and encourage friends to promote their products to each other in order to ensure that their group is cooler than others. They also know that it is the parents who often stand between their wish to sell their products and successfully driving a kid's desire to purchase. The answer is simple and cynical. As Susan Linn from the Campaign for a Commercial-Free Childhood puts it, "They denigrate adults and exploit children's desires to fit in with their peers and rebel against authority figures as a selling point for their products." The message that adults are out of touch or stupid and must be defied for a kid to be able to fit in and be accepted is played over and over to kids. This generation of children is, more than any before, acutely brand conscious. Teens between thirteen and seventeen have 145 conversations about brands per week, around twice as many as adults. In other words, this kind of marketing sets parents and kids on a collision course.

How Screens Affect Discipline and Guidance

Anything that you do repeatedly becomes a part of you. It forms part of the filter through which you see yourself and take in and process what's out there in the world. Every parent, teacher, or coach knows this. In sports, for example, a coach will have kids practice a skill over and over (hopefully in a fun way) so that it becomes automatic and the children or teens do not even have to think about it as they execute a play. Likewise, a parent will again and again correct a child who chews with his or her mouth open. We do this because we want our kids to have basic table manners, but we also instinctually know that if we make this correction repeatedly, a more appropriate way of eating will develop.

What happens in the freewheeling online world will likewise become a part of a child's social and emotional habits. When they go online, kids are doing the same thing they do in sports, at school, and at home in terms of training. But what is it they are training at? We have become somewhat delusional as a society if we assume that the Internet world our kids inhabit for so many of their daytime hours does not affect how they see themselves and how they relate to the world. In fact, our kids' online interaction incorporates four major training attributes:

1. Repetition
2. Challenge via reward and punishment
3. Pushing of boundaries
4. Automatic response

As our kids navigate the digital world, they are developing social, emotional, and behavioral responses much as an athlete develops automatic muscle-memory responses in training. And we, as parents, are on the front lines, bearing the brunt of these responses, because we— more than anyone else in our child's or teen's life—are at the receiving end. What we allow our kids to repeat over and over becomes a huge part of the way in which they relate to us. This is why we need to pay close attention to what is going on with screens and discipline. Not all of the screen world is bad or wicked, but it is potent, and it can set the tone of your relationship with your son or daughter if he or she is overexposed and you are undervigilant.

The Flight Response and Screens

What has this got to do with discipline? In Chapter One, we took a look at the activation of the fight-or-flight response in our kids and how it so easily triggers us as parents. Let's look into what in particular can cause the flight part of this response to become habitual. There are several ways kids go into flight response. They may simply flee from a room if they feel threatened. Or they may withdraw emotionally. Another flight possibility that's now becoming widespread is the retreat into social media. This form of escape interferes with the development of person-to-person-based problem-solving skills, which are crucial to healthy brain development and success in life. The online world can be moderated, so if a kid doesn't like the direction in which a virtual relationship is going, he or she can simply "unfriend" the person who is causing discomfort and, hey, presto, no more problem.

Things clearly don't work this way in the real world or in a real family, and yet this pseudo-social process is reinforced as kids repeatedly "friend" and "unfriend" each other.

As a result, parenting becomes much more challenging. If your kid spends hours online in chat rooms or on Facebook, Twitter, Pinterest, Instagram, and assorted virtual messaging machinery, where he has the power of a CEO or demigod, he will find it very difficult to recognize your authority. After all, he is the ruler of his own private social pleasure dome for many hours a day. You are now doing the unthinkable. You are shattering his power base and causing him distress. His reaction is predictable. He will most likely "unfriend" you by ignoring you and may not even be capable of having a discussion with you. He has become practiced in the art of "discipline aikido," in which he deflects or shifts away from any uncomfortable conversation. You have to turn up the heat in order to break through. This cyclical dynamic plays out over and over in families all over the world and is a major cause of fiery disciplinary scenarios that benefit no one.

The Friendly vs. Friending Confusion

Here's what one dad told me he overheard at his child's basketball game: "I was sitting with my daughter and a few of her friends. Two of her teammates were discussing problems they were having with their parents. Not at all unusual. But what caught my attention was when one of them said, 'You know what's so totally weird? My mom tried friending me on Facebook.' Her teammate responded, 'If you think that's bad, my mom tried to become one of my Twitter followers.' Their faces contorted as they called out in unison: 'Ewww, creeeepy!'"

We struggle to understand where being a warm and friendly parent ends and being an adult who "friends" a child or teen begins. While screens may not have caused this misunderstanding, they have opened up a whole new way of confusing our relationship with our kids that makes it very hard to discipline and guide them, especially if they see us less as parents and more as weird peers.

What our kids really need is for us to take a leadership position. They feel safe and trustful if they know we are "covering home," as well-known author, educator, and baseball fan Jack Petrash says. Or as family therapist Todd Sarner said to me, "It's so important that your child receive the message 'You are safe here; this is a place from which you can grow, go out into the world, and return to safety.'"

Kids need to know their place in the order of things. And parents need to be, well, *parents* and provide a secure base for the child. Dr. John Bowlby pioneered a way of explaining this primal need, calling it the Attachment Theory. The insights he developed treating emotionally disturbed children led him to focus on the link between early infant separations with their mothers and later maladjustment. He found that children come into the world biologically preprogrammed to form attachments with others, because this will help them to survive and navigate life's challenges. If a child's attachment figure (that is, the parent) does not represent a place the child can retreat to when he or she feels unsafe or needs to make meaning of experiences, he or she will seek to create this in other ways. In today's digital age with all it offers in terms of social networking and friending, the default attachment figure can become a kid's screen. This creates a troubling disconnect between the parent and the child. It means peers and screens become a primary way a child learns values and seeks support.

In their insightful book, *Hold On to Your Kids: Why Parents Need to Matter More Than Peers,* Gordon Neufeld and Gabor Maté shed new light on this understanding of a child's needs. In it, they raise the concern that children are splitting off from their families at far too young of an age and seeking answers and relationships online and that many parents see this as being a positive sign of autonomy. The effect of this can be that children do not accept, or even recognize, the directions of their parents. Neufeld writes, "Our society is so topsy-turvy that we may actually come to value the child's willingness to separate. . . . Unfortunately, we cannot have it both ways. Parents whose young children are not properly attached face a nightmare scenario just keeping the child in sight." But, he assures us, "Like a . . . mother goose with goslings, we can let attachment do the work of keeping our young close instead of having to herd them or put them in pens."

The Dangerous Interruption of the Three Phases of the Norming Process

There are four essential stages to a child's exploration of his or her place in the world—known as the norming process. In a healthy family, infants and young children take their cues from parents or guardians. The child watches and imitates all the little things we do and learns from the corrections we make.

Though family influence persists, the elementary school environment begins to reshape the child's world. As one father told me, "I remember my daughter correcting us at the dinner table. Citing her class teacher, she announced, 'Mrs. Synder says we should hold our knife and fork like this.' The child learns new games and gains a little more independence. Many parents find that new, even edgy playground vocabulary creeps into a child's speech patterns.

The third stage of finding one's place in the world is shaped by peer influence, which alters our kids' musical tastes, speech patterns, choice of attire, and attitudes.

This is the *typical* or healthy picture. Remember that the child does not move from one stage to the next as if they were separate countries. These phases are cumulative, but the foundation of them all is family life. The child launches further out into the world with each new phase, but he or she must regroup, refresh, and resupply from time to time at family base camp.

Severe adjustment problems can occur when heavy screen use, particularly social networking, is prevalent among younger kids who should be in the family and elementary school norming phases. Kids are becoming social-networking users at ever younger ages. ComScore, a firm that measures Internet traffic, estimates that 3.6 million of Facebook's 153 million monthly visitors in America are under twelve years of age. Entire social-networking sites, such as Togetherville, which was recently acquired by Disney, are designed for children under the age of ten. Disney also operates Club Penguin, which targets children as young as six years old.

If we give our kids access to social networking too young, they may simply circumvent the crucial family and school influence stages that help them build up the ability to cope with the powerful influences of peer groups. It is family in the early years and the combined influence of family, parents, and teachers in the later years that shape our preteen kids' judgment skills and empathy for others. When a teenager stands on such solid ground, he or she has the strengthened moral qualities (such as empathy) that can influence him as his thumb hovers over the

"Send" button when a demeaning, hurtful photo of a classmate is cued up to be publicly displayed. Providing a young child with access to social media is like giving her the keys to a powerful SUV and hoping she will drive home safely from her playdate.

When the Screen Is Supreme

The family *medium* needs to be more important than the social *media* in a child's life. Otherwise, the danger is that it is the children who are bringing up children and the teaching of family values is displaced by the passing fads on social media. Every parent wants to inculcate in his or her child good moral values: We want our children to be strong, kind, and considerate of others. These fundamental values are strengthened whenever we affirm the little kindnesses our children show and every time we correct their disrespectful behavior. These values need careful parental nurturing because they develop slowly and cannot compete with the fast-paced, relentless, manipulative marketing forces unleashed through screens. It is important that we parents understand that kids who are bombarded with screen values don't reject a parent's discipline and guidance but, rather, simply deem it boring and irrelevant to their situation. How bitterly ironic that, in this brave new world in which the screen is supreme, the very digital devices that we gift to our children serve to bankrupt our parental authority.

The Alluring World of No Boundaries

When you request anything of a child, tween, or teen who is interacting with a screen, you are asking them to break away from a world of near-total acceptance. A screen does not judge you or ask you to do anything. You are in charge. You create your avatar. You develop your own profile. You post the pictures you want your virtual friends and followers to see. Your "likes" increase, your thoughts are tweeted, and you are happy to see that your followers respond and affirm you. You affirm them right back. It is a buy-in-one-quick-click world. To put the contrast in simple terms:

The online world has few boundaries.

Whereas

Family life has boundaries.

———

The online world affirms you over and over, and if it does not, you delete the cause of displeasure in one quick click.

Whereas

Family life does not always affirm your every action, and "deleting" or ignoring a parent does not necessarily cause him or her to go away.

———

The online world takes you wherever you want to go.

Whereas

Family life exists in the here and now.

———

In the online world, there are few consequences for actions.

Whereas

Family life involves constantly facing the results of your actions and seeing how you affect other humans.

———

The online world is largely free of enduring responsibilities to others. . . . Family life is about being a long-term team player.

A fine young man deep in the grip of heroin addiction once told me, "It's so hard to be in 'low' world, man, because in my 'high' world, I am a god." It is not at all surprising that Internet addiction camps and centers are opening up around the world and psychology courses and counseling programs that train professionals about Internet addiction are becoming very popular. When there is a choice between living with few or many boundaries, the direction that children choose is not often in their best developmental interest.

When we discipline and guide our children, they are challenged to *do* something or take responsibility for something they may have said or done that needs to be put right. But when a child is used to spending hours online in a free and feral world, we might as well be trying to haul him or her out of a pleasure dome. Inevitably, the parent becomes strongly associated with being the cause of displeasure. We become the Grim Reaper rather than the Team Coach. If this pattern goes on long enough, children start to distance themselves from us physically and emotionally. As Attachment Theory tells us, when a child avoids connection with a parent, he or she may fail to develop the secure base we explored earlier in this chapter, and that can trigger a range of emotional and mental health problems. While the Internet appears to offer security on the surface, even an ardent online defender would be hard pressed to argue that anyone can truly bond with the Internet and depend on computers for deep and enduring emotional well-being.

The Culture of Disrespect

Parents often voice their concern about how disrespectfulness in screen-media content has become habitual and is strongly affecting the way their kids speak. One mother put it succinctly when describing how her sons interact: "It's like verbal sword fighting: They circle each other, looking for a place to attack."

South Park, Beavis and Butt-Head, and *The Simpsons* are the TV programs most often referenced by parents who speak to me about shows that teach their kids disrespect. In a thesis undertaken at Cleveland State University, Amy Brown found that in the popular children's television programing she surveyed there was one disrespectful act per minute and that there were very few attempts to correct these behaviors within the episodes' dialogue or action.

Here are some examples of the way in which characters in *The Simpsons* speak:

- "Oh yes, Marge, I think I'll be nice to your sisters, and then I think I'll hug some snakes! Yes! I will hug and kiss some poisonous snakes!"
- "No, I get my news from the Internet, like a normal person under seventy. Farewell, dinosaur."
- "Family, religion, friends—these are the three demons you must slay if you wish to succeed in business."
- "Just because I don't care doesn't mean I don't understand."

Sarcasm, as C. S. Lewis put it, "builds up around a man the finest armour-plating . . . that I know." Nowadays many children employ "dissing" habitually as a way of keeping the world and all its pressures at bay. If you treat everything as a joke, then nothing much can affect you. A father I worked with described an "aha" moment for him: "When we cut back on the pace of life and especially a lot of the TV and computer stuff, our son and daughter started dropping a lot of the comeback ways they spoke to each other and to us."

Some parents feel this kind of negative interaction is inevitable—it's just the way kids speak now. That's a fair point, because speech patterns shift and change over time and across cultures. If you watch movies from the forties or fifties, you immediately notice how differently people spoke. And obviously what is thought to be disrespectful in one culture or subculture may not be offensive in another. When this point was raised in a workshop, one dad responded, "Yeah, but in any culture, there is a line that can get crossed. If my kids cross that line, I tell them so!" Maybe this is also true for family culture. When a child is corrected because he is fresh or disrespectful and he responds,

"But, Dad, everybody speaks like that," it's okay for the parent to answer, "I understand, but we don't speak like this in *our family*." When you do this, you are not judging others; you are clarifying what is okay and not okay within your family state.

Family Takes Time

For every hour our kids spend on a computer, they spend one hour less engaging with real people and, most important, with their family. What's more, while it's a cliché to say kids grow up fast, we know very well we won't end up on our deathbeds saying, "I wish I had made more time for my kids to watch TV and play videogames."

A number of parenting experts advise that parents *connect and then direct.* Before we can properly *direct* our kids, we first have to *connect* with them. In both the Simplicity Parenting and Attachment Parenting models, connection and bonding with a child are core practices.

When we stop and think, it's quite clear that if we want our kids to respond to our guidance we have to spend time building a strong connection with them. Screens rob us of this connection-building time. If we want to improve on the difficult moments in family life—when we need to discipline and guide our kids—then we have to keep these time bandits we call screens at bay.

At a college child development class, a young woman in her early twenties wrote this story in her journal assignment: "I grew up in a regular home where the TV was on all the time and we all used computers a lot. Then, when I was twelve, my dad got into a serious car accident in which he was nearly killed. He was, in fact, pronounced dead, but he came back. When he got out of the hospital he announced that 'every minute was going to count.' On the very first day home he hobbled around the house and—with the help of my mother—carried every one of our four TVs and three computers out the door and put them in the back of our van to be taken away. I was so grateful to have my dad home that I didn't say anything, and anyway, I could tell I needed to keep quiet as he had 'that look' on his face that meant 'Don't mess with me, girl.'

"Everything changed that day. It's not that we did a lot of super exciting things together—we couldn't because my dad was still badly injured—but the house got quiet and we learned about spending time *with* each other just hanging out with no distractions. This was very different from being vaguely 'around' each other as we had been in the past. Looking back on it now, I can see that what the TV, computer, and all that other stuff did meant that although we were in the same house—the same space—we were miles apart. I know without any doubt at all that I am closer to my parents now because of my dad's determination that 'every minute would count.'

"Even now, when I visit my parents, I leave my laptop and phone in my apartment. I just love the feeling of peace I get when I walk into my family home. I know that we will talk and read and just hang out, with no distractions. I visit with them often—particularly when things get a little crazy in my life—because every time I leave I feel a little calmer and stronger. When I get back to my apartment and check my phone and email, there's hardly anything that really matters and yet I know if I'd had my phone with me at my parents' place, I would have been on it quite a bit. Having one place in my world where *human connection* matters more than *Internet connection* has helped me know when I am getting too involved with all that media has to offer and losing touch with myself and the people I care about." (Reproduced with permission.)

Parents Portrayed as Stupid or Negligent

It seemed to start with the movie *Home Alone,* although there were certainly other movies that represented adults as out of touch, superficial, self-interested, naïve, and just plain stupid. An entire genre of movies and sitcoms known as family comedy portrays parents this way. To be sure, there are some really funny exchanges in these shows, but viewed through a lens of deeper care for parents and discipline, these shows are truly problematic.

Perhaps filmmakers are picking up on a child or teen perspective that has a vein of truth to it. Maybe seeing that the adult world can be self-indulgent and superficial is not a bad thing. But the problem is that I am not the generic "adult world," and neither are you. If you are reading this book, you are a parent who consciously strives to nourish your child's or teen's deeper needs and provide the essential boundaries that are so important to raising healthy kids. In a world where almost everyone is a writer or content developer, it takes an act of humility and intent to become a reader. It is not okay to be labeled dumb and out of touch by our kids. What parent does not have doubts and fears that he or she is not doing well enough? But our children should not be privy to the world of adult self-doubt, striving, falling back, and trying again. That is our private domain, and it doesn't do our kids any good to have it caricatured on a screen as a source of mockery and amusement.

In fact, allowing our kids access to the kind of screen content that ridicules parents and makes them seem goofy and out of touch with a child's needs may make our children feel fundamentally unsafe on a deeper level, even as they laugh at what they see.

TWO OTHER CONCERNS

1. **Powerlessness:** First, if your child sees the parental figure depicted as vulnerable, easily manipulated, and essentially powerless, it becomes harder for you to maintain an authoritative position, which is critical to your ability to discipline and guide him or her.

2. **Kids will fill the leadership vacuum:** Second, if a child believes parents are not in charge, a leadership vacuum is created within the family. When kids perceive this, they jump in, unconsciously, because a lack of leadership is discomforting and even scary for them. However, the problem does not end there when there is more than one child in the family, because kids will fight each other for the boss's role. So much bitter and long-term sibling conflict comes about because of a family's leadership-vacuum dynamic. When movies and TV programs depict adults as stupid, naïve, and self-indulgent and show children stepping into the leadership vacuum, the narrative result is often wild parties, peer conflict, and chaos. And this is portrayed as funny and desirable!

The Beginning Point for Change

My not-so-subtle aim in presenting these perspectives about screen use is to try to give some possible reasons why so many parents have an instinct that something is not right about the central place screens are now occupying in many kids' lives. If this has fueled your unease in any way, you shouldn't feel hopeless or negative; you may be standing right on the brink of bringing a major shift to your family. Put simply, we need to name our discontent before we can begin the process of change.

Here is a great tool called the Change Formula, which was first devised by David Gleicher, that embraces dissatisfaction as an essential element in making changes:

$$D \times V \times FS > R$$

Dissatisfaction multiplied by Vision multiplied by First Steps must be greater than Resistance.

Dissatisfaction

Gut-level intelligence comes first. When it comes to our kids' screen use, we have to listen to our instinct: Something is not right. Let the question about the amount of time our kids spend online surface. Give it some space to expand. The new and disturbing *normal* is that the average American kid between eight and eighteen years old spends some seven and a half hours watching a screen *per day.* Most parents wince at this statistic, but even if your kid is not engaged in that much screen time, you should be worried because this is the direction we are going in as a society.

With so many of society's norms driven by marketers and screen folk—who keep telling us that this is the new normal and that, unless our kids are semi-permanently plugged in, they will somehow be disadvantaged—our *D* of Dissatisfaction has an uphill battle to wage. But the truth is parenting instincts die hard. We have fire in our bellies. We want to protect our kids, and our gnawing concern about the huge role of screen media in the lives of our families is growing. A large part of the problem may be that no one asked our parental permission before providing our kids with access to so much content that doesn't square with our family values. We never really stopped and made a decision. It all just kind of happened.

The rubber-hits-the-road moment in this debate about screens and their relationship to discipline occurs when we as parents discover that going low or no screen actually strengthens our family values and that our kids begin to hear us and connect with us and their siblings in a more profound and natural way. Screens convey many messages. That's why an estimated $1.88 trillion (yes, *t-r-i-l-l-i-o-n*) is spent worldwide on children's purchases every year. And marketers know that children are often the early adopters of many digital and direct-media technologies, according to a report by David Buckingham in *The Guardian.*

If we want our children to absorb the principles on which we raise them, we have to do away with the incessant barrage of contradictory messages they get from TVs and computers. We want our kids to grow up to live principled, ethical lives and care for others as well as themselves. Screens want kids to buy stuff. Lots of it.

We don't have to join some protest march against the dark forces of digital media. All we have to do is give ourselves permission to feel that "something is wrong." If we, as parents, allow ourselves this rumble of dissatisfaction, we are taking a small but significant step toward finding a family space in which we no longer need to battle with our kids.

A big part of being able to change anything is recognizing and accepting your *dissatisfaction* with the present situation. Next you can conjure up a *vision* for a more connected, less screen-filled family life. And finally, you can work out what your *first steps* might be to reduce screen time in your family.

The Sausage Ad Story

I once saw a funny advertisement for meat products that involved a dad's exchange with his kids and screens. Here is how I remember it: A dad arrives home looking like he's had a hard day at the office. As he approaches the house, he sees that the lights are on inside. He smiles at the thought of seeing his kids after being out in the hard-edged world all day doing what he needed to do to provide for them. He opens the door and calls out that he is home. No response. He walks through the house and sees that his three kids *are home*. They are each at a screen, earbuds in, and greet him with a grunt or a distracted "Hi" while their eyes remain glued to their screens. He stands and looks dejectedly at his family . . . until he gets an idea. He goes down into the basement and turns off the main electricity switch. All the power goes off in the house. Groans of disappointment can be heard as screens go blank. The kids presume there has been a power outage in the town.

The next scene depicts the dad with his entire family happily grilling at the barbecue (this is where the sausages make their grand entrance). The kids are laughing and relating to each other. The dad, all smiles, is at the grill cooking (close-up of the sausages here) for his kids. Stories are shared. Everyone laughs. There is not a TV, computer, or phone in sight. All is well until his youngest son (an eight-year-old) says, "Hey, Dad, if the power has gone down everywhere, how come our neighbor's lights are on?" The whole family freezes. Everyone looks over at the neighbor's place. They all realize that something is not quite right with Dad's story. But quickly the laughter resumes. They simply don't want the great time they are having to end.

One couple wrote, "We used to really beat ourselves up about not being good enough at raising a family and we started blaming each other, which put a serious strain on our relationship." Then they realized that much of their kids' aggressive, distracted, and disrespectful behavior was being caused by screen exposure. When they cut their kids' screen time dramatically, they saw that all the "weird stuff that kids get drilled into them online has a powerful influence on them. It drowned us out." They ended the note by saying, "It's not perfect now, but we feel a lot more confident about our abilities as parents and we are much closer as a couple and as a family."

Given the direction of modern society, it's understandable that many parents believe that smartphones, tablets, televisions, and computers are an essential part of a child's, tween's, or teen's life. But I am heartened to report that, as I've been crisscrossing the country, I've met countless parents from all walks of life who are experiencing a strong visceral reaction to the dominant influence that such devices have on all aspects of family life. In the interest of our children's hearts, minds, and souls, we must do our best to tame this digital dragon.

Parenting That Builds
a Better World

We cannot separate the way we raise our kids and run our families from other major influences in the world. What if the way we parent could build our capacities to be more inquisitive and less accusative of our leaders and the global events that affect us? Wouldn't it be valuable to have a simple framework that you developed in your day-to-day parenting that helped you to see where someone outside your family was coming from, rather than feeling unease or even antipathy because his or her view differed from yours? While we know that we want to raise children who will make the world a better place, can the very *way* we raise our kids help them and us become more tolerant and less prone to polarizing judgments?

The Soul of Discipline approach seeks to meet the challenges of raising children in a healthy, flexible way. It does not support developing a single, well-cultivated or fixed view of parenting and discipline at the exclusion of other points of view.

So how does our view of discipline relate to the big social and po-

litical situations of our time? In the field of positive psychology, there
is an attempt to move beyond the increasing political left-right divide
that is so divisive and destructive in modern society. It is important to
consider Jonathan Haidt's perspective, presented in his book *The Righteous Mind: Why Good People Are Divided by Politics and Religion.*
Rather than think about people on the political right as backward-
looking and narrow-minded, he puts forward the view that, generally,
these folks are more "localist" in their principles. At the top of their
values are family, the rule of law, and issues that are close to home.
Most people on the political left are not so much anarchists as folks
who value global issues and tend to be more "universalist." They prefer to be more widely socially inclusive and look for "emergent" and
unstructured ways of making decisions. It even seems to me that the
so-called centrists could be termed "regionalists," because their interest
can move beyond local concerns but may not stay fully focused in
global issues. Regionalists prefer some degree of structure but are open
to listening to the arguments of the left and the right before making a
decision.

The term "echo chamber" has been used to describe a tendency society is falling into where we increasingly cluster more tightly together
in groups, locations, and even towns where we will hear opinions that
are the same as ours. This has a polarizing effect and leads to more tensions and narrowly defined and supported belief systems.

It may seem strange to see the politics of left and right mentioned in
a book on discipline and guidance, but the Soul of Discipline approach
states very clearly and simply that there are times when a parent needs
to move between being a Governor/Localist, a Gardener/Regionalist,
and a Guide/Universalist. In other words, sometimes your kid may
need you to be a localist and pull in the boundaries. When you do this,
it isn't because of a rigid, one-size-fits-all worldview; you do it because
your son or daughter needs this type of boundaries and support. There
are other times when being local, or even regional, in how you disci-

pline will create problems because your child is ready for and needs the freedom offered by the more universalist Guide to see what is emergent in his or her capacities.

As you practice this kind of discerning flexibility in your life inside and outside the family, there may be times when a burning local issue trumps the concerns you have about its larger implications for the country or world. Or the opposite may be true at another decision-making crossroads. What is assured is that children who grow up in this kind of flexible environment will absorb, in a subtle way, an attitude that is fundamentally healthy and balanced. As they mature, it will be a powerfully positive influence on them and, through them, on the world.

When we parent using the Soul of Discipline approach, our inner and outer attitudes will shift and our flexibility increase, even in the face of strong opposition from our kids. As a result, we will develop a finer capacity to sense what is needed rather than placing our focus on one fixed belief system. It is my sincere hope that this approach to discipline may even guide us as parents, as well as our children, toward more open minds and more responsive hearts.

Acknowledgments

With deep gratitude to . . .

The team at the Simplicity Parenting Project, whose servant leadership humbles and inspires.

The many workshop organizers of my visits to their communities, who so selflessly open up the space for the dear parents and me to meet, share, commiserate, and celebrate our parenting.

Our Dear Davina, for shining a clear and loyal light that shows us where we need to go.

To Almuth, our children's Nana, who shows us the simple beauty of a life lived with soul and spirit.

To Harry, our children's grandpa, who passed away as this book was being written. Even through his suffering, he smiled and asked how the writing was coming along.

Special thanks to Luis Fernando Llosa, whose astute and elegant pen and patient feedback were so important in helping shape this book.

And, of course . . .

To Katharine, the love of my life, and to Johanna and Saphira, the loves of our lives.

Notes

Chapter 1: Disobedient or Disoriented?

26   **how brain science affects parenting and discipline**   D. Coulter, *Original Mind: Uncovering Your Natural Brilliance* (Boulder, CO: Sounds True, 2014).

Chapter 2: The Three Phases of Discipline

31   **"Good fences make good neighbors"**   R. Frost, *Collected Poems, Prose, and Plays* (New York: Library of America, 1996).

36   **"speech powers of those cells"**   D. Coulter, *The World of Inner Speech,* workshop pamphlet (1986).

42   **phases of child development**   R. Steiner, *The Kingdom of Childhood: Introductory Talks on Waldorf Education* (Fair Oaks, CA: Association of Waldorf Schools of North America Publications [Anthroposophic Press], 1995).

43   **three distinct capacities**   R. Steiner, *Study of Man: General Education Course* (Sussex, UK: Rudolf Steiner Press, 2011).

Chapter 3: The Governor: The Five Essentials to Healthy Boundaries and Compliance

59   **a book that fully supports the parent being in charge**   R. Morrish, *Secrets of Discipline: For Parents and Teachers* (Fonthill, ON: Woodstream Publishing, 1998).

60   **"collect then direct"**   G. Neufeld and G. Maté, *Hold On to Your Kids: Why Parents Need to Matter More Than Peers* (Toronto: Vintage, 2004).

63   **get off the dance floor of daily life**   R. Heifetz and M. Linsky, *Leadership on the*

Line: Staying Alive Through the Dangers of Leading (Boston: Harvard Business School Press, 2002).

68   **Virtual reality and videos are shadowy substitutes**   S. Blakeslee, "Cells That Read Minds," *New York Times,* January 10, 2006, www.nytimes.com/2006/01/10/science/10mirr.html?pagewanted=all&_r=0.

69   **a mantra-like unchanging tone of voice**   J. Petrash, *Covering Home: Lessons on the Art of Fathering from the Game of Baseball* (Beltsville, MD: Robins Lane Press, 2004).

Chapter 4: Practical Strategies for Building Healthy Compliance

93   **bullying, teasing, and their effects**   K. Rigby, *Bullying in Schools: And What to Do About It* (London: Jessica Kingsley Press, 1997).

93   **sustained future success**   D. Goleman, *Emotional Intelligence: Why It Can Matter More Than IQ* (New York: Bantam, 1995).

97   **"Hairy Maclary from Donaldson's Dairy bedtime story"**   L. Dodd, *Hairy Maclary from Donaldson's Dairy* (Berkeley: Tricycle Press, 2001).

Chapter 5: Directions and Instructions vs. Suggestions and Requests

110   **"collecting and connecting"**   G. Neufeld and G. Maté, *Hold On to Your Kids: Why Parents Need to Matter More Than Peers* (Toronto: Vintage, 2004).

122   **one of many forms of intelligence**   H. Gardner, *Intelligence Reframed: Multiple Intelligences for the 21st Century* (New York: Basic Books, 2000).

123   **torrents of words**   A. Weisleder and A. Fernald, "Talking to Children Matters: Early Language Experience Strengthens Processing and Builds Vocabulary," *Psychological Science* 24, no. 11 (2013): 2143–2152.

124   **"read our minds"**   S. Blakeslee, "Cells That Read Minds," *New York Times,* January 10, 2006, www.nytimes.com/2006/01/10/science/10mirr.html?pagewanted=all&_r=0.

126   **higher social and emotional development**   E. Erikson, *Childhood and Society* (1950; repr. New York: Norton, 1993).

Chapter 6: The Tween Years and the Gardener

139   **tweens tend to be conformist**   A. Clifford-Poston, *Tweens: What to Expect From—and How to Survive—Your Child's Pre-teen Years* (Oxford: Oneworld, 2005).

140   **Seventy-seven percent of tweens**   Ibid.

141   **"Tween self-esteem is in development and fragile"**   Aeffect Inc., *Review of Literature to Support Development of the Youth Media Campaign: Exploring How to Motivate Behavior Change Among Tweens in America* (Lake Forest, IL: Department of Health and Human Services' Centers for Disease Control and Prevention, 2000), www.cdc.gov/youthcampaign/research/PDF/LitReview.pdf.

144 **11.5 percent had been drunk at least once in the past year** L. Johnston, P. O'Malley, P. Bachman, and J. Schulenberg, *Monitoring the Future: National Results on Adolescent Drug Use; Overview of Key Findings* (Ann Arbor, MI: Institute for Social Research, The University of Michigan, 2011).

144 **five times more likely to develop alcohol dependence** J. Gfroerer, "Re: Alcohol initiates under 16 use," email message communication to Jernigan D., Baltimore, MD, Substance Abuse and Mental Health Services Administration, August 30, 2010, cited in "Prevalence of Underage Drinking," Johns Hopkins School of Public Health, last modified July 2011, www.camy.org/factsheets/sheets/prevalence _of_underage_drinking.html.

144 **thirteen years old** J. Gfroerer, *National Survey on Drug Use and Health* (Rockville, MD: Substance Abuse and Mental Health Services Administration, 2004).

145 **able to get marijuana within a day** *Adolescent Substance Use: America's #1 Public Health Problem* (New York, NY: National Center on Addiction and Substance Abuse at Columbia University, 2011), www.casacolumbia.org/addiction-research /reports/adolescent.

145 **A study conducted by Just Kid Inc.** P. Novelli and Just Kid Inc., "Life's First Great Crossroad: Pre-teens Make Choices That Affect Their Lives Forever" (Norwalk, CT: Just Kid Inc., 2000), www.porternovelli.com/intelligence/cate gory/global-health-and-wellness/.

163 **90 percent of all our communication is conducted nonverbally** A. Mehrabian, *Silent Messages: Implicit Communication of Emotions and Attitudes,* 2nd ed. (Belmont, CA: Wadsworth, 1981).

Chapter 7: The Teen Years and the Guide

177 **"being sleepy in the daytime"** J. Frieden, "Teen Sleep Deprivation a Serious Problem," *Medical News, WebMD,* August 21, 2000, www.teens.webmd.com/common -sleep-disorders-teens.

177 **"a physiologic burden"** M. Trudeau (writer/narrator), "Skimping on Sleep Can Stress Body and Brain," radio broadcast, *Morning Edition,* National Public Radio, July 17, 2014, www.npr.org/blogs/health/2014/07/17/332058265/skimping-on -sleep-can-stress-body-and-brain.

179 **Sleep consolidates learning** "Sleep: Expert Q&A," M. Walker, PBS, July 16, 2007, www.pbs.org/wgbh/nova/body/walker-sleep.html.

185 **the three stages outlined in Betty Staley's wonderful book** B. Staley, *Between Form and Freedom: A Practical Guide to the Teenage Years* (Stroud, UK: Hawthorn Press, 2009).

194 **The average age of first sexual intercourse** New Strategist Publications, *American Sexual Behavior: Demographics of Sexual Activity, Fertility and Childbearing* (Amityville, NY: New Strategist Publications, 2006), www.newstrategist.com /store/files/Sex.SamplePgs.pdf.

194 **helpful insights for teens navigating the crosscurrents of sexuality** C. S. Lewis, *The Four Loves* (New York: Harcourt Books, 1960).

Chapter 9: Avoiding Discipline Fads

234 **a way to haul your kids back in line**   B. Skinner, *About Behaviorism* (New York: Vintage Press, 1976).

236 **expressed serious concerns with Dr. Skinner's emerging brand**   N. Chomsky, "The Case Against B. F. Skinner," *New York Review of Books,* December 30, 1971, 18–24.

247 **They can develop an acute fear of failure**   C. Dweck, *Self-Theories: Their Role in Motivation, Personality, and Development* (Philadelphia: Psychological Press, 2000).

248 **One of the key markers of success**   D. Goleman, *Working with Emotional Intelligence,* 2nd ed. (New York: Bantam Books, 2006).

248 **the widespread use of overpraising**   A. Kohn, *Punished by Rewards: The Trouble with Gold Stars, Incentive Plans, A's, Praise, and Other Bribes* (Boston: Houghton Mifflin, 1993).

Chapter 10: Discipline and the Four Pillars of Simplicity

255 **The limbic system is critical for emotional processing and behavior**   American Academy of Pediatrics, Committee on Public Education, "Children, Adolescents, and Television," *Pediatrics* 107, no. 2 (February 2001): 423–426.

Chapter 11: Discipline in the Digital Age

268 **Researchers from Brown University School of Medicine**   S. Donaldson-Pressman, R. Jackson, and R. Pressman, *The Learning Habit: A Groundbreaking Approach to Homework and Parenting That Helps Our Children Succeed in School and Life* (New York: Perigee, 2014).

270 **they believe that it is beneficial to their children's brain development**   F. Zimmerman, D. Christakis, and A. Meltzoff, "Television and DVD/Video Viewing in Children Younger Than 2 Years," *Archives of Pediatric & Adolescent Medicine* 161, no. 5 (May 2007): 473–479.

270 **there is no credible evidence**   G. Schurgin O'Keeffe, K. Clarke-Pearson, and Council on Communications and Media, "The Impact of Social Media on Children, Adolescents, and Families," *Pediatrics* 127, no. 4 (April 2011): 800–804, published online March 28, 2011, Pediatrics.aappublications.org/content/127/4/800 .abstract.

270 **excessive screen time is linked to increased psychological difficulties**   A. Page, A. Cooper, P. Griew, and R. Jago, "Children's Screen Viewing Is Related to Psychological Difficulties Irrespective of Physical Activity," *Pediatrics* 126, no. 5 (October 2010): 1011–1017.

270 **poor school performance**   J. Johnson, J. Brook, P. Cohen, and S. Kasen, "Extensive Television Viewing and the Development of Attention and Learning Difficulties During Adolescence," *Archives of Pediatric & Adolescent Medicine* 161, no. 5 (2007): 480–486.

270 **instant stimulus of screens can cause children to become impatient**   J. Healy,

Your Child's Growing Mind: Brain Development and Learning from Birth to Adolescence (New York: Broadway Books, 2004).

270   **the trancelike state they bring about**   D. Siegel and M. Hartzell, *Parenting from the Inside Out: How a Deeper Self-Understanding Can Help You Raise Children Who Thrive,* 10th anniversary ed. (New York: Tarcher, 2013).

272   **four will be heavily into screens**   V. Rideout, U. Foehr, and D. Roberts, *Generation M2: Media in the Lives of 8- to 18-Year-Olds* (Menlo Park, CA: Kaiser Family Foundation, 2010), kff.org/other/event/generation-m2-media-in-the-lives-of/.

272   **national average of seven and a half hours a day**   T. Lewin, "If Your Kids Are Awake, They're Probably Online," *New York Times,* Jan. 20, 2010, www.nytimes.com/2010/01/20/education/20wired.html?_r=0.

273   **Emerging research challenges the belief**   C. Borch, H. Antonius, and N. Cillessen, "The role of attractiveness and aggression in high school popularity," *Social Psychology of Education* 14, no. 1 (2011): 23–39.

273   **kids who can regulate their emotions and impulses**   C. Peterson and M. Siegal, "Mindreading and Moral Awareness in Popular and Rejected Preschoolers," *British Journal of Developmental Psychology* 20, no. 1 (2002): 205–224.

273   **Making kids aggressive**   T. Greitemeyer and D. Mügge, "Video Games Do Affect Social Outcomes: A Meta-analytic Review of the Effects of Violent and Prosocial Video Game Play," *Personality and Social Psychology Bulletin*, January 2014.

274   **Poor empathy and lower social skills**   J. Healy, *Your Child's Growing Mind: Brain Development and Learning from Birth to Adolescence* (New York: Broadway Books, 2004).

274   **Poor impulse control**   S. Donaldson-Pressman, R. Jackson, and R. Pressman, *The Learning Habit: A Groundbreaking Approach to Homework and Parenting That Helps Our Children Succeed in School and Life* (New York: Perigee, 2014).

277   **"an increasing and compulsive tendency"**   F. Vogt, *Addiction's Many Faces: Tackling Drug Dependency Amongst Young People; Causes, Effects and Prevention* (Stroud, UK: Hawthorn Press, 2002).

278   **"In every school there are the cool and popular kids"**   Salon.com, January 24, 2006, www.salon.com/2006/01/24/jeffries/.

278   **ensure that their group is cooler**   B. Horovitz, "P&G 'Buzz Marketing' Unit Hit with Complaint," *USA Today,* October 19, 2005.

278   **"a selling point for their products"**   S. Linn, *Consuming Kids: The Hostile Takeover of Childhood* (New York: New Press, 2005).

278   **145 conversations about brands**   L. Johnston, P. O'Malley, J. Bachman, and J. Schulenberg, *Monitoring the Future: National Results on Adolescent Drug Use; Overview of Key Findings* (Ann Arbor, MI: Institute for Social Research, The University of Michigan, 2011).

281   **"covering home"**   J. Petrash, *Covering Home: Lessons from the Art of Fathering from the Game of Baseball* (Beltsville, MD: Robins Lane Press, 2004).

281   **Attachment Theory**   J. Bowlby, *A Secure Base: Clinical Applications of Attachment Theory* (London: Routledge, 1988).

282   **shed new light on this understanding of a child's needs**   G. Neufeld and G. Maté,

Hold On to Your Kids: Why Parents Need to Matter More Than Peers (Toronto: Vintage, 2004).

286 **one disrespectful act per minute** A. Brown, "Promoting Children's Disrespect Through Television" (master's thesis, Cleveland State University, 2011), academic .csuohio.edu/kneuendorf/c63311/Brown11.pdf.

287 **"builds up around a man the finest armour-plating"** C. S. Lewis, *The Complete C. S. Lewis Signature Classics* (New York: HarperCollins, 2007).

291 **Dissatisfaction multiplied by Vision multiplied by First Steps** R. Beckhard and R. Harris, *Organizational Transitions: Managing Complex Change,* 2nd ed. (Reading, MA: Addison-Wesley Publishing Company, 1987).

292 **$1.88 trillion** L. Cooper, "Brand Loyalty Starts from a Very Early Age," *Marketing Week,* June 8, 2010, www.marketingweek.co.uk/brand-loyalty-starts-from-a -very-early-age/.

292 **children are often the early adopters** D. Buckingham, "Children: Victims in the Marketplace?" *Guardian,* December 15, 2009, www.guardian.co.uk/commentis free/2009/dec/15/children-marketplace-commerce-obesity-sexualisation.

Epilogue

296 **"emergent" and unstructured ways of making decisions** J. Haidt, *The Righteous Mind: Why Good People Are Divided by Politics and Religion* (New York: Vintage, 2012).

Index

KIM JOHN PAYNE, M.ED., is the author of the number one bestselling book *Simplicity Parenting*. A consultant and trainer to over 250 North American independent and public schools, Kim has been a school counselor, adult educator, consultant, researcher, educator, and private family counselor for over thirty years. He trains and certifies Parent Guidance Coaches and regularly gives keynote addresses at international conferences for educators, parents, and therapists, and runs workshops and trainings around the world. In each role, he has been helping children, adolescents, and families explore issues such as social difficulties with siblings and classmates; attention and behavioral issues at home and school; emotional issues such as defiance, aggression, addiction, and self-esteem; and the vital role of living a balanced and simple life.

He has also consulted for clinics, training centers, and educational associations in South Africa, Hungary, Israel, Russia, Switzerland, Ireland, Canada, Australia, and the United Kingdom. Kim has worked extensively with the North American and U.K. Waldorf educational movements. He has served as director of the Collaborative Counseling program at Antioch University, New England. He is director of the Simplicity Parenting Project, a multimedia social network that explores what really connects and disconnects us to ourselves and to the world. Kim is the founding director of the Center for Social Sustainability.

In addition to authoring *Simplicity Parenting: Using the Extraordinary Power of Less to Raise Calmer, Happier, and More Secure Kids,* published by Ballantine Books/Random House in 2009, he also authored *The Games Children Play* (1996), published by Hawthorn Press, *The Compassionate Re-*

sponse (2016), Shambhala Publications, and co-authored *Beyond Winning: Smart Parenting in a Toxic Sports Environment* (2013), published by Lyons Press.

He has appeared frequently on television, including ABC, NBC, CBS, and Fox; on radio, for the BBC, Sirius/XM, CBC, and National Public Radio; and in print, including being featured in *Time, Chicago Tribune, Parenting, Mothering, Times Union,* and the *Los Angeles Times.*

Kim strives to deepen understanding and give practical tools for life questions that arise out of the burning social issues of our time. He is based in Northampton, Massachusetts, with his wife and two children.

simplicityparenting.com

@KimJohnPayne